THE
NEXT
AMERICA

THE
NEXT

★ *AMERICA*

BOOMERS, MILLENNIALS, *AND THE* LOOMING GENERATIONAL SHOWDOWN

PAUL TAYLOR

PUBLICAFFAIRS
New York

To Andy and Stefanie

PublicAffairs books are available at special discounts for bulk purchases in the U.S. by corporations, institutions, and other organizations. For more information, please contact the Special Markets Department at the Perseus Books Group, 2300 Chestnut Street, Suite 200, Philadelphia, PA 19103, call (800) 810-4145, ext. 5000, or e-mail special.markets@perseusbooks.com.

Book design by Cynthia Young

Library of Congress Cataloging-in-Publication Data
Taylor, Paul, 1949–
    The next America : boomers, millennials, and the looming generational showdown
    / Paul Taylor.—First edition.
        pages cm
    Includes bibliographical references and index.
    ISBN 978-1-61039-350-8 (hardcover)—ISBN 978-1-61039-351-5 (electronic)
1. Baby boom generation—United States.   2. Generation Y—United States.
3. Conflict of generations—United States.   4. Generations—United States.
5. United States—Population.   I. Title.
HN59.T39 2014
305.20973—dc23

                                                          2013036139

First Edition

10 9 8 7 6 5 4 3 2 1

CONTENTS

PREFACE

Once you get far enough along in life, you're likely to be struck by the distance between the views in front of you and the ones you can still dimly make out in your rear-view mirror. I turn 65 this year. The America of my childhood—with its expanding middle class, secure jobs, intact nuclear families, devout believers, distinct gender roles, polite politics, consensus-building media—is nothing like the country my year-old granddaughter will inherit. Our political, social, and religious institutions are weaker, our middle class smaller, our cultural norms looser, our public debate coarser, our technologies faster, our immigrant-woven tapestry richer, and our racial, ethnic, religious, and gender identities more ambiguous. As a society, we've become more polarized *and* more tolerant—and no matter what we're like today, we're going to be different tomorrow. Change is the constant.

We're also getting a whole lot older, as is almost every other nation on the planet—the fruits of longer life spans and lower birthrates that are each unprecedented in human history. These new demographics of aging mean that pretty soon we won't be able to pay for all the promises we've made to oldsters like me. So we'll have to either shrink their social safety net or raise taxes on their children and grandchildren. This reckoning has the potential to set off a generation war, though it doesn't have to.

This book applies a generational lens to explore the many ways America is changing. It pays particular attention to our two outsize generations—the Baby Boomers, fifty- and sixty-somethings having trouble coming to terms with getting old, and the Millennials, twenty-somethings having trouble finding the road map to adulthood. It looks at their competing interests in the big showdown over entitlement reform that our politicians, much as they might try, won't be able to put off for much longer. It also examines how the generations relate to one another not only as citizens, voters, and interest groups, but as parents, children, and caregivers in an era when the family itself is one of our institutions most buffeted by change.

I don't presume to know how my story ends. Years ago when I was a political reporter I had a weakness for trying to forecast election outcomes. I was about as reliable as a coin flip. Eventually it dawned on me that the future was going to arrive anyway, unbidden by me, and that prediction was something of a mug's game. The only forecasts I'll venture in this book will be about the future we already know—the parts baked in by the demographics and the data. Mostly my aim is to be a tour guide who explains how our nation got from the middle of the last century to the present, then provides some insights about what this breathtaking journey tells us about the changes yet to come. I'll conclude with some thoughts on how to renegotiate the social compact between the generations on equitable terms for all.

Be forewarned: There are a lot of data in this book. Numbers are the coin of the realm at the Pew Research Center, where I've worked since we opened our doors a decade ago. Our staff is a mix of public opinion survey researchers, political scientists, demographers, economists, sociologists, and ex-reporters like me. We call ourselves a "fact tank" and we're fond of the aphorism attributed to Senator Daniel Patrick Moynihan: "Everyone is entitled to his own opinions, but not his own facts." We think good data make good facts, and we're just idealistic enough to believe that a common foundation of facts can help societies identify problems and discover solutions.

We know, of course, that numbers aren't omniscient. And we're aware that public opinion surveys, in particular, can sometimes convey a false certitude that disguises ambiguities of heart, soul, and mind. If you ask Americans whether they favor more assistance to the poor, 65% will say yes. If you ask them whether they favor more spending on welfare, just 25% will say yes. Which finding is "true"? Probably both. "Do I contradict myself?" Walt Whitman once asked. "Very well then, I contradict myself. I am large, I contain multitudes." I sometimes wonder whether he had a peek at our survey findings.

But while we're well acquainted with the limitations of survey research, we also appreciate its value. In the shout-fest that passes for public discourse these days, politicians and pundits frequently claim to speak for the public. Opinion surveys allow the public to speak for itself. Each person has an equal chance to be heard. Each opinion is given an equal weight. That's the same noble ideal that animates our democracy.

Introduction

D EMOGRAPHIC TRANSFORMATIONS are dramas in slow motion. They unfold incrementally, almost imperceptibly, tick by tock, without trumpets or press conferences. But every so often, as the weight of change builds, a society takes a hard look at itself and notices that things are different. These "aha" moments are rare and revealing. One occurred on November 6, 2012, the night of President Barack Obama's reelection victory in a campaign that, given the political headwinds stirred by four years of high unemployment, he had every reason to lose.

Instead he won, and rather handily, an outcome that caught a lot of smart pundits and pols by surprise. Republican operative Karl Rove succumbed to a live, on-air mini-meltdown on Fox News that night when he couldn't bring himself to accept the finality of the people's verdict. Michael Barone, the conservative analyst and longtime coauthor of the *Almanac of American Politics,* who probably knows more than anyone else alive about voting patterns down to the county and precinct level, had only a few days earlier predicted an Electoral College landslide for Mitt Romney. So had George Will, the eminence gris of the op-ed pages. As the scope of the Obama victory sunk in, three of the most animated conservative voices on the airwaves—Dick Morris, Bill O'Reilly, and Rush Limbaugh—drew the same conclusion. "This is not your father's United States. This is a United States with a permanently high turnout of blacks, Latinos, and young people," said Morris, who had also forecast a Romney blowout. "The white establishment is now the minority," said O'Reilly. "We're outnumbered," said Limbaugh.

Their demography-is-destiny despair arose from some pretty compelling arithmetic. Had the election been held only among voters ages 30 and older, Romney would have won by 2 million votes instead of losing by 5 million. Had it been held only among men, he would have won by 4 million votes. Had it been held only among whites, he would have won by 18 million votes. Romney carried the white vote by the identical 20 percentage-point landslide that George H. W. Bush had run up among whites a generation earlier. That haul netted the elder Bush 426 electoral college votes in 1988 and Romney just 206 in 2012. So in the 24 years separating those two elections, whites lost more than half of their electoral college clout. Aha.

The voters in 2012 were the most racially and ethnically diverse in our nation's history, a trend driven mainly by the tens of millions of Hispanic and Asian immigrants (and their children) who've come across our borders in the past half century and are now showing up at our polling places. But this new multi-hued electorate is actually a *lagging* indicator of the nation's demographic transformation. In 2012 some 26% of voters were nonwhite—a record—but so was 37% of the population as a whole. Even with their turnout gains, nonwhites still punch well below their weight on Election Day. Many are still too young to vote, many aren't citizens, and many aren't politically engaged. Over time, a mix of demographic and behavioral change is likely to shrink all of these deficits. The US Census Bureau projects that nonwhites will become the majority of the US population in 2043, and by that time, it's a good bet that their voter participation will have closed the gap with their population count.

Romney captured just 17% of the nonwhite vote in 2012, leading one wag to refer to the GOP as the "pale, male, and stale" party, and the Republican leadership itself, in a notably blunt official postelection autopsy, to acknowledge that it too often appears to be a "narrow-minded" collection of "stuffy old men." Elder statesman Bob Dole weighed in with a suggestion that his party hang a "closed for repairs" sign on its front door, and former Florida governor Jeb Bush lamented, "Way too many people believe Republicans are anti-immigrant, anti-woman, anti-science, anti-gay, and the list goes on and on."

The GOP's demographic predicament calls to mind German playwright Bertolt Brecht's puckish advice to his government when it faced similar troubles: dissolve the public and elect a replacement. Political parties can't fire the voters, of course, so they adapt—or try to. Ever since the electoral shock of 2012, Republicans have been engaged in an intra-party civil war, which reached a fever pitch when their congressional Tea Party faction shut down the government for 16 days in the fall of 2013 in an unsuccessful bid to defund

Figure 1.1

The Changing Face of America, 1960–2060

% of the total population

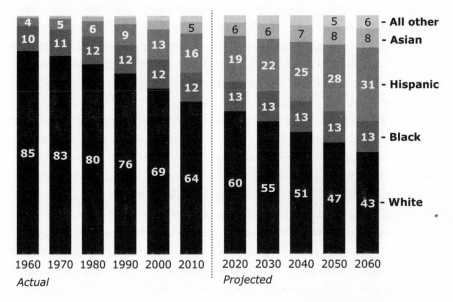

1960 1970 1980 1990 2000 2010   2020 2030 2040 2050 2060
Actual   *Projected*

Note: Data labels not showing if less than 5%. White, black, Asian and "all other" include only non-Hispanics who identify as a single race. Hispanics are of any race. Asians include Native Hawaiians and Pacific Islanders. All other includes American Indians/Alaska Natives in all years and those who reported two or more races beginning in 2000.

Source: Pew Research Center historic population estimates for 1960–1990 (Passel and Cohn, "US Population Projections: 2005–2050," Feb. 11, 2008). Census Bureau population estimates for 2000–2010 and projections for 2015–2060

Obama's signature legislative accomplishment, the Affordable Care Act. The GOP needs to get past this destructive infighting, and if it wishes to be a party that is competitive in future presidential elections, it also needs to figure out how to become more appealing to the nation's newly diverse electorate. In the meantime, if history is a guide, the demographically ascendant Democrats— now winners of the popular vote in five of the last six presidential elections— have no guarantee of smooth waters ahead. They may find themselves hurt by having to dispense bad medicine in an age of austerity. They may discover their multiracial base has fissures. Or that the troubled launch of Obamacare creates turbulence for their candidates in 2014, and perhaps beyond. The most reliable rule of American politics is that nothing is static. The pendulum swings.

This book will keep an eye on these partisan dynamics, but its main ambition lies elsewhere. Using a generational frame, it aims to illuminate the demographic, economic, social, cultural, and technological changes that are remaking not just our politics but our families, livelihoods, relationships, and identities. These shifts have left no realm of society untouched. As a people, we're growing older, more unequal, more diverse, more mixed race, more digitally linked, more tolerant, less married, less fertile, less religious, less mobile, and less confident. Our political and media institutions have become more polarized and partisan; so has the public itself. Our economy is producing more low-wage and high-wage jobs, but fewer in between. Our middle class is shrinking. Our median household income has flatlined. Our social class divisions are wider than they've been since the Gilded Age. Wealth gaps between young and old are at levels never before seen in modern times; so are the economic divides between whites, blacks, and Hispanics, and so, of course, is the gap between rich and poor. Our neighborhoods have become more integrated by race but more segregated by income. And more sorted by party. Women have become more economically independent, men less. Gender roles are converging, both at work and at home. Marriage is in decline. The nuclear family is losing its pride of place. The fastest-growing household type in America contains just one person. Not far behind are multigenerational households, in which two or more adult generations live under the same roof, often because that's the only way to make ends meet. More than 4 in 10 newborns have an unwed mother. Half are nonwhite. A teenager has less chance of being raised by both biological parents in America than anywhere else in the world. Young adults are taking longer to grow up; the middle-aged longer to grow old; and the elderly longer to depart this vale of tears. Biases against minorities and gays are diminishing. Today's immigrants—nearly 9 in 10 of whom are not Europeans—look very different from the previous waves of settlers and immigrants who created America. But when it comes to embracing what we think of as traditional American values, it's hard to find more fervent devotees.

Some of these changes are for the better, some for the worse—and some people no doubt will differ over which is which. Most are mutually reinforcing. And all, in one way or another, will have an impact on the immense national challenge that's the central focus of this book: namely, as our population ages, how do we keep our promises to the old without bankrupting the young and starving the future? When we built the social safety net in the twentieth century, the math was easier. We had more workers per retiree, fewer people living to be very old, an economy that seemed to generate new jobs on autopilot; and health care costs that hadn't escalated beyond control. The politics were easier, too. Back then, except for the gray hair and crow's feet, young and old pretty much looked and thought alike. No more. Our older generation is predominantly white; our younger generation increasingly nonwhite. They have different political philosophies, social views, and policy preferences, as they made clear in 2008 and 2012, when the young-old voting gaps were the widest on record. Many of the young are big government liberals; most of the old are small government conservatives (but hands off Social Security and Medicare!). The young are comfortable with the dizzying array of new lifestyles, family forms, and technologies that have made the start of the twenty-first century such a distinctive moment in human history; the old for the most part are disoriented by them. The young are the least religiously connected generation in modern American history; the old are the most devout believers in the industrialized world. The young have been starting their working and taxpaying lives in the worst economy since the Great Depression; the old are finishing theirs off having run up $17 trillion in government IOUs that their children and grandchildren will spend their lives paying off. "Mugging Our Descendants," is how a headline on a George Will column toted up the math.

It sounds like the script for a fiscal horror flick, pitting parent against child in offices, hospitals, legislatures, and homes. In the concluding chapter, I'll argue that the drama doesn't have to end in tragedy. If the generations bring to the public square the same genius for interdependence they bring to their family lives, the policy choices become less daunting and the politics less toxic. But this optimistic scenario is by no means preordained. Social Security and Medicare are the most popular, successful domestic programs the federal government ever created. They are a profound expression of the idea that as a nation, we are a community, all in this together. For the best and most compassionate reasons, Americans of all ages oppose reducing benefits to the elderly. Yet as our population grows older and these programs consume an ever larger share of our federal budget, they pose increasingly difficult questions of generational equity. Today's young are paying taxes to support a level of benefits for today's old that they themselves have no realistic chance of receiving when *they* become old. Meantime, the cost of these programs is crowding out investments in the economic vitality of the next generation—and the entire nation. Rebalancing the entitlement programs to adapt to the demographic realities of the twenty-first century will be a massive political challenge. Even more, it will be a test of social cohesion at a time when our generations are divided by race, politics, values, religion, and technology to a degree that's rare in our history.

The story is best told through the prism of the two big generations with competing interests: the Baby Boomers, who'll be crashing through the gates of old age in record numbers for the next two decades, not nearly as well fortified financially for the journey as they'd hoped; and the Millennials, twenty-somethings who have landed back in their childhood homes in record numbers because they haven't been able to get launched in a hostile economy. In the pages ahead, you'll also meet the Gen Xers, who are navigating middle age with mounting economic anxieties about their own old age; and the Silents, the oldest and most financially secure of our four adult generations, but also the cohort most unsettled by the pace and magnitude of social change.

LONGER LIVES, FEWER BABIES, MORE IMMIGRANTS

The fundamentals of our demography are these: in 2014, about 4 million Americans will be born, roughly 1 million will arrive as immigrants, and about 2.5 million will die. "Generational replacement" is the demographer's term of art for the population change produced by this churn. In some eras the process can be relatively uneventful, but not so in the America of the early twenty-first century, when young and old are so different from each other. Of the myriad forces that bear on these numbers, none has been more inexorable or important than the rise in human longevity. Advances in health care, nutrition, and sanitation have increased life expectancy at birth in the US from 47 years in 1900 to 62 years in 1935 (the year Social Security was enacted) to 79 today to a projected 84.5 by 2050. In the first part of the twentieth century, most of the gains came as a result of improvements in the survival rate of newborns; in the second half, most gains came from medical advances that have prolonged the lives of older adults. And there's more to come. While it sounds like the stuff of science fiction, some biomedical researchers believe that by mid-century, bionic bodies embedded with computer chips and fortified by as-yet-uninvented medications will make life spans of 120 or more years attainable, perhaps even commonplace. If so, just imagine the quality-of-life issues—to say nothing of the retirement finances!—that future generations will need to sort out.

Longer life spans beget lower birthrates. As living standards improve and people grow more confident that their children will survive to adulthood, succeeding generations reduce the number of children they have. In the twentieth century, the world's population grew by nearly fourfold. In this century, however, it is expected to grow only by about another 50% before eventually stabilizing at roughly 10 billion.[1] Over the long haul, this is good news for all who worry about the sustainability of the earth's resources. But in the short and medium term, it can create social, economic, and political dislocations, especially in countries like the US that have large cohorts entering old age and smaller cohorts in the workforce. However, all of our biggest economic competitors face even more challenging age pyramids. China's median age will rise from 35 now to 46 by 2050, surpassing the projected median of 41 in the US. Germany's will be 52. And in Japan, where birthrates have been among the lowest in human history for the past generation, the market for adult diapers now exceeds the market for baby diapers. Japan's median age will be 53 by 2050. If present trends continue, there won't be nearly enough Japanese youngsters to care for its oldsters, which helps explain why Japan is the global leader these days in the development and manufacture of caretaker robots.

One way for nations to prevent the economic sclerosis that can occur when their populations age is to replenish their workforce with immigrants. In this realm, the US boasts the world's most enviable demographics. The third great wave of immigration to the US, which began when Congress reopened America's doors in 1965, is now more than 40 million strong. Based on current mortality-fertility-immigration trends, roughly 90% of the growth in the US labor force between now and mid-century will be from new immigrants and their children. Immigration waves always produce political and cultural backlashes; this one has been no exception, especially since more than a quarter of the modern-era immigrants are living here illegally. As columnist Fred Barnes has written, we have a history of hating immigrants before we love them.[2] But no nation has been better served than ours by immigration, and judging by the tens of millions of people from all over the world still clambering to come here, there's every reason to expect our long winning streak to continue.

RACE AND RELIGION

The modern immigration wave has done more than boost our economy. It has given us a racial makeover. Until the middle of the last century, our racial checkerboard was white with a smattering of black. Now it's multicolored, and whites are on a long, steep slide toward losing their majority status. Moreover, in today's America, our old racial labels are having trouble keeping up with our new weddings. More than a quarter of all recent Hispanic and Asian newlyweds married someone of a different race or ethnicity; so did 1 in 6 black and 1 in 11 white newlyweds. Not too long ago these marriages were illegal and taboo; now they barely raise an eyebrow. As these couples procreate, what race will society call their children? What will the children call themselves? For centuries we've used the "one-drop rule" to settle such questions—if you're not all white, you're not white at all. Going forward, we'll need a more nuanced taxonomy. America isn't about to go color-blind; race is too hardwired into the human psyche. But race is becoming more subtle and shaded, and most Americans (especially the young) are at ease with the change.

As noted, the new rainbow America has had a big impact on presidential politics. There's an interesting history here. After he lost the Hispanic vote in 1980, Ronald Reagan described Hispanics as "Republicans who don't know it yet." Three decades later they apparently *still* haven't figured it out. To the contrary, they've grown even more Democratic. In 2012, 71% voted for Obama (up from the 56% who voted for Jimmy Carter over Reagan in 1980), as did a record 73% of Asian Americans. Block voting is nothing new among minority groups in America; blacks have supported Democrats by even more lopsided margins for generations. But these new patterns are ominous for the GOP. Hispanics and Asians today compose 22% of the US population; by 2060 they will make up nearly 40% (while blacks will remain constant at about 13%). They embrace values common to immigrant groups—they're hardworking, family-oriented, entrepreneurial, and freedom loving—all of which, as Reagan rightly observed, could easily make them natural Republicans. Yet they also favor an active government and tend to be social liberals. And many have been put off by the anti-immigrant rhetoric of the GOP in recent years. "If we want people to like us, we have to like them first," said Bobby Jindal, the Indian-American Republican governor of Louisiana, after the 2012 election. The growing partisan divisions by race and ethnicity coincide with the growing divisions by ideology and age. These deep divisions aren't healthy for the polity; they're especially perilous for the Republicans, who find themselves on the wrong side of the new demography.

Race isn't the only demographic characteristic changing before our eyes. Religion is another. In 2012, for the first time ever, not one of the four major party candidates for president and vice president was a white Anglo-Saxon Protestant (one was black, one Mormon, two Catholic). Nor was the Speaker of the House (Catholic), the majority leader of the Senate (Mormon), or any of the nine justices of the US Supreme Court (six Catholics, three Jews). WASP dominance of our nation's political institutions pretty much peaked at the opening bell in 1776, when 55 of the 56 signers of Declaration of Independence were white Protestants. It has been falling ever since, and the pace of decline has ramped up in the half century since John F. Kennedy became the first non-WASP president in 1960 and Congress was still three-quarters Protestant (as opposed to 56% now). However, it's not just that the American public is becoming less white and less Protestant—it's also becoming less attached to religious denominations in general. A record 1 in 5 American adults today—and fully a third under the age of 30—is religiously unaffiliated. Of these so-called "nones," roughly a quarter describe themselves as atheists or agnostics; the remainder believe in God but have no religious affiliation. The US is still the most religiously observant nation among the world's great powers. But led by today's young, it's growing more pluralistic and less connected to traditional religious institutions.

A HOLLOWING OF THE MIDDLE

For the past decade and a half, America's middle class has suffered its worst economic run since the Great Depression. It has shrunk in size, fallen backward in income and wealth, and shed some—but by no means all—of its characteristic faith in the future.[3] Median household income in this country peaked in 1999 and still hasn't returned to that level, the longest stretch of stagnation in modern American history. As for median household wealth—the sum of all assets minus all debt—it has fallen by more than a third since peaking at the height of the housing bubble in 2006. Not surprisingly, an overwhelming share of Americans—85%—say it has become tougher to live a middle-class lifestyle than it was a decade ago. Yet most middle-class Americans say they have a better standard of living than their parents had at the same stage of life (the economic data bear them out) and a plurality expect their children will do even better than them. The trademark optimism of the American middle class may not be as robust as it was a decade ago, but it hasn't disappeared. It may, however, not be as well founded as it used to be.

This hollowing out of the middle has been accompanied by a sharp rise in income inequality. One standard measure is known as the Gini Index, which ranges from 0 to 1, with 0 representing perfect equality (everyone has equal income) and 1 perfect inequality (one person has all the income). In the US, the index rose to .477 in 2012 (the latest year for which such data are available) from .404 in 1980, an increase of 18%.[4] On the global scale, this means we're not as unequal as many African and South American countries, but we're more unequal than most European and Asian nations. We still think of ourselves as the land of opportunity, but a child born into poverty in Canada and most Western European countries has a statistically better chance of making it to the top these days than does a poor kid in the US.[5] The two decades after World War II were a period of declining inequality in the US—all income groups did well, but in relative terms, those at the bottom did best. Since then, all groups have done less well, and in relative terms, those at the top have done best.

Moreover, when one looks at wealth rather than income, the gaps since the 1980s have ballooned into chasms and are starkly aligned with race and age. As of 2011, the typical white household had 14 times the wealth of the typical black household (up from 7 times in the mid-1990s) and the typical older household had 26 times the wealth of the typical younger household (up from 10 times in the mid-1980s).[6] There's little evidence from public opinion

Figure 1.2

Average Annual Change in Mean Family Income, 1950–2010

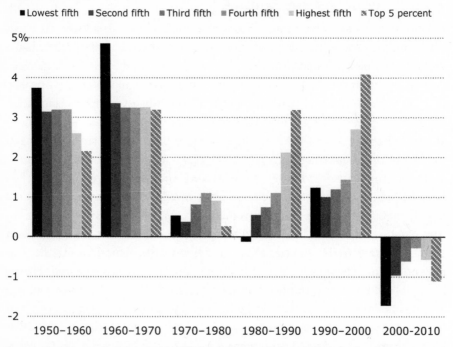

■ Lowest fifth   ■ Second fifth   ■ Third fifth   ■ Fourth fifth   ▦ Highest fifth   ▧ Top 5 percent

Source: Pew Research Center analysis of US Census Bureau, Historical Family Income Tables, Table F-3 for 1966 to 2010, and derived from Tables F-2 and F-7 for 1950 to 1965

surveys that Americans resent the rich. But in growing numbers, they resent the policies and institutions—political as well as economic—that they believe are rigged in favor of the rich.

The rise in inequality is driven in large measure by a workforce that has begun to resemble an hourglass—bulging at the top and bottom; contracting in the middle. The leading culprit is technology. Whole categories of good-paying midlevel white- and blue-collar jobs have been wiped out in recent decades, first by computers and more recently by robots. "The factory of the future will have just two workers," goes the gallows humor in manufacturing towns. "A man and a dog. The man is there to feed the dog. The dog is there to make sure the man keeps his hands off the equipment." This pessimism may prove overwrought. Over time, technological revolutions typically create more jobs than they destroy, and in a 2013 paper, economists Frank Levy and Richard

Murnane counted 3.5 million jobs—software engineers, systems analysts, data experts, and so on—created by computer technology. Most, however, demand more advanced skills and training than the middle-level jobs they replace. In America the key to preserving social and civic cohesion among a diverse population is a dynamic economy that offers plenty of work for a sprawling middle class, with lots of on-ramps from below. Today there are fewer such jobs and on-ramps. At least so far, the digital revolution has left the middle class in worse shape than it found it.

CULTURE, GENDER, MARRIAGE, FAMILY

When the Baby Boomers came of age with a great primal scream of social protest in the 1960s, the electoral backlash was immediate and enduring. In 1968 Richard Nixon won the presidency as the champion of the "silent majority"—by which he meant all the folks who *weren't* protesting. In 1972 he was reelected in a landslide over a Democratic opponent he mocked as the candidate of "acid, amnesty, and abortion." In the ensuing decades the GOP's most effective alliterative attack lines migrated a few notches down the alphabet—to god, guns, and gays—but the basic political calculus never changed. Whenever culture wars flared, Republicans profited—that is, until 2012. In that election

Figure 1.3

Views of Legalizing Marijuana: 1969–2013

% saying marijuana should be...

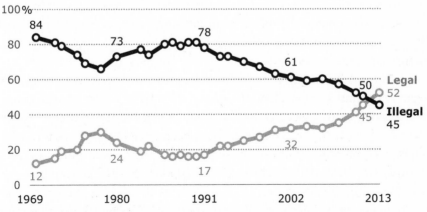

Source: Pew Research Center surveys, 2010–2013; 1973–2008 data from General Social Survey; 1969 and 1972 data from Gallup

year, gay marriage state ballot initiatives, after having gone 0-for-32 during the previous decade, went 4-for-4. Also, voters in Washington and Colorado became the first to legalize the recreational use of marijuana. And in Missouri and Indiana, Republican candidates lost eminently winnable US Senate races because of their tone-deaf remarks about rape and women's reproductive rights. To be sure, the culture wars are far from over. The landmark 2013 Supreme Court rulings that struck down the federal Defense of Marriage Act left the same-sex marriage issue to be fought out state by state, likely ensuring it will be contested terrain for a long time to come. That has been the pattern with abortion. Four decades after the court's landmark *Roe v. Wade* decision, abortion is still fiercely contested; in 2013 alone, legislatures in several dozen states tested the limits of that ruling by passing bills to tighten restrictions on abortion. But even as these moral issues continue to play differently in different states and regions, the overall trends in public opinion have put social conservatives on notice. As younger adults age into the electorate and older adults age out, the old wedge issues simply don't work the way they once did. "It's not that our message didn't get out," R. Albert Mohler Jr., president of the Southern Baptist Theological Seminary, told the *New York Times* a few days after the 2012 election. "It did get out. It's that the entire moral landscape has changed. An increasingly secularized America understands our positions, and has rejected them."[7]

One casualty of the new economic and cultural order has been traditional marriage, which has suffered a dramatic loss of market share. In 1960, 72% of all adults ages 18 and older were married; by 2011, just 51% were. In the old days, people in all social classes married at roughly the same rate; today marriage is much less prevalent at the bottom than the top. Pew Research surveys find that adults on the lower rungs are as just likely as others to say they want to marry, but they place a higher premium than others on economic security as a precondition for marriage—a threshold they themselves are unable to cross. These attitudes are self-fulfilling. Marriage brings economies of scale and a heightened commitment to financial responsibility, which means that the growing marriage deficit among poorer adults both reflects and reinforces their growing income deficits. This is worrisome for society. A large body of social science research shows that children born to single parents tend to have a more difficult path in life, even when one holds constant other socioeconomic factors.[8] The same holds for elderly adults who don't have a close relationship with their children.

As marriage has declined, gender roles have converged. Today women are the sole or primary breadwinners in 4 in 10 households with children; a half century ago, this was the case in just 1 in 10 such households. A majority of these "breadwinner moms" are unmarried, but a significant share (37%) are wives who earn more than their husbands. Men are having a tougher time than women adjusting to the demands of the modern knowledge-based economy, and it shows in the way they rank their life priorities. A 2011 Pew Research poll found that 66% of young women say that being successful in a high-paying career or profession is a very important life priority for them. That number may not seem remarkable, except for this: just 59% of young men said the same.

This reversal of traditional gender aspirations comes at a time when nearly 6 in 10 college and graduate students are female; nearly half the labor force is female; and working fathers are just as likely as working mothers to say they find it difficult to balance work and family—and more likely to say they don't spend enough time with the kids. The public overwhelmingly supports the trend toward more women in the workforce and more egalitarian marriages. Nonetheless, Americans are cross-pressured on these topics, and many traditional gender norms endure. For example, a 2013 Pew Research survey found that about half of respondents say that children are better off if the mother stays at home and doesn't hold a job, while just 8% say the same about the father. Also, twice as many Americans say it is very important for a prospective husband to be a good provider than say the same about a prospective wife.[9] In sync with those norms, the decline of marriage has been greatest in the communities where women have the greatest potential to outearn men. For example, fewer than a third of black adults today are married, down from 61% in 1960. As men and women navigate a brave new world of gender convergence, it's not clear how well the institution of marriage will survive.

Figure 1.4

Women and Men Approach Parity in Labor Force

Share of labor force that is men, women, 1970–2011

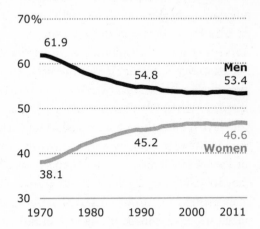

Note: Annual averages based on civilian noninstitutional population age 16 and older. For changes to the Current Population Survey (CPS) over time, see www.bls.gov/cps/eetech_methods.pdf.

Source: Pew Research Center analysis of US Bureau of Labor Statistics, "Women in the Labor Force: A Databook," Table 2, Feb. 2013

Families and living arrangements have changed, too. Nearly 3 in 10 house-holds in America today contain just one person, double the share in 1960. Among American women in their early 40s, 1 in 5 have never had children, double the share of 30 years ago. A 2013 memoir by comedian Jen Kirkman, *I Can Barely Take Care of Myself: Tales from a Happy Life Without Kids*, serves up an amusing string of anecdotes from the front lines of childlessness. ("Who'll take care of you when you're old?" "Servants!") Demographer Joel Kotkin has coined the term "post-familialism"; others talk about "the new singleism." It's a global phenomenon, having taken root not just in the US but in Canada, much of Europe, and the wealthy countries of East Asia. It's linked to urbanization, secularism, women's economic empowerment, and higher standards of living. There's a lively debate among cultural arbiters over whether it will deliver more or less happiness over the long haul for the people who make these choices. Clearly, though, it poses a dilemma for humankind as a whole. Societies with fewer young people tend to have less energy, dynamism, and innovation. Soci-eties dominated by the old risk becoming sclerotic. The old require the care of the young. If fewer people form families to play that role, then governments will need to fill more of the gap—but this is a burden they already struggle to bear.

POLARIZED POLITICS, PARTISAN MEDIA

One reason elected leaders keep postponing their rendezvous with entitlement reform is that the issue is so partisan and divisive. These days, of course, so is our entire political system. There's no evidence from decades of Pew Research surveys that public opinion, in the aggregate, is more extreme now than in the past. But what *has* changed—and pretty dramatically—is the growing ten-dency of people to sort themselves into political parties based on their ideolog-ical differences. There was a time when our big-tent political parties had room for elected officials who were liberal Republicans and conservative Democrats; nowadays, such political moderates are all but extinct. There are many causes of this political "big sort"—among them the growing tendency of people to live in economically, culturally, and politically segregated neighborhoods; the proliferation of safe-seat congressional gerrymandering; and the rise of a partisan amen chorus in the news media and twittersphere. There's also one unmistakable consequence: government gridlock. The two most recent ses-sions of Congress have by several measures been the most politically polarized and least productive in modern history, as members (especially Republicans, with their Tea Party base) worried more about staving off ideological challeng-ers from within their own parties than about forging bipartisan compromises across the aisle.[10]

RED TRUTH, BLUE TRUTH. Republicans and Democrats have always had different opinions, but these days they also seem to have different facts. Pew Research surveys in recent years have found a growing partisan gap within the public on such empirical questions as whether the world's climate is getting warmer; whether the national economy has been getting better; whether one's personal finances are improving; and whether the wars in Iraq and Afghanistan were going well.[11] Perception gaps are as ancient as the shadows on the wall of Plato's famous cave. But lately they've taken on an explicitly partisan cast—a development fueled by a change in the norms of journalism, from an era when neutral fact-based reporting was the highest calling to one in which the brightest stars in the media firmament are paid to deliver their facts premixed with partisan commentary. Why were so many smart conservative pundits flummoxed by the outcome of the 2012 election? Perhaps because they'd spent so much time during that campaign in today's version of Plato's cave, trading their "facts" back and forth in a media-saturated echo chamber of think-alike colleagues, readers, tweeters, and viewers. But to be clear, this occupational hazard isn't confined to Red Truthers. A content analysis done in late 2012 by my colleagues at the Pew Research Center's Journalism Project found that MSNBC outdid Fox News by a considerable margin in the share of its news content that was commentary rather than straight news reporting—85% versus 55%. It just so happened that, at least in 2012, the blue crystal balls had a better grip on reality than the red ones.

All these data points and trends, squeezed between the covers of one book, can create a sense of foreboding about America's future. They portray a society tugged apart by centrifugal forces. And they show that the two institutions we rely on to be repairers of the breach—the government and the family—are themselves being shaken to their core. Yet this isn't a gloom-and-doom book. There are too many findings from the Pew Research Center's surveys that give voice to the optimism, pragmatism, and resilience of the American public, even in the teeth of dysfunctional politics, rising inequality, frayed families, and anemic labor markets. America *isn't* breaking apart at the seams. The American dream isn't dying. Our new racial and ethnic complexion hasn't triggered massive outbreaks of intolerance. Our generations aren't at each other's throats. They're living more interdependently than at any time in recent memory, because that turns out to be a good coping strategy in hard times. Our nation faces huge challenges, no doubt. So do the rest of the world's aging superpowers. If you had to pick a nation with the right stuff to ride out the coming demographic storm, you'd be crazy not to choose America, warts and all.

Millennials and Boomers

MILLENNIALS AND BOOMERS are the lead characters in the looming generational showdown by dint of their vast number and strategic location in the life cycle. But what gives the drama an almost Shakespearean richness is something more: they're also each other's children and parents, bound together in an intricate web of love, support, anxiety, resentment, and interdependence. Every family, on some level, is a barter between the generations—I care for you when you're young so you'll care for me when I'm old. Every society needs to strike a similar intergenerational compact, then renegotiate the terms if the underlying demographics shift.

That's the challenge ahead. To understand it better, and to explore how these dynamics will play out in both the family and public realms, let's start by concocting a prototypical Boomer. We'll call her Jane Smith. She turns 65 in 2014, one of 10,000 members of the jumbo-sized Baby Boom Generation who'll cross that threshold *every single day* from now until 2030. If the actuaries have her pegged right, Jane's got 20 more years ahead, most of them in good health, during which time she'll collect about half a million dollars' worth of benefits from Social Security and Medicare. Like most people her age, Jane worries about her health, her finances, and her family. But thanks to these programs, she can take comfort in knowing she'll never be penniless in her old age. She'll never fully "outlive her money." She'll never go completely without medical care. And she has a good chance of never becoming a burden to her children and grandchildren. People don't measure their lives in the vast sweep of history—they live in the here and now—so Jane probably doesn't have much occasion to dwell on her good fortune. She might even assume this is what getting old has always been like. She would be wrong. In fact, she and her progeny are about to become the beneficiaries of a radical improvement in old age that's not much older than she is: a publicly financed social safety net that eases some (though by no means all) of the frets and dreads of the golden years.

Of course, nothing in life is free. Some back-of-the-envelope calculations show just who'll be picking up the roughly $500,000 public tab for Jane's old age. During the more than 35 years she worked in various clerical jobs and earned the median wage, Jane paid the equivalent of about $180,000 in Social Security and Medicare taxes, and her employers matched that with another $180,000 (though, by standard economic theory, that share also came out of Jane's pocket in foregone wages). As for the unfunded gap of about $140,000, well, that'll have to be covered by America's taxpayers, today's and tomorrow's.[1]

As it happens, one of them is Jane's youngest child, John Jr., 29. Junior had the bad timing to start his work life just as the national economy went into a tailspin. After bouncing in and out of a run of low-wage, dead-end jobs, he's scraping together a living as a freelance website designer. In 2014 he'll take in about $22,000. Thanks to the deductions he qualifies for, Junior will owe no federal income taxes. Not a penny will come out of his pocket to pay for the nation's soldiers, veterans, food safety inspectors, border patrol agents, diplomats, spies, or cancer researchers. However, Junior *will* have to fork over more than $3,300 in Social Security and Medicare taxes this year to help underwrite the social safety net that he hopes will one day support him in his old age—but that for now supports his mother and the more than 40 million other beneficiaries her age and older.

In his own small way, then, Junior is helping to bankroll Mom. But that's only half their story. Mom is also bankrolling Junior. He boomeranged back to her home two years ago, when the mortgage insurance company where he'd been working as an appraiser's assistant succumbed to the housing bust. He's now living rent-free in his childhood bedroom, amid his faded soccer ribbons, creaky PlayStation, and zany graduation-day photos. This wasn't Plan A, but it has been a pretty useful Plan B. He gets along fine with Mom, even better now than when he was growing up. The refrigerator is stocked, the laundry service free. Plus, he's fortified by an almost eerie certitude that he'll eventually land a good job, launch a career, move into his own place, find a wife, and start a family. In short, all of Junior's dreams are still intact—but on hold.

Had he come of age a generation earlier, it would have been considered strange for Junior to be hunkering down at his mom's home at this stage of life. Nowadays, there's barely a stigma. Forty percent of all Millennial men ages

18 to 31 (and 32% of all young women that age) were living in their parents' homes in 2012, the highest share in modern history. Call it what you will—post-adolescence, pre-adulthood—it's become so hardwired into the zeitgeist of coming of age in the new millennium that it's already the subject of its own genre of books, movies, sitcoms, reality shows, and PhD dissertations.

But there's not yet a settled take on the phenomenon. Millenial novelist Haley Tanner writes gloomily about her generation "wandering in the purgatorial landscape of postgraduate inertia, premarital indecision, and proto-careerist yearning." Most commentators blame the wretched economy. Boomer author Sally Koslow sees other aggravating circumstances. She goes after Boomer parents who, she believes, are foisting onto their children their own neuroses about getting old. "Boomers' fury at the very idea that we have to age sends a subliminal message that there will always be time for our kids to get another degree or surf another couch, to break up with one more partner or employer, and to wait around to reproduce, while ignoring the reality that opportunities will evaporate," she writes. "If parents aren't old—and who among us doesn't feel 35?—if parents aren't old, with our titanium joints and botox, how can we expect our kids to grow up?" Koslow is the author of *Slouching toward Adulthood: Observations from the Not-So-Empty Nest*, and also pens advice columns for women who date men who live at home. Meantime, over at the Adult Children Living at Home website, the practical advice is for the parents, not the girlfriends. Rule one: Establish ground rules to cover who pays for what. Rule two: Decide in advance if overnight guests are permitted. Psychologist Carl Pickhardt, author of *Boomerang Kids*, reminds parents that there's a fine line between supporting and enabling. He encourages them to create an atmosphere of "constructive discomfort" by charging their Boomerangers rent and setting a departure date.

Family historian Stephanie Coontz finds some silver linings in the boomerang phenomenon; she argues that young people who postpone the major transitions to adulthood tend to wind up with more durable marriages and more stable careers than their early-maturing counterparts. That analysis gets no love from social commentator Kay S. Hymowitz, who takes a dim view of delayed adulthood, especially when celebrated in movies starring the likes of Adam Sandler, Will Ferrell, Jack Black, Luke Wilson, Vince Vaughn, Zach Galifianakis, Steve Carell, Seth Rogen, or Jonah Hill, whose characters typically flounder around without life scripts, career direction, or the wit to see women as anything other than disposable estrogen playthings. This generation of leading men is a pretty steep downgrade from the glory days of cinema, when Gary Cooper, Clark Gable, Humphrey Bogart, John Wayne, Jimmy Stewart, and Cary Grant set the cultural norms for manhood. Hymowitz, for one, is unamused. Her terse advice to today's male slackers, whether cracking wise on the silver screen or surfing on their parents' couch: "Man up!"

All of this makes twenty-something romance, courtship, and sex something of a minefield. In *F*ck, I'm in My Twenties*, author Emma Koenig bares her serial heartbreaks ("There should be some kind of loyalty rewards program for getting hurt over and over again"). But it's not just guys who can be commitment-phobic slackers. As author Donna Freitas tells it in *The End of Sex: How Hookup Culture Is Leaving a Generation Unhappy, Sexually Unfulfilled, and Confused about Intimacy*, the sex-without-attachment rules apply equally these days to young men and women—and leave both genders emotionally shortchanged. In the hit HBO series *Girls,* the opening scene of the first episode had Hannah (played by show creator Lena Dunham) throwing a fit when her parents announce they're cutting off her monthly checks. The show follows Hannah (the self-described "voice of my generation") and her angst-ridden girlfriends as they navigate awkward sex, dead-end relationships, lousy internships, and oceans of self-pity in the gritty never-never land between childhood and adulthood. For yet another pop culture exposition on growing up Millennial—this one with a quirky, intergenerational twist—there's GrannyIsMyWingman.com by Kayli Stollak. Launched as a blog in 2011, it has since morphed into a book and possible TV series. It features Stollak and her septuagenarian grandmother, Gail—a "shit-talking, straight-shooting, adventure-seeking, gossipy yenta"—dishing with one another about their romantic adventures, good and bad, online and off.

Will the Boomerangers ever grow up? Eventually, perhaps, but not just yet. More than 4 in 10 of today's twenty-somethings, like Junior, have returned home to live with their parent(s) at some stage of their young adult lives. As for marriage—for now, fuhgeddaboudit. Back when Jane was the age Junior is now, about half of all twenty-somethings in America were married. Today about 20% are. The Millennials' two seemingly incompatible characteristics— their slow walk to adulthood and their unshaken confidence in the future— are their most distinctive traits. Despite inheriting the worst economy since the Great Depression, despite rates of youth un- and underemployment that are the highest since the government began keeping such records, despite the growing albatross of student loan debt, and despite not being able to think about starting a family of their own, Millennials are America's most stubborn optimists. They have a self-confidence born of coddling parents and everyone-gets-a-trophy coaches. They have a look-at-me elan that comes from being humankind's first generation of digital natives (before them, nobody knew that the whole world wanted to see your funny cat photos).[2] And they have the invincibility of youth. For all those reasons, Millennials are far more bullish than their better-off elders about their financial future. Even as they struggle to find jobs and launch careers, even as 4 in 10 describe themselves as being in the lower or lower middle classes (a higher share than any other generation), nearly 9 in 10 say they already have or one day will have enough money to meet their financial needs. No other generation is nearly as optimistic.

Jeffrey Jensen Arnett, a psychology professor at Clark University in Worcester, Massachusetts, and an expert on twenty-somethings, ascribes their optimism to their lack of life experience. "The dreary, dead-end jobs, the bitter divorces, the disappointing and disrespectful children . . . none of them imagine that this is what the future holds for them," he writes. In an interview with Robin Marantz Henig for a *New York Times Magazine* article, Arnett elaborated: "Ask them if they agree with the statement 'I am very sure that someday I will get to where I want to be in life,' and 96 percent of them will say yes. . . . But despite elements that are exciting, even exhilarating, about being this age, there is a downside, too: dread, frustration, uncertainty, a sense of not quite understanding the rules of the game." Arnett says that what he hears most often from young adults is ambivalence; 60 percent of his subjects tell him they felt like both grown-ups and not-quite-grown-ups.[3]

When it comes to their economic prospects, are they clueless Peter Pans on course for an unhappy rendezvous with reality? There's no shortage of elders who fear exactly that. "We have a monster jobs problem, and young people are the biggest losers," says Andrew Sum, director of the Center for Labor Market Studies at Northeastern University, who predicts the specter of unemployment will "haunt young people for at least another decade. . . . It almost makes you want to cry for the future of our country." Harvard economist Richard Freeman says today's young adults "will be scarred and they will be called 'the lost generation'—in that their careers would not be the same had they avoided this economic disaster." These and other pessimists believe America's unemployment crisis is as much structural as cyclical—a by-product of a witch's brew of globalization, automation, foreign competition, and a faltering education system. Millennials, they worry, are on track to become the first generation in American history to do less well in life than their parents.

All of these challenges will be exacerbated once the nation has to start coping with the full cost of the retirement of 76 million Boomers. The oldest turned 65 in 2011. By the time the youngest cross that threshold in 2030, America's age pyramid will take on a shape it has never had before. About 1 in 5 Americans will be 65 or older, up from 1 in 7 now. The number of retirees on Social Security and Medicare will rise to about 80 million by 2030, roughly double the figure in 2000. Among them, the fastest growing cohort will be the "old-old." The number of seniors ages 85 and older is expected to more than triple between now and 2050, to 19 million. Fewer workers supporting more of the old and old-old isn't much of a formula for economic growth, standard of living gains, or social comity. "It's like a seesaw—if one side is up, the other side has to be down," says Andrew Biggs, a former deputy commissioner of the Social Security Administration, of the challenge of preserving a safety net for the old without bankrupting the young. "Nobody wants to do the actual things you have to do so you don't screw your kids on this stuff."

THE BOOMERS

At 76 million and 80 million strong, respectively, Boomers and Millennials are the biggest of the four living generations—each significantly larger than the generation that came before. In the case of Boomers, the population bulge is the product of a spike in births that began right after World War II and ended right after the introduction of the birth control pill. Those 19 years were a time when the American economy was a colossus astride the world and its middle class was living in what was then unimaginable luxury (washing machines! Levittowns! color TVs!). The typical Boomer's mother had three children—one more than the mothers of the previous generation or than any generation since. In the case of Millennials, the big numbers are the product not of high fertility rates but of renewed immigration flows (though immigrant women have about 50% more children than do native-born women, so the two phenomena are related).

As Millennials are entering the workforce, Boomers are entering retirement (although many in both generations will cross these milestones later rather than sooner, thanks to hard times, bad choices, or both). This juxtaposition alone sets up a potential conflict: some of the jobs Boomers aren't leaving are the same jobs Millennials aren't getting.

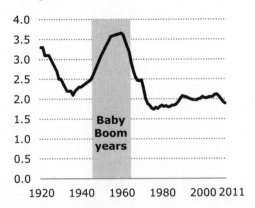

Figure 2.1

The Baby Boom

Estimated lifetime births among US women, 1920–2011

Baby Boom years

Note: Based on the Total Fertility Rate (TFR). While the TFR is extremely sensitive to shifts in birth timings, it tracks closely with the General Fertility Rate (GFR) throughout this period.

Source: Pew Research Center analysis of National Center for Health Statistics data

But the conflict has more to it than that. "Generation Screwed" was the headline on a 2012 *Newsweek* article by demographer Joel Kotkin. The sub-head: "Boomer America Never Had It So Good. As a Result, Today's Young Americans Have Never Had It So Bad." His piece used data from Pew Research and other sources to put a zero-sum-game frame around the diverging economic fortunes of the young and old, the topic of Chapter 4. For now, another element of the Kotkin critique commands attention. Boomers these days are a generation that seems to relish public self-flagellation. A brief sampler, with all of the lashes delivered by Boomers themselves:

> " . . . a grasshopper generation, eating through just about everything like hungry locusts." —Thomas Friedman, *New York Times* columnist

> " . . . squander[ed] the legacy handed to them by the generation from World War II." —Documentary filmmaker Ken Burns

> " . . . the most self-centered, self-seeking, self-interested, self-absorbed, self-indulgent, self-aggrandizing generation in American history." —Paul Begala, TV pundit and former speechwriter for Bill Clinton

> "Thanks to the '60s, we are all shamelessly selfish." —Kurt Andersen, author and social critic

For those who want more, there's always BoomerDeathwatch.com ("Because one day, they'll all be dead") or DieBoomerDie.blogspot.com ("There is no political left or right, only failed baby boomer leadership"). The bashing more typically comes from the Right than the Left, and has ever since the late 1960s, when Boomers held their famous counterculture coming-out party on Max Yasgur's farm near Woodstock, New York, an outdoor rock concert that was either "An Aquarian Exposition: 3 Days of Peace and Music" (so said the iconic poster) or a dystopian homage to drugs, sex, and mud (so said the critics). Boomer culture wars have flared up in fits and starts ever since. But right from the get-go, Boomers themselves have always been on both sides. The same generation that fought the war in Vietnam also stormed the dean's office to protest it (and the military draft that cast such a shadow over their coming-of-age years). The same generation that was in the vanguard of the civil rights, women's rights, and free love movements also gave more votes in 1972 (the first year 18-year-olds could vote) for conservative Richard Nixon than for liberal George McGovern. As columnist Gregory Rodriguez once drily observed, one need only glance at Supreme Court Justice Samuel Alito Jr.'s wonky 1971 Princeton yearbook photo to recall that not all Boomers back then were long-haired hippies. Now fast forward four decades later. When card-carrying Boomer Bill Keller, a columnist and former executive editor of the *New York Times*, labeled his generation an "entitled bunch" and called for them to accept cuts in their retirement benefits, he got an earful from Boomer Leonard Steinhorn, author of *The Greater Generation: In Defense of the Baby Boom Legacy*. Steinhorn wrote:

> In the early 1980s, before most Boomers started raising families, they were called too selfish to have children. Then, when Boomers turned out to be pretty good and selfless parents, they were accused of getting too involved in their kids' lives. Boomers have been accused of creating cultural chaos through moral relativism. Then, when Boomers came of age and declared bigotry of any kind immoral, they were accused of being too politically correct. . . . When the World War II generation was about to retire, no one blamed them for the Vietnam War, their discrimination against blacks, women, and gays, or their pollution of our waterways and air.

Maybe it's time we navel-gazing Boomers (myself included) declare a cease-fire and stipulate that we all have lots to be proud of—and to be embarrassed by. And to acknowledge that as we've gotten older, the most pressing debates about our generation have evolved from the personal and moral to the political and economic. Many of the old culture wars have died down—and Steinhorn gets that part of the story right. When it comes to promoting tolerance over bigotry, the Boomers won. And because we won, America won. But now the entitlement wars are heating up, and here Keller and his fellow critics have it right. When the oldest Boomers entered the workforce and started to pay taxes in the late 1960s, the national debt was measured in the mere billions. It crossed $1 trillion for the first time in 1981, just as the youngest of the Boomers were graduating from high school. Today it stands at $17 trillion and counting. (A better apples-to-apples time trend measures national debt as a share of gross domestic product. This figure peaked at 122% in 1946 as the federal government borrowed heavily to wage World War II. It subsequently dropped to 33% by 1981 but has been rising ever since. It currently stands at about 100% of GDP.) Boomers are by no means the only guilty parties. But this generation, more than any other in American history, has passed through its economically active years not paying the full tab for the goods and services it has asked for and gotten from the government. Its children and grandchildren have been left holding the bill.

A lot of Boomers are angry about this. If it was their passivity and profligacy that allowed the problem to get out of hand in the first place, it's now their frustration over the size of the federal debt that has helped to fuel the Tea Party and the rise of small-government conservatism. "It's not moral for my generation to keep spending massively more than we take in, knowing those burdens are going to be passed on to the next generation, and they're going to be paying the interest and principal all their lives," said 65-year-old presidential candidate Mitt Romney during the 2012 campaign. But as Boomers have grown more fiscally and politically conservative over time, they're also dealing with life-cycle transitions that make them unlikely warriors in the political battle to restrain the growth of the social safety net for seniors. More so than other generations, they're worried about money. And they're just plain downbeat about life.

"Baby Boomers Approach 65—Glumly" is the title of a Pew Research report published on December 20, 2010—12 days before the first of the Boomers turned 65. It began: "The iconic image of the baby boom generation is a 1960s-era snapshot of an exuberant, long-haired, rebellious young adult. That portrait wasn't entirely accurate even then, but it's hopelessly out of date now. This famously huge cohort of Americans finds itself in a collective funk as it approaches old age." The report assembled data on attitudes about life satisfaction, economic mobility, confidence in retirement financing, and optimism about the nation's economic futures to show that, across the board, Boomers were gloomier than other generations. This, despite the fact that most were at or near their peak earning years (at the time, they were ages 46 to 64).

Some of the pessimism is related to the life cycle. For most people, middle age is the most stressful time of life.[4] This has been especially true for Boomers, who are more likely than previous middle-agers to be juggling the needs of adult children and aging parents. But middle age doesn't appear to be the only culprit. Other longitudinal research, drawn from three decades of data from the General Social Survey, suggests that Boomers have experienced less happiness on average than have other generations over the entire span of their lives. One theory, advanced by University of Chicago sociologist Yang Yang and others, holds that the very size of the Boomer cohort has led to a lifetime of stressful intragenerational competition for a limited share of top spots in schools, colleges, and careers.[5]

It's also possible that the seeds of Boomers' current malaise were planted long ago, but for a different reason: they're having trouble getting their minds around the idea that they aren't young anymore. Remember, this is the only generation in history to become famous just for being born (witness the name). A 1947 *Washington Post* article heralded the start of the nation's post–World War II wave of fecundity as one of the "fruits of demobilization"—and went on to confidently but mistakenly assure readers that it wouldn't last long. Two decades later, Boomers became even more famous just for being young adults; a 1966 *Time* magazine cover story enshrined "Twenty-five and Under" Americans as the Man of the Year, a distinction typically reserved for presidents, generals, inventors, or Nobel laureates. The journalistic instinct was spot on. Back then, as Boomers reveled in their youth and idealism, they were the world's change agents. In some realms, they've succeeded. In others, life has gotten in the way. But whatever the final score, this much is clear: a generation famous for being young ain't young no more. And it's a bummer.

THE MILLENNIALS

In the decades since Boomers first came bounding onto the national stage, no generation of young adults had made nearly as loud an entrance—until now. Meet the Millennials: liberal, diverse, tolerant, narcissistic, coddled, respectful, confident, and broke.

If timing is everything, Millennials have known a mix of good and bad fortune. By lottery of birth timing, they're the world's first generation of digital natives. Adapting to new technology is hardwired into their generational DNA (more about that in Chapter 10), and while it's impossible to forecast where the digital and social media revolutions will take humankind, it seems safe to predict that Millennials will get there first. They are also the most racially and ethnically diverse generation in American history, a profile that should serve them (and the rest of the US) well in a multicolored world engulfed by cultural, ethnic, and religious divisions (see Chapter 7). On the downside, they're the first generation in American history in danger of having a lower standard of living than the one their parents enjoyed (see Chapter 5). On all these fronts, timing has played a central role.

Millennials' political views (see Chapter 4) have been forged by these distinctive identities and experiences. First, though, a few words about a debate among scholars over a related question: Are they on track to become America's next great civic generation? That was the prediction advanced by generational scholars William Strauss and Neil Howe when they published *Millennials Rising* in 2000, just as the oldest of the Millennials were turning 18. Relying on interviews with teenagers and data about decreases in teen pregnancy, alcohol and drug abuse, dropout rates, crime, and other antisocial behaviors, they posited that the new generation would resemble the Greatest Generation (born before 1928)—a pattern foreordained by the authors' four-phase cycle of history. Millennials would be conformist, socially conservative, involved in their communities, and interested in government. Their book started a genre. Since then numerous journalists and authors have promoted this civic portrait of Millennials, exemplified by such books as *Generation We* by Eric Greenberg and Karl Weber.

But it hasn't taken long for revisionism to set in. A *Time* magazine cover in 2013 pegged Millennials as "The Me Me Me Generation"—"lazy, entitled narcissists still living with their parents." (In classic newsmagazine style, the cover added a cheeky hedge: "Why they'll save us all.") The "me me me" meme isn't new. It was first put forth nearly a decade ago by psychologist Jean Twenge, a San Diego State University psychology professor whose 2006 book, *Generation Me*, analyzed surveys of young people dating back to the 1920s and showed a long-term cultural shift toward high self-esteem, self-importance, and narcissism. In follow-up work, she found that Millennials are less likely than Boomers and Generation Xers had been as young adults to exhibit values such as social trust and civic engagement and behaviors such as contacting public officials or working on political, social, or environmental causes. She did find an overall increase in volunteerism, though she noted it has come at a time when more high schools are requiring their students to do some sort of community service to graduate. Twenge expanded her critique in a 2009 book, *The Narcissism Epidemic,* cowritten with W. Keith Campbell. It cast a jaundiced eye across all precincts of the modern celebrity culture but reserved a particularly disapproving glare for the everyone-gets-a-trophy school of child rearing that has come into vogue in the modern era. Twenge's research found that college students in 2009 were significantly more likely than their counterparts in 1966 to rate themselves above average in writing and math skills—despite the fact that SAT scores decreased slightly during that same period. As she and many others have noted, the parental coddling often persists beyond adolescence. College deans nowadays complain that the hardest part of freshman orientation week isn't getting the new students to feel comfortable staying—it's getting the "helicopter parents" to feel comfortable leaving. Some schools even provide separation-anxiety seminars for Mom and Dad, but that doesn't keep some from calling professors during the academic year to complain about their child's grades.

I'll leave it to the experts to untangle the psychological roots of such behaviors. My own guess is that the mix of global terrorism, digital "stranger danger," the Columbine school shooting, 9/11, Newtown, media hype, and fewer kids per family have thrust parents' biologically normal protective instincts into overdrive. These same factors may also be responsible for the low levels of social trust among Millennials themselves. If you were born in 1984, you were in middle school when the Columbine massacre happened; in high school on 9/11/01; and perhaps just about to become a parent for the first time when the young children of Newtown were struck down. Evil of that magnitude leaves a mark.

Then there's the Internet and social media—the first communication platform in human history that enables anyone to reach everyone. Suppose your buddy shot a video of you bouncing so high on your backyard trampoline that you got stuck briefly in a tree? Back in the dark ages (pre-2005 or so) you might have shown it to a few friends as you yukked it up over some beers. Now you post it on YouTube and Facebook and hope it goes viral. At which point hundreds may see it. Or thousands. Or tens of millions.[6] This outlet for personal expression and empowerment may help to explain their look-at-me tendencies—which find an offline analog in their fondness for tattoos. Back in the day, tattoos were the body wear of sailors, hookers, and strippers. Today they've become a mainstream identity badge for Millennials. Nearly 4 in 10 (38%) have at least one. Gen Xers are not far behind; 32% say they have a tattoo. Only 15% of Baby Boomers and 6% of Silents wear body art. And by the way, for Millennials, one tattoo often isn't enough. Half of all tattooed Millennials have 2 to 5, and 18% have 6 or more.

When it comes to civic engagement, the data on Millennials are mixed. They match their elders on some measures of volunteering and contacting public officials, but lag behind on voting. The voter turnout deficit is largely a life-stage phenomenon; previous generations of young adults also turned out at much lower rates than their elders. In 2008 and 2102, Millennials narrowed the turnout gap—a testament to Obama's strong personal appeal to the young. But in the midterm election of 2010, with Obama not on the ballot, the young stayed home in droves.

As for volunteering, a 2010 Pew Research survey found that 57% of Millennials said they had done so in the past 12 months, compared with 54% of Gen Xers, 52% of Baby Boomers and 39% of Silents.[7] Pew Research surveys also find that Millennials are about as likely as other generations to say they had signed some sort of petition in the past year, but are less likely than Boomers and Xers to say they'd contacted a government official. Once again, there's a life-cycle effect; people start reaching out to their elected officials when they have families, children, jobs, and homes. Lots of Millennials aren't there yet.

That's true of nearly all aspects of this generation's life story. It's still a work in progress. The question is whether their futures will be enhanced or encumbered by choices their elders are making now.

Generation Gaps

YOUNG AND OLD IN AMERICA are poles apart. Demographically, politically, economically, socially, and technologically, the generations are more different from each other now than at any time in living memory. Let us count (some of) the ways:

- *They have a different racial and ethnic makeup.* Nearly half of all children in America today are nonwhite. So are 4 in 10 members of the Millennial Generation—but just 1 in 5 members of the Silent Generation and about 1 in 4 Baby Boomers.
- *They vote differently.* In 2012 Obama won 60% of the Millennial vote and just 44% of the Silent Generation vote. This young/old voting gap was just a few notches below its historic peak of 21 percentage points in 2008. Throughout the 1980s and 1990s, the age gap was either small or nonexistent. And in the 1992 and 2000 presidential elections, oldsters actually voted slightly more Democratic than youngsters.
- *Their economic fortunes have diverged.* In 1984 the typical household headed by someone 65 or older had 10 times the net worth of the typical household headed by someone under the age of 35. By 2011 that ratio had ballooned to 26:1.
- *Their families are different.* In 1960, 6 in 10 twenty-somethings were married. Today just 2 in 10 are married. In 1960 just 5% of children were born to an unmarried mother. Today 41% are.
- *Their gender roles are converging.* Until a few decades ago, becoming a man meant becoming the family breadwinner. Today some

4 in 10 children have a mother who is either the family's sole or primary breadwinner, up from 11% in 1960. Nearly 60% of college students are women, and in a knowledge-based economy that pays no premium for male strength, women are now nearly half of the labor force, leaving many young men struggling to find careers and life scripts—and many young women faced with a choice of "marrying down" or staying single.

- *They have different ideas about the role of government.* Six in 10 Silents prefer a smaller government that provides fewer services to a bigger government that provides more services. Just a third of Millennials agree.
- *They have a different view of religion.* A third of Millennials are unaffiliated with any religion, compared with 9% of Silents, 15% of Boomers, and 21% of Gen Xers. Millennials are the least religiously connected generation in modern American history.
- *They have different views about American exceptionalism.* Two-thirds of Silents say the US is the greatest country in the world; just one-third of Millennials agree. However, Millennials are much more likely than Silents to say that life in America has improved in the past half century.
- *They have a different take on the digital revolution.* Eight in 10 Millennials say the Internet has changed life for the better. Fewer than half of Silents agree.
- *They have different appetites for news.* On a typical day, Millennials spend only about half as much time as Silents consuming news (46 minutes versus 84 minutes). While this is related in part to their phase of the life cycle, Millennials are consuming less news than older generations did when they were younger.

Generation gaps are hardly a novelty. Nearly two centuries ago Alexis de Tocqueville marveled that in America "each generation is a new people." Perhaps more so perhaps than any society in history, our country has always embraced change, making it a hothouse for young adults who have a different worldview from their parents and grandparents. But the current gap is unusually large—and for the reasons spelled out in the previous chapter, potentially fraught. This chapter will look at the new generation gaps through the prism of today's four living generations: the Millennials (born after 1980), the Gen Xers (born from 1965 to 1980), the Baby Boomers (born from 1946 to 1964), and the Silents (born before 1946).

Figure 3.1

The Young/Old Voting Gap, 1972–2012

% voting for Democratic candidate

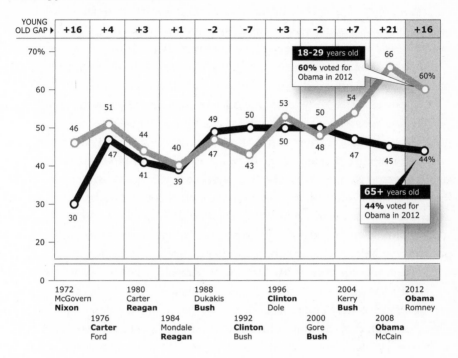

YOUNG OLD GAP ▶	+16	+4	+3	+1	-2	-7	+3	-2	+7	+21	+16

Note: From 1972 through 1988 oldest age category is 60 and older.

Source: Based on exit polls. 1972 and 1976: CBS. 1980–1988: CBS/New York Times. 1992: Voter Research & Surveys. 1996 and 2000: Voter News Service. 2004–2012: National Election Pool

GENERALIZATIONS ABOUT GENERATIONS

As a branch of demography, generational analysis has always been a bit of a step-child. It rests on the premise that members of the same generation experience the same historical events at roughly the same stage of their life cycle, and as a result share what might loosely be called a generational persona, one that's also shaped by (and in reaction to) the persona of their parents' generation. In the early twentieth century, Hungarian-born sociologist Karl Mannheim wrote a seminal essay that helped to legitimize generational analysis as a scholarly pursuit. In modern times, American historians Neil Howe and William Strauss expanded on Mannheim's theories by compressing 500 years of Anglo-Saxon history into an overarching generational frame. In their schema, four archetypal generational personas (idealist, reactive, civic, and adaptive) recur in repeating 80-year cycles, with each holding sway for about 20 years before yielding to its successor. They categorize Millennials—America's 14th generation—as civic; Xers as reactive; Boomers as idealistic; and Silents as adaptive. Their work has been popular in part because it helps employers and educators anticipate and plan for the distinctive characteristics of their future workers and students. But it has also attracted critics who find it too rigid and formulaic.

As long as one acknowledges the obvious—that there are as many different personality types *within* a generation as across generations—I see some value in generalizations about generations. All of us know people who bear the marks of their distinctive coming-of-age experiences: the grandmother raised during the Depression who still reuses her tea bags; the uncle who grew up in the 1960s and still sports a ponytail; the kid sister who sends 200 texts a day to her many, many best friends. At the same time, one should bring healthy doses of humility and caution to the exercise. That's because in one sense, it's too easy, and in another, too hard. It's too easy because no one needs a scientific survey to persuade them that the typical 20-year-old, 40-year-old, 60-year-old, and 80-year-old are different from one another. They already know. It's too hard because we can never completely disentangle the many reasons for the differences. At any given moment, they can arise from any of three overlapping processes.

1. Life cycle effects. Young people may be different from older people today, but they may become more like them tomorrow, as they themselves age.
2. Period effects. Major historical events (wars, social movements, booms, busts, religious awakenings, medical, scientific, and technological breakthroughs) affect all age groups, but the depth of impact may differ according to where people are located in the life cycle.
3. Cohort effects. Period events often leave a particularly deep impression on the young, who are still forming their core values and worldviews.

Pew Research surveys allow for comparisons between today's young and today's old. And because we've asked the same questions over many years, we can also compare today's young with yesterday's young. We can do the same with census, economic, and election data. Taken together, these numbers paint a picture of a society not with generation gaps but with generation chasms. To understand it better, let's start with thumbnail sketches.

THE MILLENNIALS (born after 1980). Empowered by digital technology; coddled by parents; respectful of elders; slow to adulthood; conflict-averse; at ease with racial, ethnic, and sexual diversity; confident in their economic futures despite coming of age in bad times. Icons: Mark Zuckerberg, Lena Dunham, LeBron James, Carrie Underwood, Jennifer Lawrence, Lady Gaga.

GEN XERS (born from 1965 to 1980). Savvy, entrepreneurial loners. Distrustful of institutions, especially government. Children of the Reagan revolution—and the divorce revolution. More comfortable than their elders with an increasingly diverse America. Icons: Quentin Tarantino, Will Smith, Adam Sandler, Tiger Woods, Robert Downey Jr.

BABY BOOMERS (born from 1946 to 1964). As exuberant youths, led the countercultural upheavals of the 1960s. But the iconic image of that era—long-haired hippie protesters—describes only a portion of the cohort. Now on the front stoop of old age, Boomers are gloomy about their lives, worried about retirement, and wondering why they aren't young anymore. Icons: Bill and Hillary Clinton, George W. Bush, Barack Obama, Steve Jobs, Tom Hanks.

SILENT GENERATION (born from 1928 to 1945). Conservative and conformist, Silents are uneasy with the pace of demographic, cultural, and technological change—and with the growing size of government. But hands off their Social Security and Medicare! Icons: Clint Eastwood, Neil Armstrong, Marilyn Monroe, Tom Brokaw, Hugh Hefner.

Most members of each of these four age groups say their own generation has a unique and distinctive identity, according to a 2010 Pew Research Center survey. But each gives a different set of reasons for their distinctiveness. In response to an open-ended question, Millennials stressed their use of technology. Gen Xers did as well, but many fewer offered that explanation. Boomers cited their work ethic and Silents their shared coming-of-age experience in the Depression and World War II.

A different Pew Research survey, this one taken in 2009, asked Americans of all ages whether they saw a generation gap in America between young and old. About 8 in 10 said yes, nearly identical to the share that had said the same back in 1969, when the generations were famously at each other's throats. But

Figure 3.2

What Makes Your Generation Unique?

Millennial

Technology use (24%)

Music/Pop culture (11%)

Liberal/Tolerant (7%)

Smarter (6%)

Clothes (5%)

Gen X

Technology use (12%)

Work ethic (11%)

Conservative/Traditional (7%)

Smarter (6%)

Respectful (5%)

Boomer

Work ethic (17%)

Respectful (14%)

Values/Morals (8%)

"Baby Boomers" (6%)

Smarter (5%)

Silent

WWII, Depression (14%)

Smarter (13%)

Honest (12%)

Work ethic (10%)

Values/Morals (10%)

Note: Based on respondents who said their generation was unique/distinct (n=1,205). Items represent individual, open-ended responses. Top five responses are shown for each age group.

Source: Pew Research Center survey, Jan. 2010, N=2,020 US adults

in the modern era, as follow-up survey questions in 2009 and 2012 made clear, the generation gap isn't seen as a source of great friction. Many fewer Americans said they see strong conflicts between young and old than said the same about conflicts between immigrants and the native-born, rich and poor, black and white, and Republicans and Democrats. And what generation gaps they do see tend to be focused on technology and lifestyle rather than on the more polarizing terrain of politics (see appendix Figure 3A.1).

THE POLITICS OF THE GENERATION GAP

In the past four national elections, generational differences have mattered more than at any other time in modern history. In each election since 2004, younger people have voted substantially more Democratic than other age groups, while older voters have cast more ballots for Republican candidates in each election since 2008. The greater liberalism of the young and conservatism of the old in part reflect the differences in their racial and ethnic profiles. Young voters are more likely than older ones to be nonwhite, and nonwhites are more likely to be Democrats and liberals. Political polls also find that older generations—Boomers and especially Silents—do not fully embrace racial diversity. For many Silents in particular, President Obama himself appears to be an unwelcome symbol of the way the face of America has changed. Surveys taken in 2011 and 2012 found that feelings of "unease" with Obama, along with higher levels of anger toward government, are the emotions that most differentiate the attitudes of Silents from those of the youngest generation. Here's a look at the political views of the four generations:

THE SILENT GENERATION

The Silent Generation came of age in the Truman, Eisenhower, and Kennedy years. They had divided partisan allegiances in the 1990s but have become much more Republican in recent years. As the nation's current cohort of older adults, they have all but "replaced" the Greatest Generation (born before 1928), who were more reliably Democratic voters throughout their political lives, but who have now largely passed from the scene.

Silents hold the most consistently conservative views among any generation about government, social issues, and America's place in the world. An overwhelming majority of Silents say they are either angry or frustrated with government. They are a generation that strongly

Figure 3.3

Group Conflicts

% saying there are "very strong/strong conflicts" between...

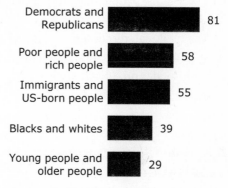

Democrats and Republicans	81
Poor people and rich people	58
Immigrants and US-born people	55
Blacks and whites	39
Young people and older people	29

Source: Pew Research Center survey, Nov.–Dec. 2012, N=2,511 US adults

Figure 3.4

The Silent Generation

Born: 1928 to 1945

Turned 18 in: 1946 to 1963

Age on Jan. 1, 2014: 68–85

- Conservative views on government and society for most of their lives
- Once one of the most Democratic generations, today they are the most Republican
- More uncomfortable than younger people with many social changes, including racial diversity and homosexuality
- Highly engaged in 2012 election, as in 2010
- More likely to rate Social Security as top voting issue
- Favor Republicans on most issues, but not Social Security

Source: Pew Research Center surveys and US Census Bureau data disapproves of Barack Obama, for whom most did not vote. Silents also are the most politically energized generation, as demonstrated by their heavy turnout, relative to other age groups, in the 2010 midterm election.

More often than the younger generations, Silents take the American exceptionalist view that the United States is *the* greatest nation in the world. But fewer older people than young people think that "America's best days are ahead of us."

The political discontent of the Silent Generation is not economically based. A greater proportion of Silents than younger people say they are financially satisfied, and Silents are less likely to say they often don't have enough money to make ends meet.

Race is a factor in their political attitudes. Silents are the whitest of the generations and are the least accepting of the new face of America. Compared with younger generations, relatively few Silents see racial intermarriage and the growing population of immigrants as changes for the better (see appendix Figure 3A.2).

Silents cite Social Security as often as they name jobs as their top voting issue. And while Silents tend to favor the Republican Party on most issues, they are as likely to favor the Democrats as Republicans on Social Security.

Figure 3.5

Percent "Angry" With Government

23 Silent
23 Boomer
18 Gen X
13 Millennial

'97   '01   '05   '09   '13

Source: Aggregated data from surveys conducted by the Pew Research Center for the People & the Press, 1997–2013

THE BABY BOOMERS

Baby Boomers came of age under presidents Lyndon Johnson, Richard Nixon, Gerald Ford, Jimmy Carter, and Ronald Reagan. They had very little allegiance to the GOP during the 1960s and 1970s but were increasingly drawn to the Republican Party starting in the 1980s. In more recent elections, they've divided their votes between the two parties, with no strong tendency in either direction.

Historically, there has been an age gap within the Baby Boom Generation. Older Boomers, who cast their first ballots in the Nixon elections of 1968 and

1972, have voted more Democratic than have younger Boomers who came of age under Ford, Carter, and Reagan. In 2008, for example, Obama performed better among older Boomers than younger ones.

Over the course of several decades, a rising share of Boomers have come to call themselves conservatives, and a majority now favor a smaller government that provides fewer services. When they were in their 20s and 30s, most Boomers preferred big government. On most social issues, their opinions generally fall

---

Figure 3.6

The Boomer Generation

Born: 1946 to 1964

Turned 18 in: 1964 to 1982

Age on Jan. 1, 2014: 49–67

- Now express as much frustration with government as the Silents
- Particularly concerned about their own financial future
- Uncertainty about retirement security has many planning to delay retirement
- Older Boomers are somewhat more Democratic than younger Boomers
- Nearly half say life in US has gotten worse since the 1960s

Source: Pew Research Center surveys and US Census Bureau data

---

between those of the Silents and the younger age cohorts. And many Boomers express reservations about the changing face of America.

Most Boomers say they are dissatisfied with their financial situation and many are anxious about their retirement. In 2012 nearly 4 in 10 (38%) said they aren't confident that they will have enough income and assets to last through their retirement years.

Like other generations, Boomers oppose cutting entitlement benefits to reduce the budget deficit. They are also part of a multigenerational majority that supports reducing Social Security and Medicare benefits for seniors with higher incomes. However, unlike Silents, Boomers oppose raising the eligibility age for Social Security and Medicare.

GENERATION X

Generation X is the in-between generation. They represent the dividing line on many issues between young and old. They came of age politically in the Reagan, George H. W. Bush, and Clinton years, and have never shown a strong allegiance to either party. In 2000 they split their votes between George W. Bush and Al Gore; they narrowly supported Bush in 2004, favored Obama by a clear margin in 2008, but were evenly divided in 2012.

On a range of social issues Gen Xers take a more liberal position than do older voters. They are more likely than both Boomers and Silents to favor legalizing gay marriage and marijuana, and Gen Xers are far more comfortable with

Figure 3.7

Generation X

Born: 1965 to 1980

Turned 18 in: 1983 to 1998

Age on Jan. 1, 2014: 33–48

- Similar to Millennials on social issues
- Grown more critical of government over the last decade
- Since '09, sharp drop in financial satisfaction
- Older Xers tend to vote more Republican, younger Xers vote more Democratic

Source: Pew Research Center surveys and US Census Bureau data

the social diversity of twenty-first-century America.

As is true of Millennials and Boomers, jobs have been the number-one voting issue for Gen Xers in recent years. And they are increasingly anxious over their financial futures. Fully 46% say they are not confident they will have enough income and assets to last through their retirement years—the highest percentage in any generation.

THE MILLENNIALS

Millennials have voted more Democratic than older voters in the past five national elections. They came of age in the Clinton and Bush eras and hold liberal attitudes on most social and governmental issues, as well as America's approach to foreign policy.

Just as members of the Silent Generation are long-term backers of smaller government, Millennials, at least so far, are strong supporters of a more activist government.

They are a racially and ethnically diverse generation, and this diversity helps to explain some

Figure 3.8

The Millennial Generation*

Born: 1981 to _____

Turned 18 in: 1999 to _____

Age of adults on Jan. 1, 2014: 18–32

- Voted for Obama by two-to-one in 2008, the largest margin within any age group since 1972
- Much less politically engaged than in 2008
- Consistently liberal views on many social and governmental issues
- Experiencing high rates of unemployment, but still upbeat
- Welcome the new face of America

* The cut-off year for the Millennial Generation is not yet determined.

Source: Pew Research Center surveys and US Census Bureau data

but not all of their liberalism on a range of issues. For example, while 57% of all Millennials favor a bigger government with more services, just 44% of white Millennials do. But only about a quarter of whites in older generations (27%) support an activist government.

It's an open question whether the liberalism of Millennials is "baked in" for the long haul or will succumb to the disillusionment many Millennials already feel as a result of their difficult economic circumstances. Polls taken since the 2012 election show falling Democratic allegiance, rising political cynicism, and growing frustation over the troubled roll-out of Obamacare. Millennials were 26% of the age-eligible electorate in 2012, but through the inexorable churn of generational replacement, they will peak at about 36% in 2020.

GENERATIONAL TRENDS IN RED AND BLUE

One way to look at the political leanings of generations is to sort people by the political environment when they became politically engaged. For example, not so long ago, voters 65 and older were predominantly members of the Greatest Generation. Most came of age during Franklin Roosevelt's presidency and were fairly reliable supporters of Democrats even into their later years. As recently as 2004, members of the older cohort supported John Kerry by a greater margin than did all voters in that election. Now, however, the Greatest Generation has mostly passed from the scene, and members of the Silent Generation—most of whom came of age politically during the Truman and Eisenhower presidencies—have come to make up the lion's share of voters 65 and older. They have long voted less Democratic than the Greatest Generation; in 2008 and 2012, both Truman- and Eisenhower-era Silents voted more Republican than did the electorate as a whole.

The Baby Boomers span many presidencies. The oldest, who turned 18 when Lyndon Johnson was president, voted more Democratic than others when they were young, but have become more Republican than average as they have aged. Those Boomers who came of age when Richard Nixon was president for the most part have retained a Democratic leaning. Their votes closely mirrored those of the overall electorate in 2006, 2008, and 2010, but they tilted more Democratic once again in 2012. The youngest Boomers, who mostly came of age in the Ford and Carter years, have been among the most reliable Republican voting groups.

Internal divisions within Generation X are even more notable. The older portion of Generation X who came of age during the Reagan and George H.W. Bush presidencies have voted more Republican than the electorate. In contrast, younger Xers, who became active politically during the Clinton administration, mostly have voted more Democratic than average. Millennials largely came of age during George W. Bush's presidency and have consistently voted more Democratic by large margins.

Figure 3.9

Generational Voting History

If you turned 18 under president...	Your age in 2012	Your Generation	Compared with the national average, your cohort was more likely to vote ...									
			'94	'96	'98	'00	'02	'04	'06	'08	'10	'12
Roosevelt	85+	Greatest	D	D	D	D		D				
Truman	78–84	Silent	R			D			D	R	R	R
Eisenhower	70–77	Silent				R	D	R		R	R	R
Kennedy/Johnson	62–69	Boomer	D		D	R				R		R
Nixon	56–61	Boomer	R			D	D	D				D
Ford/Carter	50–55	Boomer	R	R		R	R		D	R	R	R
Reagan/Bush	38–49	Gen X	D	R	R	R		R	R	R		R
Clinton	30–37	Gen X					D	R	D	D	D	D
Bush/Obama	18–29	Millennial						D	D	D	D	D

Note: Light grey boxes represent years in which an age group's vote was roughly equal to the national average. Data from some years not available for oldest and youngest generations due to small sample sizes. Based on likely voters in pre-election polls conducted in each election year. "Your Generation" shows where the majority of that age group is traditionally categorized (e.g., most people who turned 18 under Clinton are Gen X, though the very youngest are classified as Millennials).

Source: Pew Research Center pre-election surveys, 1994–2012

SOCIAL VALUES

On the young-to-old continuum, the younger the generation, the more likely it is to self-identify as liberal, and the older it is, the more likely to identify as conservative. As Figure 3.10 shows, these gaps have been fairly consistent since at least 1996, suggesting that they are driven more by a cohort than a life-cycle difference. The same pattern appears in appendix Figure 3A.3, which shows trends over 25 years in generational attitudes on an index of questions about family, homosexuality, and civil liberties. Once again, the oldest generation has been the most conservative throughout, and the youngest the most liberal.

VIEWS OF BUSINESS

Millennials' views of business are not substantially different from those of older generations. On a three-question index of attitudes about business power and

Figure 3.10

Self-Reported Ideology by Generation: 1997–2013

%

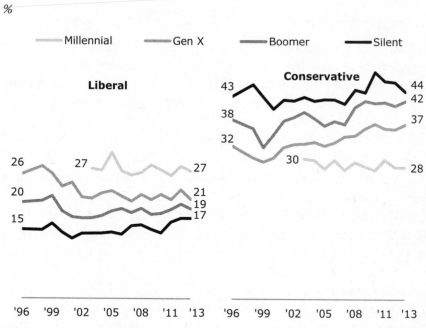

Millennial   Gen X   Boomer   Silent

Liberal

Conservative

26
27   27
20   21
          19
15   17

43   44
          42
38   37
32
          30
                   28

'96 '99 '02 '05 '08 '11 '13   '96 '99 '02 '05 '08 '11 '13

Note: Based on registered voters.

Source: Aggregated data from surveys conducted by the Pew Research Center for the People & the Press, 1996-2013; 2013 data is for January-July only

profits, Millennials' opinions mirror those of Gen Xers and members of the Silent Generation and are slightly less critical of business than are the views of Baby Boomers (see appendix Figure 3A.4). Also, Millennials are about as likely as other cohorts to agree that the country's strength is built mostly on the success of American business.

SOCIAL SAFETY NET

Millennials are less skeptical than older age groups about the effectiveness of government, but they are not particularly supportive of an expanded government social safety net. There have been few differences by generation over the past quarter century in views about whether the government has a responsibility to help those in need. Since 2007 there has been a modest decline in the overall proportion favoring more generous assistance for the poor, a downturn that was true for Millennials as well as for older groups.

NATIONAL SECURITY

Members of the Silent Generation tend to be more supportive than other age groups of an assertive approach to national security. At times, Baby Boomers have been more hawkish than the two younger generations, though often the differences among the cohorts have been quite small (see appendix Figure 3A.5).

One of the key questions driving the pattern in the index asks people to agree or disagree with the statement that "the best way to achieve peace is through military strength." With only a few exceptions, Generation X has been significantly less likely than the two older cohorts to agree with this statement. The Millennials first appeared in the 2003 survey, when 47% agreed. That was close to the 45% among Gen Xers who agreed and lower than the 55% of Boomers and 60% of the Silent Generation who did so (see appendix Figure 3A.6).

Another dimension of attitudes about America's relationship with the rest of the world has to do with immigration. Pew Research Center surveys in recent years have found that older adults are more likely than younger adults to say that immigrants have a negative impact on American customs and values.

VIEWS OF THE NATION

Not surprisingly, older generations are also having a harder time than younger ones processing the dramatic demographic, social, and technological changes of the past half century. Among older adults, there is a tension between their belief that America is the greatest country in the world and a sense of pessimism about the country's future. Younger adults are less convinced of America's greatness but more comfortable with the path the country is on.

Figure 3.11

Generational Divide Over American Exceptionalism

% saying US is "the greatest country in the world"

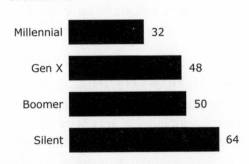

Source: Pew Research Center survey, Sep. 2011, N=2,003 US adults

Overall, 48% of all adults say America is the greatest country in the world, and an additional 42% say it is one of the greatest countries in the world. Fewer than 1 in 10 (8%) say the US is not one of the greatest countries in the world.

There are sharp differences across generations on this question. Millennials are the least likely to say the US is the greatest country in the world—only 32% hold this view. The share rises with each older generation. Nearly two-thirds of Silents (64%) say the US stands above all other nations, a conviction they adhere to despite the discomfort many feel with the societal changes they have witnessed in the past 50 years. Within the Silent Generation it is the oldest members who feel most strongly about America's greatness—fully 72% of those ages 76 to 83 in 2011 said the US is the greatest country in the world.

MORAL VALUES; AMERICA'S FUTURE

The vast majority of American adults—9 in 10 or more across generations—believe that moral values in this country have changed in the past 50 years. However, the generations differ over whether this change has been for the better or the worse. A lopsided majority of Silents (78%), Boomers (77%), and Gen Xers (70%) say it has been a change for the worse, a view shared by about half of Millennials (54%).

There's also a generation gap—albeit a smaller one—on the question of whether America's best days are ahead or behind. Once again, the more upbeat assessments come from the younger generations, with an identical 55% of Millennials and Gen Xers saying our nation's best days are ahead, a view shared by 48% of Boomers and 47% of Silents. The overall balance of opinion tilts positive on this question—with 51% of the American public saying our best days are ahead, 39% saying they are behind us, and the remaining 10% not expressing an opinion one way or the other. That may not be an overwhelming vote of confidence in the future. But neither is it the voice of a public that has lost faith in the national enterprise.

NEWS CONSUMPTION, BY GENERATION

Today's younger and middle-age adults consume much less news in a typical day than do their older counterparts, and long-term trends suggest that they may never match the avid news interest of the generations they will replace, even as they enthusiastically transition to the Internet as their principal platform for news consumption.

A 2012 Pew Research survey found members of the Silent Generation spending 84 minutes watching, reading, or listening to the news the day before the survey was conducted. Boomers did not lag far behind (77 minutes), while Xers and Millennials spent much less time with the news: 66 minutes and 46 minutes, respectively.

Historically, the pattern has been that a generation's news consumption increases as it ages. Pew Research surveys give little indication that this has been happening with today's younger generations. In 2004, Xers reported following the news about as often as they did in 2012. The eight-year trend for Millennials has also been flat.

This persistently low level of news consumption among the younger generations is likely the result of a variety of factors—such as having more activities and entertainments that compete with the news or

Figure 3.12

Generational Gaps in Time Spent Following the News

*Average number of minutes per day following the news by age group**

	Silents	Boomers	Xers	Millennials
2004	88	75	63	43
2006	80	71	63	45
2008	82	72	64	43
2010	83	79	71	45
2012	84	77	66	46

*On the day prior to the survey.

Source: Pew Research Center News Consumption surveys, 2004–2012

fewer compelling major historical events during childhood and adolescence. But one key factor that emerges from our surveys is that older people simply *enjoy* the news more than the young do. Some 58% of Silents and Boomers report they enjoy following the news a lot, compared to 45% of Xers and just 29% of Millennials.

Social media looms as a potential booster of news consumption among the younger generation, albeit a modest one so far. Pew Research's 2012 survey found that a third of Millennials and 20% of Xers said they regularly see news or news headlines on social-networking sites. (For more on this, see Chapter 10.) However, only about 35 percent of those who get news from social network sites say they follow up and seek out full news stories.

Traditional news organizations have been forced to cut their reporting staffs by more than a third over the past decade because these changing news habits have eroded their revenue base. Figuring out how to thrive on digital platforms and social media will be essential to their economic survival. But these surveys suggest they may never regain the dominance they once enjoyed in the information ecosystem. The most important raw ingredient—high levels of news engagement among younger generations—isn't there, at least not so far.

Battle of the Ages?

IF EVER THERE WAS A MOMENT to gird for a generation war, now would seem to be it. The unsparing arithmetic of a graying population is about to force political leaders to rewrite the social contract between young and old. This will lead to tax increases, benefit cuts, or both. Taking stuff away from people is never popular in a democracy, but it's particularly fraught on this issue at this time, because old and young in America are so different—racially, ethnically, politically. "The question is, how do we re-imagine the social contract when the generations don't look like one another?" asks Marcelo Suarez-Orozco, codirector of immigration studies at New York University.[1] Political analyst Ronald Brownstein worries that the challenge will split the country along a great "gray-brown" age and race divide that could "rattle American politics for decades."[2]

I'm an optimist—not, however, a blinkered one. So let it be said that the pessimists have a pretty strong case, especially when one also considers the diverging economic fortunes of the generations. "Older Americans do not intend to ruin America, but as a group, that's what they're about," writes veteran economics columnist Robert Samuelson, who over many decades has chronicled the way older Americans have used their political clout to grab a growing share of government largesse. Absent changes to current law, more than half of the federal budget will go to Social Security, Medicare, and the non-child portion of Medicaid by 2022, up from 11% in 1960 and 30% in 1990, according to an Urban Institute study.[3] The federal government now spends nearly $7 per capita on programs for seniors for every $1 it spends per capita on programs for children. But even as spending priorities have migrated toward the top of the age pyramid, economic need has settled toward the bottom. In 1967, just as the oldest of the Baby Boomers were making their way into the workforce, the poverty rate was nearly three times higher among households headed by an adult age 65 or older than among households headed by an adult below the age of 35 (33% versus 12%). Since then, the ratio has flipped. Today poverty is twice as high among the young as the old (22% versus 11%). The reduction in elderly poverty is largely the handiwork of Social Security and Medicare, and stands as one of the great triumphs of public policy. The benefits of those programs flow to all generations of Americans. But they won't be sustainable unless today's young have the same chance their parents and grandparents did to lead economically productive lives.

So is a Battle of the Ages looming on our horizon? Anything's possible, but there's a lot of evidence to the contrary. In their family lives, the generations are more interdependent now than at any time in modern history. In their attitudes toward the social safety net for seniors, the young are every bit as supportive as the old. And in their basic outlook on life, Millennials seem much more disposed toward cooperation than conflict, perhaps because of the nurturing parental norms that guided their upbringing. In response to a survey question, parents of Millennials said they are only about half as likely to report they often had disagreements with their children as they are to say that, as children themselves, they often fought with their own parents. Our surveys also find that Millenials have a great respect for their elders. Asked which generation has the better moral values, 8 in 10 Millennials pick older adults (as do 9 in 10 Boomers).

It's hard to imagine the Boomers, back when they were coming of age with a great roar of countercultural protest, delivering a similar verdict about their elders. The campus upheavals and street rallies of the late 1960s carried a whiff of generation war. "Never trust anyone over 30," went the popular rallying cry. "We were certain in our convictions, and never more so than in our conviction that our parents were foolish to be certain in theirs," recalled Mark Salter, a longtime speechwriter for Senator John McCain. Those grievances had nothing to do with economic hardship. How could they? In 1969 the US had experienced a record 106 consecutive months of economic expansion. The unemployment rate stood at 3.5%. "I didn't have to look for a job," recalled sociologist Alan Wolfe. "The job looked for me." That was then. In recent years a smaller share of young adults has been employed than at any time since the Bureau of Labor Statistics started tracking such trends in 1948. So it's not surprising that this generation of youthful protesters has a different focus for their grievances: the economy, stupid. But notice the targets they've chosen to demonize. It's all about class, not age. It's 1% versus 99%, not young versus old. Occupy Wall Street, not Occupy Leisure World.

INTERDEPENDENCE

There's another reason this war may never be fought: It would be awkward to storm the ramparts against Mom and Dad when you're a twenty-something still living in your childhood bedroom. The multigenerational family household—an age-old living arrangement that began falling out of favor when the federal government began creating social safety-net programs in the twentieth century—has come roaring back. Some 54 million Americans now live in such households, double the number in 1970. The home construction industry, among others, has taken note. Builders like the Lennar Corporation of Florida and Standard Pacific Homes of California are now promoting multigen floor plans that feature self-contained suites for Grandma or Junior. Boomers and their live-in Boomerangers aren't the only new family ensemble driving this new market. It also encompasses hard-pressed middle-age adults moving in with relatively well-off elderly parents. Or it's widows in declining health moving in with an adult child. Or it's the new generation of immigrants, who—like their frugal counterparts from other continents and previous centuries—are living in the same house with their extended families, an arrangement that many of them imported from their home cultures. In some cases, multigenerational households are an emergency accommodation to financial hardships or health setbacks. But there's also a happier explanation: longer life spans. According to sociologist Peter Uhlenberg, it's more likely today that a 20-year-old has a living grandmother than it was in 1900 for a 20-year-old to have a living mother.

Even when multiple generations don't live in the same home, they look after one another in other ways. Millions of middle-age adults provide various forms of caregiving to elderly parents, which is one reason the share living in nursing homes has declined over the past several decades. At the same time, millions of well-to-do seniors provide financial assistance to adult children buying homes or to grandchildren going to college. And even if they're not in a position to help out with money, millions of grandparents pitch in with time. An estimated 24% of children under the age of 5 are cared for regularly by a grandparent, and about 1 in 10 live with a grandparent.[4] All of these arrangements spread well-being up and (more typically) down the family tree—almost always in the direction of need. Then, of course, there's the biggest intergenerational family transfer of all—inheritance—which happens when the benefactors are no longer around to take pleasure in the gift of giving. A 2010 study by the Center for Retirement Research at Boston College estimated that Boomers had already inherited $2.4 trillion from their Greatest Generation parents and are in line to eventually take in an additional $6 trillion. And a 2012 report from Accenture calculated that the Boomer themselves, once they go on to their greater rewards, will be in a position to pass along up to $30 trillion to their children and grandchildren.

Those are eye-popping numbers, but they come with equally big qualifiers. The distribution of inheritance is highly skewed toward folks at the upper end of the income and wealth curve. The typical Boomer will receive an inheritance of $64,000, not exactly a ticket to financial paradise. The timing of the receipt is always uncertain; often the money arrives too late to change one's life course. And once you take into account the long-term increases in the cost of living, the gigantic numbers become less impressive. A more downbeat portrait of the financial well-being of Boomers comes from the Employee Benefits Research Institute, which has estimated that nearly half of all Boomers are at risk of not having enough income for basic living and health care expenses in retirement. Boomers themselves share this concern. A 2012 Pew Research survey found that 40% say they aren't confident they'll have enough income and assets to last throughout their retirement years. Yes, some of them eventually will be rescued by fat inheritances. The vast majority won't. Meantime, boomers are the most "sandwiched" generation in human history—more likely than any previous cohort in its middle age to have (and be supporting or caring for, in some capacity) parents as well as children. Indeed, demographers have a new coinage—"club sandwich"—to evoke the four generations of family members that Boomers can find themselves helping. It's one of the reasons they are staying active in the workforce for an average of three or four years longer than their parents did. And that, in turn, may be one of the reasons Boomerangers are having so much trouble finding jobs and starting careers.

AS THE WORLD TURNS . . . GRAY

Financing the retirement of the Boomers without bankrupting the Boomerangers isn't only an American problem. If it's any solace, the global population boom of seniors will pose far greater stresses in Europe and East Asia. The rolling European financial and unemployment crisis has already forced austerity cuts to the social safety net at the worst possible time, especially in the continent's hard-hit southern nations. Unemployment among young adults hovers around 20% in many countries and tops 40% in Spain and Greece. *Mammismos* (mama's boys) who live at home well into their thirties have been a fixture of family life in Italy and other southern European countries since long before the current economic meltdown, but now the costs to parents and grandparents are spiking as a result. In 2012 the Spanish polling firm Simple Logica found that 40% of Spaniards ages 65 and older said they were supporting at least one younger relative; in 2010 just 15% had said the same.

These age-based economic, social, and political challenges will continue to mount as populations keep growing older. By 2050, half a dozen European nations will have a median age of 50 or older. So will Japan and South Korea. China won't be quite that old, but by 2050 it will be home to 438 million people over the age of 60. If those people were a country unto themselves, they'd trail only India and China itself in population. Some of the same analysts who once foresaw a century of unrestrained economic expansion ahead for China now wonder whether the country will "get old before it gets rich." In the coming decades it will have to cope with the economic and social consequences of its one-child policy, which has created a nation of "inverted family trees" (or, in the Chinese vernacular, 4-2-1 families—four grandparents, two children, one grandchild). In 1975 there were 12 Chinese children for every 2 seniors; by 2035, there will be just 1 Chinese child for every 2 seniors.

As these families age and as China modernizes, the obligations of filial piety so central to the Confucian social order are being severely tested. In 2013 the Chinese government toughened up its "call your mom" law with a stipulation that "family members living apart from the elderly should frequently visit or send greetings." Chinese parents, most of whom still live in rural poverty, now have the right to take legal action against their grown children, most of whom work in urban factories, if they don't stay in touch or send money. In nearby South Korea, Shin Kyung-Sook's bestseller, *Please Look after Mom*, explored filial guilt in children who fail to care for their aging parents; it sold 2 million copies. Countries as diverse as Italy, Spain, Japan, and Russia also confront upside-down family trees—in those cases, driven not by state edict but by a mix of globalization, urbanization, education, and changing gender roles and cultural mores. Fertility rates have plunged to levels never before seen in human history—sinking below 1.5 per woman in many of the world's wealthy nations. Russia is already experiencing the steepest population decline of any major country since the fourteenth century's bubonic plague. In an effort to stem the decline, President Vladimir Putin in 2012 announced he was extending the government's "baby bonus" payments of $8,300 to cover a mother's third child (previously the program had been limited to the first two). After decades of deline, fertility rates have ticked up a bit in recent years in Russia, as they have in countries such as France, Norway, Sweden, Denmark, and Singapore that have also adopted aggressive cash incentive programs for childbearing. (Singapore's package, believed to be the world's most lucrative, is estimated to be worth the equivalent of $135,000 in the first seven years of a child's life.)[5] But even with the increases, the rates in all those countries still fall well short of population replacement level.

PUBLIC ATTITUDES ABOUT SAFETY NETS

In the United States, public opinion surveys offer scant support for the notion that policy challenges presented by an aging society will lead to a generational conflict. Like middle-age and older adults, most Millenials say the government does *too little,* not too much, to support seniors. And young and old alike are more concerned that Social Security and Medicare will run out of money for benefits than about the burden that maintaining current benefit levels puts on future generations of workers and taxpayers (see appendix Figure 4A.4).

Those two programs are among the most popular the government ever created. Nearly 9 in 10 Americans say they have been good for the country, and this includes at least 8 in 10 across all generations, young and old (see appendix Figure 4A.1).

However, the generations do differ in their evaluations of the effectiveness of these programs and in their receptivity to changes. A majority of the Silent Generation says they do a good job of serving the people they cover, while most Millennials, Generation Xers, and Boomers rate them as doing only a fair or poor job. Because few in these younger generations are currently drawing benefits from these programs, it's likely that their impressions have been shaped at least as much by media reports and political commentary as by direct experience.

Most Millennials (56%) and Gen Xers (66%) say Social Security needs major changes or a complete overhaul, while most in the Silent Generation (62%) say the system works pretty well. Boomers, many of whom are on the cusp of receiving Social Security themselves, are divided—45% say they think only minor changes are in order, while 50% say major changes need to be made.

Fully 86% of Millennials support changing the system so younger workers can invest their Social Security taxes into private retirement accounts. And 74% of Millennials favor changing Medicare so future participants can use the benefit toward purchasing private health insurance. Support for both of these ideas drops off among older generations and they garner a decidedly mixed reaction from those in the Silent Generation.

When it comes to proposals to gradually raise the eligibility age for these programs, there is substantially more support from those who have already reached retirement age than from those who haven't. About half in the Silent Generation favor gradually raising the Social Security retirement age and the Medicare eligibility age. Majorities across all younger generations oppose this idea. These generational patterns have a distinct flavor of self-interest—cut someone else's benefits, not mine.

A third set of proposals for entitlement changes—means-testing benefits to reduce the amounts that high-income seniors receive—divide the country, but not along generational lines. About half (53%) of Americans favor reducing Social Security benefits for seniors with higher incomes as a way to address financial problems with the system, and there is no difference in levels of support across generational lines. Similarly, 55% of the public, including nearly identical percentages across generations, favor reducing Medicare benefits for higher-income seniors (see appendix Figure 4A.2).

By 58% to 35%, the public says that keeping entitlement benefits as they are is more important than reducing the budget deficit. And by an almost identical 59% to 32% margin, more say that higher priority should be placed on avoiding future Social Security benefit cuts than on avoiding any Social Security tax increases for workers and employers (see appendix Figure 4A.3).

Resistance to benefit cuts increases across generations, but with some variances. Boomers and Silents favor preserving entitlement benefits by a ratio of least 2 to 1, while Millennials are more evenly divided.

One factor strongly related to attitudes about entitlements is people's reliance—or expected reliance—on these programs. A majority of retired adults (56%) say that Social Security is their main source of income. But among those who are not yet retired, two-thirds (65%) say Social Security will *not* be their main source of income in retirement, while only a 32% minority say that it will. When probed further, nearly a third (31%) of non-retired adults think they will end up getting no money from Social Security in their retirement.

Not surprisingly, experiences with and expectations about Social Security vary significantly across generations. Among those in the Silent Generation—84% of whom are retired—58% cite Social Security as their main source of retirement income. Among these, 28% say it is (or will be) their only source of income in retirement, while 30% have other sources to supplement Social Security.

Millennials have starkly different expectations. More than 7 in 10 (72%) Millennials do not expect Social Security to be their main source of retirement income. In fact, 42% of Millennials think they will get no retirement income from Social Security at all, as do 35% of Generation Xers.

While around 1 in 5 Baby Boomers (22%) say they are already retired, most are not, and their expectations about Social Security are mixed. Fewer than half (42%) of Boomers say that Social Security is or will be their main source of income in retirement, with about a quarter (24%) saying it is or will be their only source of income. A majority (56%) says they will have other sources of income that are more important during retirement, though most of these (35% of all Boomers) say they expect to get at least some income from Social Security to supplement their other sources.

People's dependence, or expected dependence, on Social Security has a significant effect on their attitudes about Social Security policy. In particular, those who say Social Security is or will be their main source of income in retirement overwhelmingly favor maintaining entitlement benefits over deficit reduction as the bigger policy priority. This is particularly true among those in the Silent Generation, who have mostly retired already, but also true among Boomers and younger people as well.

Similarly, those who are counting on Social Security as their own primary income source are far more opposed than others to raising the retirement age for Social Security eligibility. The link between personal need and attitudes on this issue is notably strong among Baby Boomers. Boomers who say Social Security is or will be their main source of income oppose raising the retirement age by more than 2 to 1 (69% oppose, 29% favor) while Boomers who say other sources of income will be more important are divided (52% oppose, 47% favor).

LOOKING AHEAD

Across generations, there is considerable concern that in the future there may not be enough money to provide Social Security and Medicare benefits at their current levels. By contrast, the possibility that keeping these benefits at their current levels may put too much of a financial burden on younger generations is less of a concern—even among young generations themselves.

Majorities of Gen Xers (70%) and Millennials (57%) say they are very concerned that financial shortfalls in Social Security and Medicare may lead to reduced benefits. Fewer Gen Xers (45%) and Millennials (41%) are very concerned that maintaining current benefits may excessively burden young people.

In this regard, Gen Xers and Millennials are in sync with Boomers and Silents; among both groups, more are very concerned about possible benefit reductions than about the possibility that keeping benefits at current levels may place too much burden on younger generations (see appendix Figure 4A.4).

IS THE GOVERNMENT DOING TOO MUCH, OR NOT ENOUGH, FOR SENIORS?

The fact that federal government spending priorities over time have come to favor the old at the expense of the young isn't a concern that registers with the public. To the contrary, a majority of Americans (60%) say the federal government isn't doing *enough* for older people. They say the same about what they consider to be inadequate government spending on programs for the middle class (58%), poor people (57%), and children (57%). On the other hand, nearly two-thirds (64%) say the government does *too much* for wealthy people.

There are few differences by age in these views. More than half of each generation agrees that the government does not do enough for older people, including 64% among Baby Boomers and those in Generation X, 55% of Millennials, and 52% of Silents. Notably, majorities of Democrats (69%), Republicans (52%), and independents (56%) agree that the federal government does not do enough for older people.

The Silent Generation is least likely to say the government does not do enough for children. Just more than 4 in 10 (44%) say this, compared with 64% of Gen Xers, 59% of Baby Boomers, and 57% of Millennials.

On the other hand, the youngest generation is the most likely to say that the government does not do enough for the poor: 62% of Millennials express this view, compared with 53% of the Silent Generation. Nearly 6 in 10 Boomers agree (57%), as well as 54% of those in Gen X (see appendix Figure 4A.5).

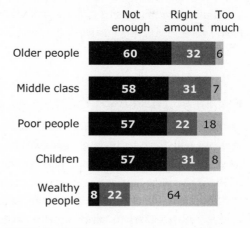

Figure 4.1

Government Seen as Shortchanging Old, Young, Middle Class and Poor

% saying government does ...

	Not enough	Right amount	Too much
Older people	60	32	6
Middle class	58	31	7
Poor people	57	22	18
Children	57	31	8
Wealthy people	8	22	64

Source: Pew Research Center survey, Sept.–Oct. 2011, N=2,410

WHO SHOULD LOOK OUT FOR OLDER PEOPLE?

The public is divided over whether the government or individuals and their families should be mainly responsible for making sure that retired older adults

have at least a minimum standard of living. The differences between generations on this question are relatively small.

Among the public as a whole, about 4 in 10 (43%) say the government is
mainly responsible for ensuring at least a minimal standard of living for older
people, while 40% say individuals and their families are mostly responsible.
Some 14% volunteer that both are equally responsible (see appendix Figure
4A.6).

Millennials and Boomers are nearly evenly divided. The balance among
Gen Xers tilts toward the government (47% versus 34%), while the Silents tilt
slightly more toward individual responsibility (44% versus 36%).

On this question, the divides are greater across income levels than across
generations. Among those with household incomes of $75,000 or more, 51%
say individuals should be mainly responsible for making sure older adults
are getting a basic level of care, while 33% say the government should be.
The numbers are reversed among those with household incomes of less than
$30,000 (53% say the government should be mainly responsible, 29% say indi-
viduals and their families). Those with incomes between $30,000 and $74,999
are evenly divided (42% each).

When those who say that individuals are mainly responsible are questioned
further about whether the government should be responsible if individuals fall
short, most agree that the government should be the ultimate backstop. Lopsided majorities across all generations say the government should be mainly or
partly responsible for ensuring that retired people have a minimum standard
of living.

HOLES IN THE FAMILY NET

Come the inevitable day when entitlement programs for seniors are trimmed,
families will have to reclaim some of the caregiving ground they've surren-
dered to the state. These challenges will be daunting, because the architecture
of the American family has changed dramatically since presidents Roosevelt
and Johnson built these programs in the twentieth century. As noted earlier,
we are now a society in which more than 4 in 10 children are born out of wedlock, and in which a teenager has less chance of being raised by both biological
parents than in any other country. Between non-marriage, divorce, and short-
term cohabiting unions, family life here is subject to a vast amount of churn.
Our nuclear families now share the stage with a wide assortment of stepfam-
ilies and kin networks. What impact will all this have on the bonds of intergenerational family obligation? If fathers aren't around to take care of children
when they are young, who'll take care of these absent fathers when they're old?

Will they become a generation of elderly orphans? "Over the course of our lives we're accumulating more and more kin to whom we owe less and less," says sociologist Andrew Cherlin, who believes our society is entering uncharted waters. Families are famously adaptive and resilient, but their future is hard to divine. Will kin networks replace nuclear families? Might friends become the new family? Can marriage mount a comeback? How Americans respond—in their public choices as well as their private behaviors—will go a long way toward determining whether the generations spend the coming decades at war or in harmony. And that, in turn, will help shape our nation's destiny in the twenty-first century.

Money Troubles

I F JANE SMITH, OUR PROTOTYPICAL BOOMER, is going to have the life-style in retirement that she's been hoping for, she'll need something more than the safety net of Social Security and Medicare. Happily, she's got something more—a 401(k). Unhappily, it won't be enough.

Jane is retiring with $120,000 in her 401(k) account. When she combines that with her Social Security check, she'll be able to draw about $24,000 a year in retirement. Trouble is, before she retired, Jane was pulling down the US median annual wage of $41,600. Financial planners say that if you want to enjoy the same standard of living in retirement that you had during your working years, you need to be able to replace roughly 80% of your annual pre-retirement income. Depending on your circumstances, maybe you can get by on 70%. But once you fall below that level, you'll have to start seriously scaling back. Jane is at 58%.

People tend to have fewer wants, needs, and expenses as they grow older (except, of course, for health care—about which more later). Many can down-size their lifestyles without feeling much of a pinch. But for those, like Jane, who've looked forward to their golden years as a reward after the hard slog of their work lives, it's bound to be a bit of a downer. Before we consider what Jane can do about this, let's first understand why she isn't in better financial shape as she begins this next chapter of her life.

Around the time Jane entered the workforce full time—in 1984, after the birth of her third child—a pension revolution was just getting under way in America's workplaces. The 401(k), a new retirement savings account known by the section of the IRS code that created it, enabled employees and their

employers to contribute money on a pretax basis toward the employee's retirement and have it earn interest, dividends, or capital gains on a tax-deferred
basis. Initially the idea was that employers would offer these "defined contribution" plans as a supplement to their traditional "defined benefit" pension
plans. The traditional plans guaranteed employees a fixed annual income from
retirement until death, typically derived from a formula based on the employee's salary and years of service. But it didn't take long for employers to start
treating 401(k)s as a replacement rather than a supplement. These new plans
were not only much less expensive than the traditional plans, they also enabled
employers to avoid the uncertainties associated with determining how much
money to set aside for their obligations to future retirees (risks that many
employers have managed spectacularly poorly—witness the more than a trillion dollars' worth of unfunded pension liabilities now on their books). The
transition from defined benefit to defined contribution has been anything but
smooth; over the years it has been the source of countless labor disputes. But
for the most part, it's over. In 1983, among all workers who had some kind
of pension coverage, 62% had a defined benefit plan only and just 12% had
a defined contribution (401(k)-type) plan only; the remainder had both. By
2010 these shares had flipped—69% had only a defined contribution plan and
just 19% had only a traditional defined benefit pension (a smaller remainder
had both).[1] Nowadays, traditional defined benefit plans are pretty much confined to the public employee sector, and many of those are being scaled back
or eliminated—witness Detroit's petition for bankruptcy, a step that the city
hopes will enable it to reduce its pension payments to retired city employees.
Within the next generation, Social Security is likely to be the only defined benefit revenue stream to the vast majority of America's retirees.

During her 35-year career, Jane worked for three small companies, none
of which offered a traditional pension plan. So she spent her entire working
life determined to take full advantage of her 401(k)s. She's frugal, has a good
head for math, and was quick to grasp the value of using tax-deferred dollars
to build her nest egg. Plus, her various employers were contributing 50 cents
for every dollar she invested in her plan, so the financial incentives were substantial. But life kept getting in the way—a costly divorce; college tuition for
the kids; her daughter's wedding; unexpected medical bills. There were lots of
years when she wasn't able to contribute enough of her own money to qualify for the full employer match—meaning she left a chunk of her employer's
money on the table. One year she had to take out a hardship loan from her
401(k) savings, subjecting herself to a tax penalty and joining the estimated
1 in 4 workers with such plans who've done the same thing. On top of that,
Jane isn't the world's greatest investor. She would periodically move her money

into or out of various stock funds in her 401(k) portfolio at what she thought were the market's peaks and valleys, only to find herself wrong-footed. Jane's story, alas, is pretty typical. (Sorry, Jane, that's your fate!) Despite the many attractive features of 401(k)s (tax breaks; personal choice; employer matches), the evidence from the past 30 years is clear: they don't come close to replacing the security and certainty of a defined benefit pension system.

"Basing a [retirement] system on people's voluntarily saving for 40 years and evaluating the relevant information for sound investment choices is like asking the family pet to dance on two legs," writes Teresa Ghilarducci, an economics professor and retirement policy expert at the New School for Social Research. "First, figure out when you or your spouse will be laid off or be too sick to work. Second, figure out when you will die. Third, understand you need to save 7 percent of every dollar you earn. Fourth, earn at least 3 percent above inflation on your investments. Fifth, do not withdraw any funds when you lose your job, have a health problem, get divorced, buy a house or send a kid to college. Sixth, time your retirement account withdrawals so the last cent is spent on the day you die."[2]

Most people can't pull that off. As a result, among all adults who have either a 401(k), an IRA, or some similar tax-advantaged retirement plan and are approaching retirement age (and, by the way, just 60% of households headed by someone on the cusp of retirement have such plans in the first place), the typical balance in these accounts as of 2010 was Jane's $120,000. And they're much better off than those without such accounts. Indeed, if one looks at all Americans on the cusp of retirement, about three-quarters have less than $30,000 in retirement savings, according to the AARP. These levels have changed very little in recent years, despite the stock market recovery that began in 2009, and despite the fact that recent cohorts of new retirees have spent more of their working lives in a position to take advantage of 401(k) plans. How far does $120,000 go? Not very. If a 65-year-old married retiree were to convert $120,000 into a standard joint-and-survivor annuity today, it would yield a guaranteed monthly income for life of $575—not exactly a ticket to Easy Street. The modest yield is partly a function of declining interest rates and partly of rising life spans. According to the Society of Actuaries, for a married 65-year-old couple, there's a 45% chance that one of the spouses will live until age 90 and a 20% chance that one will live to age 95. That's good karma for old age, but bad for defined contribution plans. "Many participants are likely to be surprised—and disappointed—when they find out how little their 401(k) plan provides," wrote Alicia Munnell, director of the Center for Retirement Research at Boston College, in 2012. And the disappointments will grow even more acute as retirees discover that Medicare covers only about half of the overall health care bill the typical senior incurs between turning age 65 and the end of life. The rest of the tab—in the form of deductibles, coinsurance, uncovered services, and the uninsured cost of long-term care—will have to come either out of the senior's pocket or from Medicaid. But to qualify for Medicaid, the senior must either be poor or descend into poverty.

IT AIN'T EASY BEING YOUNG

Now here's the really bad news: whatever economic challenges the over-65s are facing these days, they pale by comparison with the money troubles of the young. They're being hammered on every front—a terrible job market, runaway college tuition costs, record student loan debt, and a housing market bust that has hit young homeowners much harder than older ones. Worse, this isn't just a Great Recession phenomenon. It's the continuation of a situation that has seen the old prosper relative to the young for many decades. The result has been that Millennials and Xers are not only in far worse financial shape than Boomers and Silents now, they are also in worse shape than these older generations were back when they were the age that Millennials and Xers are now.

Any generational audit should start by looking at the household wealth—the sum of all assets (house, car, stocks and bonds, 401(k)s, etc.) minus all debts (mortgage, car loan, credit card debt, student loan debt, etc.). Unlike income, which can be subject to short-term fluctuations, wealth is a stock of assets, typically accumulated over time, that provides its owner with a foundation of economic well-being—a cushion in the event of short-term economic shocks; funds to purchase big-ticket items; a source of retirement income; and social and economic capital to pass on to one's children and grandchildren. People tend to gather more wealth as they get older, so it's no surprise that there's a big age gap on this measure. What is surprising is how big it has become. In an America that's rapidly going gray, it's not just the people who are migrating north on the age pyramid. It's also money. Back in 1984, the gap in wealth between the typical household headed by an adult ages 65 and older and one headed by an adult under the age of 35 was not quite 11 to 1. By 2011 the gap had ballooned to 26 to 1. In the intervening three decades, wealth had gone up sharply for older adults, rising by 37% in inflation-adjusted dollars, and deteriorated badly for younger adults, falling by 44%. (This analysis doesn't factor in the rising share of young adults who are still living in their childhood bedrooms and thus not counted as heads of households.)

How has this happened? When it comes to wealth accumulation, today's young adults have three things going against them. First, they're having a terrible time finding work in a high-unemployment economy. Many aren't even trying. For the past four years, an average of just 63% of adults ages 18 to 29 were either employed or seeking employment, the lowest labor force participation rate for this age cohort since women began their march into the workforce four decades ago. In part these low numbers reflect the record shares of 18- to 24-year-olds enrolled in college—41% now, up from 25% in 1980. If history is a guide, today's college grads will earn anywhere from $500,000 to $1 million more over the course of their lifetimes than their buddies who never went. But at least in the short term, college has been a net financial drag on this young generation.[3]

Figure 5.1

Median Net Worth by Age of Householder, 1984 and 2011

In 2011 dollars (unless otherwise noted)

	1984	2011	Change 1984 to 2011
All	**$67,354**	**$68,828**	**2%**
Younger than 35	$11,884	$6,676	-44%
35–44	$73,362	$35,000	-52%
45–54	$117,094	$84,542	-28%
55–64	$151,884	$143,964	-5%
65 and older	$124,259	$170,516	37%

Source: Pew Research Center analysis of US Census Bureau Survey of Income and Program Participation

Average tuition and fees have nearly tripled at public and private colleges since 1980, even after adjusting for inflation. In 2010 a record 40% of all households headed by someone under the age of 35 were carrying student loan debt, up from 17% in 1989. Among households owing such debt, the average balance in 2010 was $26,682, nearly triple the figure (in inflation-adjusted dollars) from 1989.

In standard economic theory, this sort of borrowing enhances human capital and earning power. It qualifies as "good debt"—productive in the long run for both the debtor and society. But Millennials are on a slow walk to the long run. For now, about half of those with student loans say this debt has made it more difficult to make ends meet; about a quarter say it has affected their career choices or made it harder to buy a home; and a small share—about 1 in 13—say it has caused them to delay marriage or parenthood. "The next generation is starting their economic race 50 yards behind the starting line," warned the prologue to *Generation Debt: Why Now Is a Terrible Time to Be Young*, by newly minted Yale University graduate Anya Kamenetz. Her book and that of another Millennial author, Tamara Draut (*Strapped: Why America's 20- and 30-Somethings Can't Get Ahead*), were both published in 2006, *before* the Great Recession deepened their generation's debt woes. As the national economy has finally begun to recover, Millennials have led other generations in shedding

Figure 5.2

The Average Student Debt Outstanding among Households with Student Debt, 1989–2010

In 2011 dollars

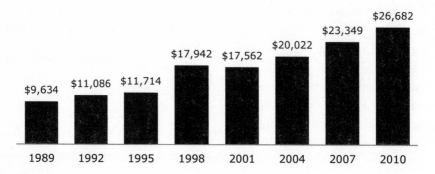

Note: Includes education loans that are currently in deferment and loans in scheduled repayment period.

Source: Pew Research Center analysis of the Survey of Consumer Finances

debt. From 2007 to 2010 their total debt went down by 29%, compared with a drop of 8% for households headed by an adult age 35 or older.[4] But even this seemingly happy statistic has a dark side. The biggest reason Millennials have less debt is that they have fewer homes and cars than their same-age counterparts had in the past. They've downsized their lifestyles.

HOUSING

When the housing bubble burst in 2006, it seized up the financial markets, wrecked lots of people's financial lives, sent millions of homeowners into foreclosure or left them with mortgages that exceeded the value of their home, and plunged the economy into a tailspin from which it is still struggling to recover. That sorry saga is pretty well known. Less well understood, however, is how much of a generational skew there has been to this housing calamity.

Housing is the most important component of wealth of the typical American. In 2011, despite the collapse of the housing market, home equity (the market value of a house minus mortgage debt) still accounted for about 75% of the total wealth of the median US household. The public's next largest asset—stocks and mutual funds—came in a distant second. But housing has been a much better investment for the old than the young—largely as a result of nothing more complicated than good timing. A majority of today's older homeowners purchased their present home before 1986, at "pre-bubble" prices. Along with every other homeowner, they've been hurt by the housing market collapse of recent years, but over the long haul, the vast majority have seen their home equity rise. Moreover, two-thirds of homeowners ages 65 and older no longer have a mortgage to pay, so they haven't had to worry about going underwater or facing foreclosure. For young adults in their 20s, 30s, and early 40s, no such luck. Among those who are homeowners, most bought at bubble-inflated prices. And when the bubble burst, many were left with negative equity in their homes. Figure 5.3 shows the time trends by age over a quarter century.

The contrast in fortunes could hardly be more stark. The typical household head ages 65 and older had 36% more equity in his home in 2011 (in inflation-adjusted dollars) than his same-age counterpart had in 1984, while the typical household head age 44 or younger had only about half the equity in his home than his same-age counterpart had in

Figure 5.3

Change in Median Home Equity, by Age of Householder, 1984–2011

% change

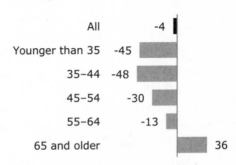

Note: Standardized to 2011 dollars.

Source: Pew Research Center analysis of the Survey of Income and Program Participation data and US Census Bureau P-70, No. 7; Household Wealth and Asset Ownership, 1984: Data from the Survey of Income and Program Participation, Table 5

1984. If there's any silver lining for the younger generation, it's that houses are still selling at a heavy discount from their market peak in 2006. That represents a potential transfer of trillions of dollars in wealth from today's homeowners (who skew old) to tomorrow's homebuyers (who skew young). Of course, as the housing market finally begins to recover, these bargains will dry up.

INCOME AND POVERTY

Median household income is yet another measure that illustrates how the old have been prospering relative to the young. Households in all age groups have made gains in annual income compared with their same-age predecessors over the course of the past half century, but the incomes of the oldest households have risen four times as sharply as those of the youngest ones. As a result, incomes of the oldest households, which had been lower than those of younger households, are catching up.

In households headed by adults younger than 35, the median adjusted annual income grew by 28% from 1967 to 2012 (from $40,650 to $51,962). By contrast, in households headed by adults ages 65 and older, median income increased by 108% during the same period (from $21,908 to $45,563; all figures expressed in 2012 dollars and standardized to a household size of three).

As these generational shifts in median income were occurring, Social Security continued to provide a bedrock of stable support for older adults. During the past three decades, it contributed a steady share—about 55%—of the rising annual median incomes of households headed by adults ages 65 and older.

Median income reflects what is happening at the middle of the socioeconomic ladder. Poverty statistics reflect what is happening at the bottom, where the divergence in economic fortunes by generation could hardly be more stark. In 1967 older households were nearly three times more likely than younger ones to be in poverty. Today they are only half as likely. In the intervening years, poverty rates have declined by two-thirds among the old while doubling among the young. These trends result from many factors—government policies that favor the old over the young; structural changes in the economy and labor force; compositional changes in the age pyramid (i.e., a rising share of young adults are historically disadvantaged minorities); and a method of counting poverty that critics say has grown outdated.[5] Whatever the causes, alleviating poverty among the elderly is one of the great success stories of the past half century. But the gains have come, at least in part, on the backs of the young.

Figure 5.4

Share of Households in Poverty, by Age of Householder, 1967–2011

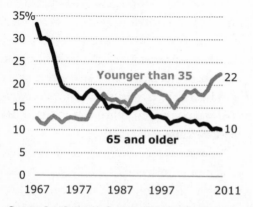

Source: Pew Research Center analysis of the Current Population Survey Annual Social and Economic Supplement, IPUMS

EMPLOYMENT

The American workforce is graying—and not just because the American population itself is graying. Older adults are staying in the labor force longer, and younger adults are staying out of it longer. According to one government estimate, 93% of the growth in the US labor force from 2006 to 2016 will be among workers ages 55 and older.

Appendix Figure 5A.1 shows the trends. Starting around 2000, the share of young adults who are employed began falling sharply while the share of older adults who are employed began rising. These were both reversals of the patterns that had prevailed in the 1970s and 1980s, when the women's revolution was bringing young women into the workforce in unprecedented numbers. At the same time, the growing aspiration of older adults to retire young was taking more and more of them out of the workforce at younger ages. But young women have reached labor force participation parity with young men, so there are no more dramatic gains to be had from changing gender work patterns. As for older adults, their aspiration to retire early has cooled off markedly in the past two decades. The average age of retirement for men fell to a modern low of 62 in 1995 but has since climbed back up to 64. For decades, the Gallup Poll has been asking working Americans when they expect to retire. In 1996, the average answer was age 60. By 2012, it was 67. Perhaps not incidentally, the age at which a worker can receive the standard Social Security retirement benefit has also been rising gradually, and will eventually reach 67 (up from the traditional 65) for those born in 1960 or later.

It's not only economic necessity that has been keeping more older adults on the job. Attitudes about work also play an important role—in particular, the desire of an aging but healthy population to stay active well into the later years of life. A 2009 Pew Research survey found that a majority (54%) of workers ages 65 and older said the main reason they continue to work is that they want to. Just 17% say the main reason is that they need the paycheck, while about a quarter (27%) say they're motivated by a mix of desire and need. Among workers ages 16 to 64, the pattern was reversed—many more say they work because they need to than say they work because they want to.

When asked to identify specific reasons for working, older workers emphasized psychological and social factors: "to feel useful"; "to give myself something to do"; "to be with other people." Younger and middle-age workers were much more inclined to cite classic pocketbook considerations: "to support myself and my family"; "to live independently"; "to qualify for retirement benefits"; "to receive health care benefits."

Figure 5.5

Work Because You Need To? It Depends on Your Age

% of workers who say they work because they ...

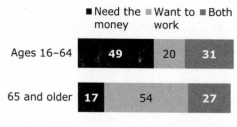

■ Need the ■ Want to ■ Both
money   work

Ages 16–64   49   20   31

65 and older   17   54   27

Note: Based on those who work full or part time.

Source: Pew Research Center survey, July–Aug. 2009, N=1,815 residents ages 16 and older

The recession-racked economy of 2009 darkened nearly everyone's calculations about the economics of old age. According to a Pew Research survey that year, nearly 4 in 10 adults who were working past the median retirement age of 62 said they had delayed their retirement because of the recession. And among workers ages 50 to 61, fully 63% said they might have to push back their expected retirement date because of current economic conditions.

Three years later, the economy was slowly climbing out of its ditch, but retirement confidence had yet to stage a recovery. To the contrary, it kept falling. In 2012, nearly 4 in 10 (38%) of all adults said they were not confident they had enough income and assets to last through their retirement years, up from 25% who felt that way in the recession year of 2009. Interestingly, the age group most concerned about financing its retirement is adults in their late 30s and early 40s. It's almost as if, having finally reached the milestones of adulthood—marriage, parenthood, homeownership—this cohort of middle-age Gen Xers suddenly started doing their retirement math and realized that it didn't add up.

Nor is this the only indication from recent Pew Research surveys of the toll the bad economy has taken on the economic self-confidence of young and middle-age adults. As noted in the last chapter, Millennials are strikingly upbeat about their long-term financial prospects; they are more likely than any other age group to say they'll eventually have enough money to live the life they want. That confidence notwithstanding, they are also more likely than any other age group to place themselves in the lower or lower-middle class. Nearly 4 in 10 (39%) do so, up from 25% who said the same in early 2008, as the Great Recession was just beginning. Indeed, Millennials are now twice as likely as adults ages 65 and older to place themselves in one of the two lower socioeconomic classes (39% versus 20%), one illustration of the way the changing economic fortunes of young and old have left a mark on the way these generations view themselves.

Every car salesman knows that Millennials' big-ticket purchasing habits reflect these changes. One of the great mysteries confronting the (otherwise recovering) auto industry these days is: How do you sell a car to a twenty-something? In 2010 adults between the ages of 21 and 34 bought 27% of all new vehicles sold in America, down from a peak of 38% in 1985. "The Young and the Carless" is how one trade publication summed up the trend. Technological change may also be playing a role. "Cars used to be what people aspired to own," says Mark Norman, president of Zipcar, the

Figure 5.6

Which Age Group in What Class?

% who say they are ...

	Upper class	Middle class	Lower class
All adults	**17**	**49**	**32**
Younger than 30	18	42	39
30–49	16	48	35
50–64	19	48	32
65 and older	15	63	20

Note: "Upper class" includes those who identify as upper or upper-middle class; "lower class" includes those who identify as lower or lower-middle class.

Source: Pew Research Center survey, July 2012, N=2,508 US adults

world's largest car-sharing company. "Now it's the smartphone."[6] Whatever the mix of reasons, Millennials are also buying fewer houses—especially in the car-centric suburbs—than their same-age counterparts did a generation ago.

Consumer spending drives between 60% and 70% of the US economy, and one reason the recovery has been so sluggish is that so few Millennials are able or inclined to open their wallets. Their low levels of income and wealth and high rates of student debt are likely to put a damper on their economic fortunes for decades to come. They're also facing trillions of dollars in taxes or foregone government goods and services, or both, to pay off the public debt bequeathed to them by their elders. And they'll spend trillions more to finance the entitlement programs for those same parents and grandparents in their old age.

Meantime, where does this leave Jane and her underfunded retirement? For starters, she can be pretty confident that her Social Security and Medicare benefits are safe. No elected official who's compos mentis could look at the public opinion survey findings about those programs and touch the current benefits of current retirees (except, perhaps, the wealthy ones). When Jane compares her economic circumstances at retirement with those of her parents and grandparents at the same stage of life, she knows she's ahead of the game. But when she looks at the economic circumstances facing her kids and grandkids, she knows they're in for a rougher financial ride than she's had. That explains why Junior is living in her house, rent free. And it's why, now that she's retired, she's spending two days a week caring for young grandchildren, as a way to free up her daughter to work part-time. This wasn't exactly Plan A for Jane's golden years. But as her children have already figured out, it's good to have a Plan B.

6

The New Immigrants

IMMIGRATION IS THE ENGINE that makes and remakes America. After a long hiatus in the middle of the twentieth century brought on by a social and political backlash, an economic depression, and a world war, the engine is roaring once again. That's good news for anyone who worries about the issue at the heart of this book—how we reengineer the compact between the generations. It's even better news for those who wonder whether the US can remain the world's indispensable nation on into another century. Immigrants are strivers. They have energy, ingenuity, a tolerance for risk, an appetite for hard work, and a faith in the future. Few if any countries have been more enriched by immigrants than ours. And not many are better at weaving them into the social, political, and economic fabric of their new home.

Even so, immigration never starts out easy. Emma Lazarus's inscription on the Statue of Liberty notwithstanding, Americans don't typically welcome newcomers with arms fully extended, especially not when they arrive in large numbers. "Going back to the Founding Fathers—with their formula of limited government, civic equality and tolerance of religious and cultural diversity—each new surge of arrivals has been greeted as a crisis without precedent, only to disappear with unexpected speed as the nation faces new challenges," writes Michael Barone, author of a 2013 book on the impact of immigrants on politics.[1] We worry that they'll take our jobs, drain our resources, threaten our language, mongrelize our race, worship false idols, and import crime and vice. People once said such things about the Irish, Germans, Italians, Poles, Greeks, Slavs, Russians, Jews, and pretty much every other immigrant wave that came ashore, just as today some say the same about Hispanics and Asians.

But still they come, chasing dreams, escaping nightmares, and in greater numbers than ever. Today the US is home to a record 42 million immigrants and 37 million US-born children of immigrants. If current birthrates and immigration flows continue, more than two-thirds of the nation's total population growth—and about 90% of the increase in its working-age population—between now and 2050 will be accounted for by immigrants and their US-born children. By midcentury an estimated 162 million Americans, or 37% of the population, will be "immigrant stock" (immigrants themselves or their US-born children). This would be the highest share in US history, surpassing the peak of 35% that prevailed in the late 19th and early 20th centuries, when previous immigration waves brought tens of millions of newcomers to a much more sparsely populated America.

Figure 6.1

"Immigrant Stock" Share of US Population, Actual and Projected, 1900–2050

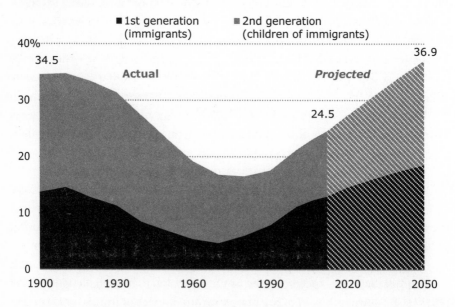

Note: Based on total population, including children and adults.

Source: 2000–2012 data and all second-generation data from Pew Research Center analysis of Current Population Survey, IPUMS; Pew Hispanic Center projections for 2020 to 2050 from Passel and Cohn, "US Population Projections: 2005–2050," Feb. 11, 2008; historical trend from Passel and Cohn (2008) and Edmonston and Passel, *Immigration and Ethnicity: The Integration of America's Newest Arrivals*, Washington, DC: The Urban Institute Press, 1994.

The big difference between now and then is who these immigrants are and where they're coming from. Half of all new arrivals in the post-1965 immigration wave have been from Latin America and just over a quarter from Asia (since 2009, though, Asians have surpassed Hispanics in new arrivals). Europe, which had sent 9 in 10 of America's immigrants during the earlier immigration eras, supplies only about 1 in 10 today. Africa, the Middle East, and other regions account for the remaining 10 or 12 percent (see appendix Figure 6A.1).

Because of this shift, immigrants in the twenty-first century are doing more than replenishing our labor force and electorate. They're changing our complexion. America is already one of the most racially and ethnically diverse nations in history, and the modern immigration wave is making our tapestry more intricate with each passing year. In 1960 our population was 85% white; by 2060 it will be 43% white. How we handle the identity issues that accompany such a sweeping racial makeover is the subject of Chapter 7. Here we focus on the economics, demographics, and politics of immigration, starting with this question: Will the great American story of generational upward mobility—wherein the children of immigrants do better than their parents, and the grandchildren do better yet—play out in the twenty-first century as it did for their counterparts in the nineteenth and twentieth?

In the modern era, lots of immigration scholars and policy-makers have been skeptical. They cite a range of factors: most of today's immigrants are non-European and thus face more deeply entrenched cultural barriers than did their predecessors; about a quarter of all immigrants (the vast majority Hispanic) arrived illegally and thus must navigate lives of stunted opportunity in the shadows of the law; globalization and the digital revolution have eliminated many of the jobs that provided ladders into the middle class for earlier generations of immigrants; the close proximity of the largest sending country (Mexico) and the growing ease of all international travel and communication have enabled today's immigrants to retain their ties to their countries of origin, thereby reducing pressures to adopt America's language, customs, values, and mores.

The worries all have a ring of legitimacy, but increasingly they compete with a growing body of facts on the ground that tell a more upbeat story. The modern immigration wave is mature enough to have produced a sizable adult "second generation" (US-born children of immigrants). In recent years the Pew Research Center has generated a trove of information about this group, some from our own surveys and some based on our analysis of US Census Bureau data. The headline findings are almost entirely positive. Second-generation Hispanic and Asian American adults are following a well-trekked path in American history—doing better than the immigrant generation on key measures of socioeconomic attainment and cultural adaptation (see appendix Figure 6A.2). Moreover, like their parents' generation, they place more importance than other Americans do on such "traditional American values" as family, hard work, education, and career success.

HISPANICS

There are some blemishes in the story, but first let's register the good news, starting with Hispanics. A decade ago the eminent Harvard historian Samuel Huntington wrote that "the single most immediate and most serious challenge to America's traditional identity comes from the immense and continuing immigration from Latin America, especially from Mexico. . . . The extent and nature of this immigration differs fundamentally from those of previous immigrations, and the assimilation successes of the past are unlikely to be duplicated with the contemporary flood of immigrants from Latin America." Huntington was primarily concerned by what he saw as shortcomings in Hispanic values and culture, which he feared over time would erode this country's Anglo-Saxon work ethic, language, rule of law, individualism—the "American creed," as he called it. Other scholars have focused on more tangible deficits. They worry that the relative paucity of human capital—money, education, job skills—that most Hispanics have brought with them across the border will consign the immigrants and their progeny to economically marginal lives in a knowledge-based economy. Three-quarters of all adult Hispanic immigrants have only a high school degree or less; half are in this country illegally; only a third speak English proficiently.

Such deficits, however, have not condemned their children to a purgatory in the underclass. The 7 million Hispanic adults in the second generation have a significantly higher median annual household income[2] than the 17.5 million in the immigrant generation ($48,000 versus $35,000), a higher share with at least some college or more (52% versus 24%), a higher homeownership rate (50% versus 43%), and a lower poverty rate (16% versus 23%). On all of these indicators, the adult Hispanic second generation still trails the overall adult population of the US, whose 2012 median income for a household of three was $58,000; share with at least some college was 57%; homeownership rate was 65%; and poverty rate was 13%. But the data suggest a classic progression toward the mean, the more notable because the second generation of Hispanic adults have a median age of just 28, nearly two decades younger than the median age (46) of all American adults (see appendix Figure 6A.3). If history is a guide, median incomes and homeownership rates of second-generation

Hispanics will rise as more become middle-age. In the meantime, for the vast majority of Hispanics—first and second generation alike—there's already a strong appreciation for the upward arc of their life journey. Seven in 10 Hispanic adults of the first (71%) and second (67%) generation say their own standard of living is better than their parents' was at the same stage of life. Among all US adults, just 60% say the same.

When it comes to basic measures of social and cultural integration—language, friends, spouses, identity—second-generation Hispanics are much more rooted than immigrant Hispanics in the US mainstream. Fully 93% say they speak English very or pretty well, compared with 48% of the immigrant generation. They are twice as likely as immigrants to say Hispanics as a group get along very or pretty well with whites, blacks, and Asian Americans (52% versus 26%). They are nearly four times as likely to marry a non-Hispanic (26% versus 7% among married adults). They are less likely to say that most or all of their friends come from their family's country of origin (49% versus 64%) and they are almost twice as likely to say they think of themselves as a "typical American" (61% versus 33%).

At the same time, however, second-generation Hispanics retain strong ties to the land and language of their ancestors. Eight in 10 say they can speak Spanish at least pretty well, and more than 9 in 10 say it is important that future generations of Hispanics living in the US be able to do so as well. A majority say they most often identify themselves by their family's country of origin (e.g., Mexican American) or by a pan-ethnic label, such as Hispanic or Latino; just 35% say they most often identify simply as American. That's more than the first generation (8%) and less than the third-and-higher generation (48%), indicating a trajectory of assimilation over time (see appendix Figure 6A.4).[3] However, with only half of third-plus-generation Hispanics saying they

Figure 6.2

Generational Differences in Intergroup Relations

% saying their group gets along with each of three other groups "very well" or "pretty well"

■ 1st generation   ■ 2nd generation

Hispanic — 26 / 52

Asian American — 49 / 64

Note: Hispanics were asked how well they get along with blacks, Asians and whites. Asian Americans were asked how well [country of origin] Americans get along with blacks, Hispanics or Latinos, and whites.

Source: Pew Research Center National Survey of Latinos, Sep.–Oct. 2012 (N=1,765 US Hispanic adults), and Pew Research Center Asian-American Survey, Jan.–Mar. 2012 (N=3,511 US Asian adults)

typically describe themselves as Americans, assimilation has come to mean something different. Our twentieth-century metaphor was "melting pot." Our twenty-first-century metaphor, in a much more racially and ethnically diverse nation, is "mosaic." Each piece contributes to a whole, but not by losing its distinctiveness.

On values related to work and family, first- and second-generation Hispanics are more similar to one another than to the general public. For example, 78% of both immigrant and second-generation Hispanics say that most people who want to get ahead in life can make it if they're willing to work hard, an optimistic outlook shared by just 58% of the full US public. Both generations of Hispanics are also more likely than the general public to say they place high importance on career success, having a good marriage, and being a good parent, and they're equally likely to place high importance on leading a religious life. In short, they're family-oriented, religious strivers. That's a pretty good summary of what most people mean when they talk about "traditional American values." Far from eroding the American creed, Hispanics are among its most ardent believers.

Not all socioeconomic and cultural indicators are positive. Hispanic educational attainment continues to lag behind that of other racial and ethnic groups by sizable margins. Just 15% of all Hispanics adults ages 25 and older (and 21% of the adult second generation) have a bachelor's degree or higher. The problem isn't aspirational—about 9 in 10 Hispanics say getting a college education is important to success in life. It's economic. Hispanics who dropped out of high school or college, when asked why they didn't continue their education, typically cite a lack of money or the need to support a family.

These education gaps have narrowed sharply in recent years. The Hispanic high school dropout rate has fallen by nearly half since 2000 (1 dropout for every 5 high school graduates now, versus 1 for every 3 in 2000). The 2012 National Assessment of Educational Progress showed that over a four-decade span, Hispanic elementary and secondary school students had closed some of their achievement gaps with whites in reading and math (even as rates for all racial groups rose). And in 2012, for the first time ever, a Hispanic high school graduate was *more likely* than a white high school graduate to enroll in college the following fall. However, for many Hispanic students, college means a two-year rather than a four-year degree. And no matter what kind of college they enroll in, a disproportionate share leave before getting a degree. But while problems remain, the long-term progress has been more impressive than generally understood.

In addition to their education deficits, Hispanics also have a deficit of social trust. A classic question in social science research asks respondents: "Generally speaking, would you say that most people can be trusted or that you can't be too careful when dealing with people?" By a whopping 86% to 12% margin (with virtually no differences between the first and second generations) Hispanics say you can't be too careful. Among the general public, caution also trumps trust, but not by nearly as much: 59% say you can't be too careful and 37% say people can be trusted (see appendix Figure 6A.5). In a heterogeneous, fast-paced, risk-taking culture such as ours, social trust helps to keep the gears from grinding.

A third and perhaps most surprising deficit among Hispanics, especially those in the second generation, has to do with the diminished link between births and marriage.

Figure 6.3

Immediate Entry into College by Race and Ethnicity, 2000–2012

% of recent high school completers enrolled in college the following October

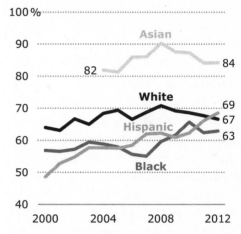

Note: White, black and Asian include the Hispanic portion of those groups. Due to the small sample size for Hispanics, blacks and Asians, a 3-year moving average is used. The 3-year moving average uses the year indicated, the year immediately preceding and the year immediately following. For 2012 a 2-year moving average is used.

Source: US Bureau of Labor Statistics, annual "College Enrollment and Work Activity of High School Graduates" news releases, and National Center for Education Statistics *The Condition of Education 2012*

More than half of all births to Hispanic women are to single mothers. Hispanics themselves disapprove in overwhelming numbers of nonmarital births (as do all Americans), but here's a case where norms are in one place and behaviors in another. As Chapter 8 describes in detail, marriage rates have been falling and non-marital births have been rising among all demographic groups in America for the past half century. The 53% nonmarital birthrate among Hispanics falls between the figure for whites (29%) and that for blacks (72%). The social science findings could not be more clear: all else equal, children born to single mothers tend to do less well in life than those born to married parents. As of 2010, a plurality of all poor children in the

US were Hispanic. That unhappy milestone is partly a function of population growth and partly of childhood poverty rates that spiked during the recession to 35% among Latinos in 2010, far surpassing that of white children (12%) and nearly equaling the 39% share among black children (see appendix Figure 6A.6).[4] Going forward, the well-being of future generations of Hispanics will depend as much on the families they form—or fail to form—as on the nation's immigration policies or economic trends.

ASIAN AMERICANS

In 2012 the Pew Research Center published a major report on Asian Americans that drew criticism from some of their leading civic and interest groups. Their complaint, in a nutshell: too much good news. Odd on its face, but less so in light of their history and culture. Aside from blacks and Native Americans, no group in this country has been the target of more official discrimination or social stigma. In the late nineteenth century all immigration from China was explicitly prohibited by act of Congress; in the early twentieth century Indian Americans had their official race designation changed from Asian to white and then back again; during World War II 120,000 law-aiding Japanese Americans were rounded up and sent off to internment camps; and it was not until 1952 that Asian-American immigrants were permitted to apply for US citizenship.

That history is enough to make any group wary, but for Asians the reticence about trumpeting success also has a cultural basis. Chinese and Japanese proverbs warn that the nail that sticks out gets hammered down, while a roughly analogous American proverb promises that the squeaky wheel gets greased. After the report came out, I had a series of spirited exchanges with community leaders. They argued that lots of Asian Americans are struggling, that their community is enormously diverse, and that the patronizing term "model minority" (which the report was careful *not* to use) paints with too broad a brush. So stipulated. But I countered that data are data. And when you gather up all the relevant numbers you can find about this remarkable immigrant group, you wind up with a story that leaps off the page. Here is a condensed version of the overview of the report, which was based on one of the most comprehensive surveys of Asian Americans ever conducted.[5]

Asian Americans are the highest-income, best-educated, and fastest-growing racial group in the US. They are more satisfied than the general public with their lives, finances, and the direction of the country, and they place more value than other Americans do on marriage, parenthood, hard work, and career success.

A century ago, most Asian Americans were low-skilled, low-wage laborers crowded into ethnic enclaves and targets of official discrimination. Today they are the most likely of any major racial or ethnic group in America to live in mixed neighborhoods and to marry across racial lines. When newly minted medical school graduate Priscilla Chan married Facebook founder Mark Zuckerberg in the spring of 2012, she joined the 37% of all recent Asian-American brides who wed a non-Asian groom.

These milestones of economic success and social assimilation have come to a group that is still majority immigrant. Nearly three-quarters (74%) of Asian-American adults were born abroad; of these, about half say they speak English very well and half say they don't.

Asians recently passed Hispanics as the largest group of new immigrants to the US. The educational credentials of these recent arrivals are striking. More

Figure 6.4

Asian Americans Lead Others In Education, Income

% with a bachelor's degree or more, among ages 25 and older, 2010

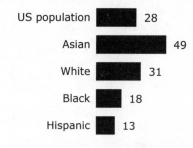

US population	28
Asian	49
White	31
Black	18
Hispanic	13

Median household income, 2010

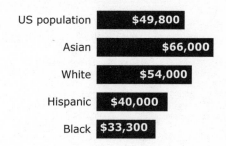

US population	$49,800
Asian	$66,000
White	$54,000
Hispanic	$40,000
Black	$33,300

Note: Asians include mixed-race Asian population, regardless of Hispanic origin. Household income is based on householders ages 18 and older; race and ethnicity are based on those of household head.

Source: Pew Research Center analysis of 2010 American Community Survey, IPUMS

than 6 in 10 (61%) adults ages 25 to 64 who have come from Asia in recent years have at least a bachelor's degree. This is double the share among recent non-Asian arrivals, and almost surely makes the recent Asian arrivals the most highly educated cohort of immigrants in US history.

Compared with the educational attainment of the population in their country of origin, recent Asian immigrants also stand out as a select group. For example, about 27% of adults ages 25 to 64 in South Korea and 25% in Japan have a bachelor's degree or more.[6] In contrast, nearly 70% of comparably aged recent immigrants from these two countries have at least a bachelor's degree (for more, see appendix Figure 6A.7).

Figure 6.5

Meet the New Immigrants: Asians Overtake Hispanics

% of immigrants, by year of arrival, 2000–2010

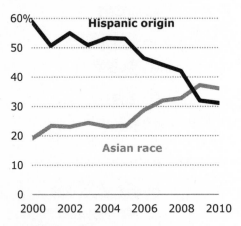

Note: Based on total foreign-born population, including adults and children. Asians include mixed-race Asian population, regardless of Hispanic origin. The 2010 ACS includes only partial-year arrivals for 2010; arrivals for 2010 adjusted to full-year totals based on analysis of 2005–2009 ACS data on partial-year arrivals.

Source: Pew Research Center analysis of 2010 American Community Survey, IPUMS

Recent Asian immigrants are also about three times as likely as recent immigrants from other parts of the world to receive their green cards—or permanent resident status—on the basis of employer rather than family sponsorship (though family reunification remains the most common legal gateway to the US for Asian immigrants, as it is for all immigrants).

The modern immigration wave from Asia is nearly a half century old and has pushed the total population of Asian Americans—foreign born and US born, adults and children—to a record 18.2 million in 2011, or 5.8% of the total US population, up from less than 1% in 1965.

Asian Americans trace their roots to any of dozens of countries in the Far East, Southeast Asia, and the Indian subcontinent. Each country of origin subgroup has its own unique history, culture, language, religious beliefs, economic and demographic traits, social and political values, and pathways into America.

But despite often sizable subgroup differences, Asian Americans are distinctive as a whole, especially when compared with all US adults, whom they exceed not just in the share with a college degree (49% versus 28%), but also in median annual household income ($66,000 versus $49,800) and median household wealth ($83,500 versus $68,529).[7]

They are noteworthy in other ways, too. They are more satisfied than the general public with their lives overall (82% versus 75%), their personal finances (51% versus 35%), and the general direction of the country (43% versus 21%).

They also stand out for their strong emphasis on family. More than half (54%) say that having a successful marriage is one of the most important things in life; just 34% of all American adults agree. Two-thirds of Asian-American adults (67%) say that being a good parent is one of the most important things in life; just 50% of all adults agree.

Their living arrangements align with these values. They are more likely than all American adults to be married (59% versus 51%); their newborns are less likely than all US newborns to have a single mother (16% versus 41%); and their children are more likely than all US children to be raised in a household with two married parents (80% versus 63%).

They are more likely than the general public to live in multigenerational family households. Some 28% live with at least two adult generations under the same roof, twice the share of whites and slightly more than the share of blacks and Hispanics who live in such households. US Asians also have a strong sense of filial respect; about two-thirds say parents should have a lot or some influence in choosing one's profession (66%) and spouse (61%).

Asian Americans have a pervasive belief in the rewards of hard work. Nearly 7 in 10 (69%) say people can get ahead if they are willing to work hard, a view shared by a somewhat smaller share of the American public as a whole (58%). And fully 93% of Asian Americans describe members of their country of origin group as "very hardworking"; just 57% say the same about Americans as a whole (see appendix Figure 6A.8).

By their own lights, Asian Americans sometimes go overboard in stressing hard work. Nearly 4 in 10 (39%) say that Asian-American parents from their country of origin subgroup put too much pressure on their children to do well in school. Just 9% say the same about all American parents. On the flip side of the same coin, about 6 in 10 Asian Americans say American parents put too little pressure on their children to succeed in school, while just 9% say the same about Asian-American parents. (Those numbers help explain why *Battle Hymn of the Tiger Mother,* a 2011 comic memoir about strict parenting by Yale law professor Amy Chua, the daughter of immigrants, touched a nerve among Asian Americans as well as other parents.)

The immigration wave from Asia has occurred at a time when the largest sending countries have experienced dramatic gains in their standards of living. But few Asian immigrants are looking over their shoulders with regret. Just 12% say that if they had to do it all over again, they would remain in their country of origin. And by lopsided margins, Asian Americans say the US is preferable to their country of origin in such realms as providing economic opportunity, political and religious freedoms, and good conditions for raising children (see appendix Figure 6A.9). Respondents rated their country of origin as being superior on just one of seven measures tested in the survey—strength of family ties. (The Pew Research survey was conducted only among Asian Americans currently living in the US. As is the case with all immigration

Figure 6.6

Who's a "Tiger Mom"?

% of US Asians saying (American parents/Asian-American parents)   *put*
... pressure on their children to do well in school

Note: For the bottom bar, respondents were asked about parents from their country of origin group (Chinese-American parents, Korean-American parents, etc.). Those who did not provide a country of origin were asked about "Asian-American parents."

Source: Pew Research Center Asian-American Survey, Jan.–Mar. 2012, N=3,511 US Asian adults

waves, a portion of those who came to the US from Asia in recent decades have chosen to return to their country of origin. However, return migration rates are estimated to be lower for immigrants from Asia than for other immigrants, and naturalization rates—that is, the share of eligible immigrants who become US citizens—are higher.)

Asian-American immigrants have set the bar of socioeconomic success so high that it will be a challenge for the next generation to surpass it. Only about half of the nearly 5 million US-born children of Asian-American immigrants have reached adulthood, so it's early to start drawing up a comprehensive generational score card. Nonetheless, some data are available, and as always, they are instructive. On basic socioeconomic measures such as median household income and college education, the adult children of immigrants resemble the immigrant generation and exceed the general public (see appendix Figure 6A.10). And when it comes to various measures of social integration, they are more likely than immigrants to say they think of themselves as "a typical American," more likely to say they have friends outside their race or country of origin group, and much more likely to marry outside their race (especially women, who are twice as likely as Asian-American men to "marry out"). Out-marriage patterns also differ by Asian country of origin group, with Japanese Americans the most likely to do so and Indian Americans the least likely, a pattern related to the fact that a much higher share of the Japanese were born in the US.

As with Hispanics, the US-born Asian-American adults are much more likely than the immigrants to have children outside of marriage. About 3 in 10 native-born Asian women (this includes both the second generation and third and higher generation) who had children in recent years were single, triple the rate among immigrant mothers. Assimilation can be a powerful force—and not always for the better.

ILLEGAL IMMIGRATION

Most of the political and media attention to immigrants in recent years has focused on those who have come illegally. Understandably so—the past few decades have seen the largest influx of such immigrants in the nation's history. The number living in the US more than tripled from 3.5 million in 1990 to a peak of 12.2 million in 2007 before declining somewhat during the 2007–2009 recession. The latest Pew Research Center estimate had 11.7 million here as of 2012,

Figure 6.7

Intermarriage Rates for Asians

% of Asian newlyweds (2008–2010) married to...

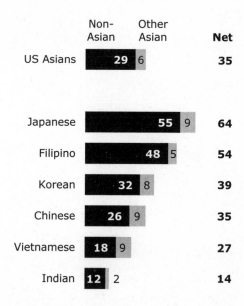

	Non-Asian	Other Asian	Net
US Asians	29	6	35
Japanese	55	9	64
Filipino	48	5	54
Korean	32	8	39
Chinese	26	9	35
Vietnamese	18	9	27
Indian	12	2	14

Note: "Newlyweds" refers to people ages 15 and older who got married in the year prior to the survey, and their marital status was "married, spouse present." US Asians and each US Asian group include non-Hispanic single-race Asians who are from only one group; "Non Asian" includes Hispanics and single- or multiple-race non-Hispanics except single-race Asians; "Other Asian" includes non-Hispanics from other single-Asian or multiple-Asian groups.

Source: Pew Research Center analysis of 2008–2010 American Community Survey, IPUMS

which means they accounted for slightly more than a quarter of the 41.7 million immigrants in the US that year.[8]

Unauthorized immigrants tend to live in the shadows and avoid contact with government agencies. How do we know how many there are? Mostly thanks to Jeffrey Passel, a brilliant former Census Bureau demographer who decades ago developed something called the "residual method" to estimate the number and characteristics of immigrants who are in the US illegally at any given time. Passel's methodology, which has since been adopted by the

Figure 6.8

Estimates of the US Unauthorized Immigrant Population, 1990–2012

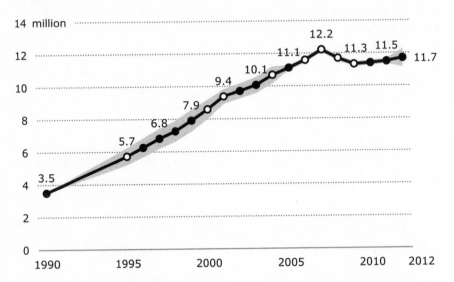

Note: Shading surrounding line indicates low and high points of the estimated 90% confidence interval. White data markers indicate the change from the previous year is statistically significant (for 1995, change is significant from 1990).

Source: Pew Research Center estimates based on residual methodology applied to March supplements to the Current Population Survey (1995–2004, 2012) or American Community Survey (2005–2011)

Department of Homeland Security and other researchers, involves totaling up the number of legal immigrants (computed from administrative data) and the number of all immigrants (computed from census data). The difference between those two numbers—the residual—is presumed to make up the universe of immigrants who are here illegally. It's a bit more complicated than that because various adjustments need to be made for undercounts. Once Passel has established the size of this universe, he can then make educated guesses about the characteristics of unauthorized immigrants. For example, if an immigrant is an accountant, a teacher, or a veteran, it's a pretty good bet he or she isn't here illegally. And so on.

Perhaps the most surprising finding from Passel's research is that a sizable share of unauthorized immigrants—nearly half—live in a household made up of an adult couple (married or not) and one or more children. This probably isn't the family constellation most people have in mind when they think about a migrant farm worker or a day laborer. However, unauthorized immigrants (46%) are much more likely to be parents of a minor child than are legal immigrants (38%) or native-born US adults (29%). The difference is driven both by the youth of unauthorized immigrant adults, who are typically in the child-rearing and -raising stage of life, and by their relatively high birth-rates. It's also a clue to their motives for coming. Yes, they come for work. But they also come to put down roots, start a family, and create a future for their as-yet-unborn children. And it's those kids who are the greatest beneficiaries of their journey. Of the more than 5 million children of today's unauthorized immigrants, about 4 in 5 were born in this country and thus are automatic US citizens, despite the illegal status of their parents. The other 20 percent—the so-called Dreamers, who as young children were brought to this country illegally by their parents—have already been spared the threat of deportation by an Obama administration policy change in 2012 and are the leading candidates to be granted a pathway to citizenship in various immigration bills Congress was considering in 2013.

As for the roughly 10 million adult unauthorized immigrants, they broke the law, which means they live under the threat of employer exploitation, government deportation, or both. Most work long hours for low wages under lousy working conditions, often doing jobs their US-born counterparts consider beneath them. Tallying up their costs and benefits to society is a complex and subjective exercise. Arguably the greatest harm they do is the illegal way they came to the country—which undermines the rule of law that helps makes the US a magnet for immigrants in the first place and is unfair to all who wait their turn to come legally. Once they get here, they tend to be more law-abiding than other Americans because they know any brush with the law could result in deportation. As for their economic impact, it's uneven. Most studies suggest that they depress wages (but only marginally) for the unskilled laborers with whom they directly compete, but raise wages for skilled laborers who benefit from the increased economic activity and productivity associated with their presence in the labor force.[9] For consumers, they're a blessing, as they lower the cost of everything from food to housing to medical care to personal services. They're a net burden on state and local governments, which by law are obligated to educate their children and provide free health care to their indigent. But they're a net benefit to the federal government, mainly because many wind up paying into the Social Security system (up to $15 billion a year, by one estimate)[10] without ever receiving benefits from it.

IMMIGRANTS AND POLITICS

Immigrants—even those who are here legally—typically become workers long before they become voters, and many never take that second step. If an immigrant wants to earn the right to vote, he or she must first become a naturalized US citizen. This is not a casual process. It requires a minimum of five years of continuous residence in the US, $680 in fees, successful completion of English tests and background checks, demonstration of an understanding of US history, government, and constitutional law, and the swearing of a loyalty oath.[11] Among all immigrants who are here legally and thus eligible to naturalize, only about two-thirds (including just 36% of legal Mexican-American immigrants) have done so. The rest remain legal permanent residents, enabling them to work, pay taxes, and receive many government benefits, but not giving them the right to vote.

So, some quick accounting: Of the immigrants currently in the country, about a quarter can't vote because they aren't here legally and an additional quarter can't vote because they aren't citizens. This cuts the potential voter pool among immigrants in half, the vast majority of whom are Hispanics and Asians.

The real electoral muscle of these new immigrant groups lies out in the not too distant future. Their children (nearly all of whom, remember, are US born and thus automatically eligible to vote) will be aging into the electorate at the rate of roughly 1 million a year for decades to come. Assuming their voter turnout rates rise over time to the levels of other native-born groups, Hispanics and Asians will be casting up to 25% of all votes in the presidential elections within a few decades, roughly double their share in 2012.

A striking feature of the politics of the modern immigration wave is that the deeper Hispanics and Asian Americans and their adult children have sunk their roots into America, the more Democratic they have become. Ronald Reagan captured 37% of the Latino vote in 1984; Mitt Romney got just 27% in 2012. Likewise, a majority of Asian Americans voted Republican in 1992 and 1996, but just a quarter did in 2012. The progression hasn't always been in a straight line—George W. Bush drew 40% of the Latino vote in 2004— and, to borrow a phrase, past performance is no guarantee of future results. Nonetheless, the trend lines are ominous for the GOP. More than any other factor, it was the big Latino vote for Obama in 2012 that led some Republicans in the US Senate to drop their long-standing opposition to immigration reform. But the politics of this issue puts the GOP in a double bind. If their conservative House members kill a bill, it will play well in their deep red congressional districts while hurting the party at the national level. On the other hand, if a bill is enacted that provides for a pathway to citizenship, it could,

Figure 6.9

Voter Turnout Rate, by Race and Ethnicity, 1988–2012

% of eligible voters

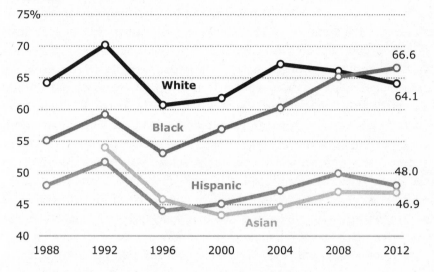

Note: Voter turnout rate for Asians not available prior to 1990.

Source: Pew Research Center analysis of Current Population Survey, November Supplements

in the (overheated) calculus of US Representative Michael Burgess (R-Texas), give "11 million undocumented Democrats" the right to vote.[12] Some GOP strategists have even argued that the party should concentrate less on trying to become competitive with Hispanic voters and more on driving up election turnout among whites, especially the lower-middle-class Republicans most threatened by immigrants. But to many party leaders, including the entire Bush political clan, that's a recipe for slow-motion political suicide. Karl Rove, the architect of George W. Bush's winning campaigns for president and for governor of Texas, wrote in 2013 that if the GOP party doesn't find a way to do better with nonwhites, it not only risks extending its losing streak in presidential races, but eventually will put its congressional base at risk as well.[13] As of now, whites make up half the population in the 201 congressional districts represented by Democrats and three-quarters of the population in the 234 districts represented by Republicans. As the nation's underlying demographics grow increasingly nonwhite, the congressional math will move in a Democratic direction unless the GOP finds a way to change the politics.

PARTY IDENTIFICATION

One reason the GOP has fallen so far out of favor with Hispanics and Asian Americans is that its candidates and elected officials sometimes seem to be in a bidding war to see who says the toughest things about illegal immigrants. In 2012 Mitt Romney called for them to "self-deport" and one of his rivals for the GOP presidential nomination, Herman Cain, proposed (in jest, he later said) that border fences be electrified. In 2013 Representative Steve King, R-Iowa, likened young illegal immigrants to "drug mules" who have "calves the size of cantaloupes." That jab drew rebukes from many GOP leaders, but epithets leave a mark. Pew Research Center surveys show that many legal Hispanic and Asian immigrants have a sense of shared identity and fate with the unauthorized, even if they disapprove of their illegal mode of entry.

Immigrants' differences with the GOP extend well beyond the issue of illegal immigration. They're broadly ideological. Both Hispanics and Asian Americans are more likely than the general public to self-identify as liberals and be supporters of big government. Second-generation Hispanics follow this pattern even more strongly than do Hispanic immigrants.

On social issues such as homosexuality and abortion, second-generation Hispanics and Asians are significantly more liberal than either the general public or the immigrants within their racial and ethnic group. Some but not all of these differences are related to age. Young adults generally are more accepting of homosexuality, but the greater acceptance of homosexuality among second-generation Asian Americans versus those in the first generation remains, even when controlling for age.

THE IMMIGRANT FUTURE

A nation's demographic future is the product of three rates: births, deaths, and immigration. The first two generally aren't susceptible to modification by public policy. The third is—at least by societies such as ours that are in the enviable position of having people from all over the world clambering to get in. With Baby Boomers retiring and birthrates declining, America's fewer-workers-per-retiree future is already upon us. Our old-age-dependency ratio will only grow more problematic with each passing year. The most direct public policy responses—social safety net cuts and tax increases—will be painful. But there's a complementary solution that needn't be: opening our borders in a rational way to more immigrants. It's akin to raising the birth-rate, but its impact is more immediate, because the newcomers arrive ready to work. They tend to have lots of babies, so they're a demographic dividend that keeps giving. Plus, our modern immigration streams are already roughly aligned with the hourglass contours of our workforce needs. We get lots of low-skilled immigrants to do the unpleasant work most native-born American won't do, and we're getting more highly skilled immigrants to pick up the slack in science and engineering, where we're not producing enough homegrown talent. For example, up to two-thirds of the workforce tending to crops and livestock—some 1 million workers—are undocumented Hispanics. (Many are relatively skilled, most have been in the country a decade or more, and some have moved into middle-management jobs.) Meantime, Asian Americans make up less than 6% of the population, but in 2010 collected 45% of all engineering doctorates and 38% of all math and computer science PhDs. Immigrants and their offspring are also heavily overrepresented in the ranks of entrepreneurs—be they sole proprietors or corporate moguls. One quarter of the high-tech firms launched in the US between 1965 and 2005 were founded by immigrants. And some 40% of all Fortune 500 companies were started by immigrants or their children (the vast bulk of them came during earlier European waves).[14]

In light of all this, it's no surprise that the most enthusiastic proponents of immigration reform are in the business community. Open borders have always been more popular with business elites (who benefit from their economic dynamism) and foreign-heritage interest groups (who want to attract more family members from their ancestral countries) than with the general public (some of whom are directly threatened by the competition for jobs).

The US is already home to four times more immigrants than any other nation in the world.[15] Political backlashes notwithstanding, we have a long and mostly happy history of bringing them in and helping them become American. If we adopt immigration policies that allow us to keep winning the global lottery for newcomers with brains, talent, and drive, we'll go a long way toward ensuring our place as the top dog in the world's economy.

Immigrants are more than units of economic output. They're also our face to the world, and their life stories embody the values our nation holds most dear: pluralism, dynamism, tolerance, entrepreneurship, achievement, optimism. At a time when a rising Asia is flexing its muscles around the globe, having so many successful Asians as part of the new American tapestry is a great calling card on the world stage. Consider the multiple messages conveyed by a small diplomatic flap between the US and China in 2012. On the eve of a visit to Beijing by then secretary of state Hillary Clinton, a Chinese human rights activist, Chen Gaungcheng, escaped house arrest and made his way to the US embassy, where he sought refuge. After a few days of tense negotiations, US authorities agreed to hand him back to the Chinese, but with the understanding that he and his family would soon be permitted to move to the US. The photo that ran in the newspapers the day the crisis was resolved probably did as much as the settlement itself to burnish the US image around the world. It showed Chen being escorted out of the embassy in a wheelchair (blind since childhood, he'd broken his foot while scaling a wall during his escape), accompanied by the two senior US diplomats who'd brokered the deal. One was Gary Locke, the US ambassador to China, a former governor of Washington, a former US secretary of commerce, and a third-generation Chinese American. The other was Harold Koh, then the senior legal adviser to the State Department, a professor of international law and former dean of Yale Law School, and a second-generation Korean American. As the saying goes, only in America.

Hapa Nation

WHEN BARACK OBAMA'S PARENTS married in 1961, the best estimates are that perhaps 1 marriage in 1,000 in the US that year was, like theirs, between a black person and a white person. Anti-miscegenation laws were still in force in 16 states, and racial intermarriage was a gasp-inducing taboo virtually everywhere else. That was then. Now 15.5% of all new marriages in the US are between spouses of a different race or ethnicity from each other. This cultural sea change has been driven not just by blacks and whites, but by a wave of Hispanic and Asian newcomers who've produced a new American tapestry more complex than anything our nation has ever known.

Few families embody this transformation better than the one that resides at 1600 Pennsylvania Avenue.[1] President Obama's wife is a descendant of an African-American slave and a white slave owner. His wife's brother is married to a white woman of Scottish/Irish heritage. His half-sister is an Indonesian American married to a Chinese Canadian. The president himself is the product of an African father raised in Kenya and a white mother raised in Kansas. According to genealogy.com, he too is the descendant of a slave— but on his white mother's side, not his black father's. Obama was born in Hawaii, America's most Technicolor state, where the word "hapa" (half or part) is meant to describe someone of mixed Asian heritage, but colloquially has come to mean a mixed-race person of any kind—a "mutt," as Obama sometimes calls himself.

The fact that no racial label neatly fits our sitting president is in its way fitting for a society that is struggling to find a modern vocabulary for race. Our labels, categories, and classification schemes haven't kept up with our behaviors, attitudes, and weddings. This is new. In one form or another, America has been confounded by race—our original sin—for four centuries. But for most of that history, racial identification had been a simple matter of black or white, with the "one-drop rule" the line of demarcation. The rigidity of this either/or formulation obscured the racial intermixing that has always been a part of our national DNA—but that, of course, was exactly the point. Mixing was deemed to be not just illegal but sinful, so it couldn't be acknowledged above a whisper. Now the stigma is receding. And so too is our exclusively black-or-white racial checkerboard, rendered obsolete by the more than 30 million Hispanic and Asian immigrants who have come to the US since 1965. Today's immigrants and their children are in the vanguard of the modern intermarriage trend. What should we call the children of such marriages? As a society, we don't yet know. No one—not the Census Bureau, not those children themselves, not Americans of different races—has come up with a common vocabulary.

Consider again the man who lives in the White House. Racially speaking, who is Barack Obama? Well, it depends on whom you ask. Given a choice between calling the president black or calling him mixed race, most blacks (55%) say Obama is black; just a third (34%) say he is mixed race. Among whites, the pattern is reversed. Most (53%) say he is mixed race, while just a quarter (24%) say he is black. And among Hispanics (who have their own unique set of challenges finding a racial label that fits their group), 6 in 10 say Obama is mixed race.

Nor is Obama the only object of semantic confusion. When a Pew Research survey asked respondents in 2009 to state what race they themselves are (the choices were white, black, Asian, or some other race) and told they could choose as many categories as they wished, just 1% chose to identify with more than one category. However, later in the same survey, when respondents were asked explicitly if they considered themselves to be mixed race, fully 1 in 6 (16%) said they did,

Figure 7.1

Do You Think of Obama as Black or Mixed Race?

% saying ...

Note: "Both/neither" and "Don't know/Refused" responses not shown. Question wording: Do you mostly think of Obama as a black person or mostly as a person of mixed race?

Source: Pew Research Center survey, Oct.–Nov. 2009, N=2,884 US adults including 8% of whites, 20% of blacks, and 37% of Hispanics. In short, responses to racial identity questions vary widely depending on wording and context—another sign that our traditional categories aren't very good at capturing our new racial landscape in all of its complexity.

Some groups are more disoriented by and disapproving of all these changes than others—and here's where a big generation gap emerges. As noted in Chapter 3, just 29% of Silents say that "more people of different races marrying each other" has been a change for the better in America. This share rises to 36% among Boomers, 47% among Xers, and 60% among Millennials. And when a similar question is posed in explicitly personal terms—how comfortable would you be if someone in your family were to marry someone of a different race?—the generational differences grow even sharper. Just 38% of Silents say they would be comfortable, compared with 85% of Millennials (see appendix Figure 7A.1).

Whether Americans are ready for them or not, racial and ethnic intermarriages are happening in record numbers.

THE RISE OF INTERMARRIAGE

Some 15.5% of all new marriages in 2011 were either interracial or interethnic, a sixfold increase over the share in 1960. Looking at all current marriages in 2011, irrespective of the year they began, 8.6% were interracial or interethnic, an all-time high.[2]

There are distinctive patterns by race and ethnicity. Among all newlyweds in 2010, 9% of whites, 17% of blacks, 26% of Hispanics, and 28% of Asians married someone whose race or ethnicity was different from their own.

Even though the rate is lowest among whites, they are still by far the nation's most numerous race group. As such, in 70% of all

Figure 7.2

Intermarriage Trend, 1960–2011

% of marriages involving spouses of a different race/ethnicity from each other

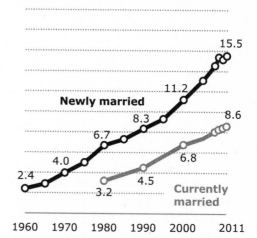

Source: Pew Research Center analysis of 1960–2011 American Community Survey and Census data (IPUMS) For 1960–2008, figures are calculated based on 1980 and 2008 data. For more details see Pew Research Center's "Marrying Out: One-in-Seven New US Marriages is Interracial or Interethnic," June 4, 2010.

Figure 7.3

Intermarriage Rates, by Race and Ethnicity, 2010

% of newlyweds married to someone of a different race/ethnicity

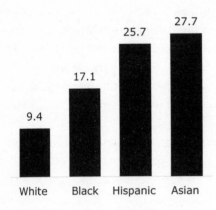

Note: Asians include Pacific Islanders.

Source: Pew Research Center analysis of 2010 American Community Survey, IPUMS

new mixed marriages, one spouse is white. Of the approximately 275,500 new interracial or interethnic marriages in 2010, white/Hispanic couples accounted for more than 4 in 10 (43%), white/Asian couples made up 14%, and white/black couples made up 12%. About 3 in 10 new intermarriages were among a mix of different non-white spouses (see appendix Figure 7A.2).

Gender patterns vary widely— and these variances are highly race-specific. Black men are nearly three times more likely than black women to "marry out." By contrast, Asian-American women are more than twice as likely as Asian-American men to marry out. Cultural norms and gender and racial stereotypes help explain these patterns. A 2013 PBS documentary, *Seeking Asian Female*, about a marriage initiated on the Internet between a 60-year-old white American man and his 30-year-old Chinese bride, sparked an animated online debate about the way American pop culture tends to sexualize Asian women and emasculate Asian men. These stereotypes, to some degree, establish the contours of the out-marriage market for Asian Americans of both genders; they also complicate romantic couplings among Asian Americans themselves. The marital dynamics between black men and women are even more fraught. Marriage rates in the African-American community have fallen to their lowest levels in modern history, a trend driven by the disparate impact of the changing economy on black men and women and exacerbated by gender tensions arising from the fact that among the declining ranks of black men who do marry, a record share (more than 1 in 5) choose a bride who is not black. Among whites and Hispanics, by the way, there is no gender difference in intermarriage rates.

There are also distinctive socioeconomic patterns among intermarried couples, based on the race, ethnicity, and gender of the partners. Some of the differences reflect the overall characteristics of these different groups in society at large, and some appear to be the result of a selection process. For example,

Figure 7.4

Intermarriage Rates of Newlyweds, by Gender, 2010

% of newlyweds married to someone of a different race/ethnicity

No gender difference for these groups ...

Big gender difference for these groups ...

Note: Asians include Pacific Islanders.

Source: Pew Research Center analysis of 2010 American Community Survey, IPUMS

among intermarried newlywed couples involving whites, white/Asian couples have the highest combined annual earnings (nearly $71,000), much higher than the earnings of white/Hispanic couples (about $58,000) as well as white/black couples (about $53,000). Also, white/Asian couples have higher combined earnings than either white/white or Asian/Asian couples. Meanwhile, the combined median earnings of white/Hispanic couples are lower than those of white/white couples but higher than those of Hispanic/Hispanic couples. The earnings of intermarried white/black couples fall between those of white/white and black/black couples (see appendix Figure 7A.3).

When it comes to education, white newlyweds who married Asians are more educated than whites who married whites, blacks, or Hispanics. More than half of the white men (51%) and white women (57%) who married an Asian spouse are college-educated, compared with only 32% of white men and 37% of white women who married a white spouse. Also, about 6 in 10 Asian newlyweds who married whites are college-educated.

Newlywed Hispanics and blacks who married a white spouse are more likely to be college-educated than those who married within their group. About 23% of Hispanic men who married a white wife have a college degree, compared with just 10% of Hispanic men who married a Hispanic woman. Likewise, 1 in 3 (33%) Hispanic women who married a white husband are college-educated, compared with about 13% of Hispanic women who "married in." The educational differences among blacks who "marry in" and "marry out" are less dramatic but follow a similar pattern.

Marrying out is much more common among the native-born population than among immigrants. Native-born Hispanics were nearly three times as likely as their foreign-born counterparts to marry a non-Hispanic in 2010. The disparity among native- and foreign-born Asians is not as great, but still significant: nearly 4 in 10 native-born Asians (38%) and nearly a quarter (24%) of foreign-born Asians married a non-Asian in 2010 (see appendix Figure 7A.4).

Among Asian newlyweds, the intermarriage gap between native and the foreign born is much bigger for Asian men than for Asian women. In 2010, native-born Asian male newlyweds were about three times as likely as the foreign born to marry out (32% versus 11%). Among newlywed Asian women, the gap between native and foreign born is much smaller (43% versus 34%). The gender differences are not significant among Hispanic native- and foreign-born newlyweds.

REGIONS AND STATES. Intermarriage in the US tilts west. About 1 in 5 (22%) of all newlyweds in western states married someone of a different race or ethnicity between 2008 and 2010, compared with 14% in the South, 13% in the Northeast, and 11% in the Midwest. At the state level, more than 4 in 10 (42%) newlyweds in Hawaii between 2008 and 2010 were intermarried; the other states with an intermarriage rate of 20% or more are all west of the Mississippi River. For new marriages between whites and Hispanics, states with the highest prevalence rates are New Mexico (19%), Arizona (12%), and Nevada (11%). The highest shares of intermarried white and Asian couples are in Hawaii (9%), District of Columbia (7%), and Nevada (5%). And the top states for white/black intermarried couples are Virginia (3.3%), North Carolina (3.2%), and Kansas (3%).

DIVORCE. Several studies using government data have found that overall divorce rates are higher for couples who married out than for those who married in—but here, too, the patterns vary by the racial and gender characteristics of the couples. An analysis conducted a decade ago found that 10 years after they married, interracial couples had a 41% chance of separation or divorce, compared with a 31% chance among couples who married within their race, according to a study based on the 1995 National Survey of Family Growth (NSFG).[3] A subsequent study that analyzed 2002 NSFG data found that "although interracial marriages overall are more vulnerable to divorce, this reflects the experience of some but not all couples." It found that after 10 years of marriage, interracial marriages that are most vulnerable to divorce involve white females and nonwhite males (with the exception of white females/Hispanic males). Conversely, there is little or no difference in divorce rates among white men/nonwhite women couples, and white men/black women couples are actually substantially less likely than white/white couples to divorce by the 10th year of marriage.[4]

Another study using 1990 to 2001 data from the Census Bureau's Survey of Income and Program Participation (SIPP) found that on the whole, interracial marriages are less stable than same-race same-ethnicity marriages, but marital dissolution was found to be strongly associated with the race or ethnicity of the individuals in the union. The authors found that "the results failed to provide evidence that interracial marriage per se is associated with an elevated risk of marital dissolution."[5] Mixed marriages involving blacks and whites were the least stable followed by Hispanic/white couples, whereas mixed marriages involving Asians and whites were more stable than same-race white marriages.

RACIAL IDENTITY AND LABELS

The US is on a demographic track to become a majority nonwhite (or, in the evocative oxymoron, "majority minority") nation sometime between 2040 and 2050. But by then, with an ever rising share of the population likely to be the product of mixed marriages, how much sense will these categories make? History offers some limited lessons. Until a few generations ago, "marrying out" mainly referred to crossing entrenched boundaries of religion or ancestry (race was still beyond the pale). Families would object to—and might sometimes block—marriages between a Protestant and Catholic, an Italian American and an Irish American, or a Jew and a gentile. Today such unions are so commonplace that they rarely set off family crises and barely attract notice of any kind in the wider society. (A 2013 survey of Jews by the Pew Research Center found that among Jews who have married since 2000, nearly 6 in 10 have a non-Jewish spouse.[6]) Yes, these "mixed" couples and their children have to figure out where to worship and which relatives to visit on which religious holidays, but they don't typically have to confront existential questions about who they are, where they fit, and how society labels them. So one lesson of our history is that identity markers that once seemed impenetrable have a way of becoming porous. And people have a way of adapting.

Race, however, poses a more profound identity challenge than does religion or ancestry. In America, it comes freighted with centuries of slavery and other forms of state-sanctioned discrimination; no other group cleavage in our national life is as deep or painful—or visible. Few people in this country wear their religion in public, but there's no hiding one's race. And nowadays, few seem to want to. Our culture has traded the melting pot for the mosaic. We glory in our distinctive hues. In this new milieu, being mixed race—a stigma not just in our society but in most societies for most of human history—now carries cultural cachet. Pick your favorite mixed-race celebrity, it's quite an A-list: Halle Berry, Beyoncé, Keanu Reeves, Salma Hayek, Derek Jeter, Mariah Carey, Norah Jones, Tiger Woods, Barack Obama.

To be sure, there are still plenty of holdouts from this new racial kumbaya. When General Mills ran a television commercial in 2013 that featured a little girl with a white mom and black dad (the cute plot line had the girl, upon hearing that Cheerios are good for the heart, dumping a bunch of them on the chest of her napping father), two interesting things happened. The first was that the interracial marriage and biracial child were presented without gawking or editorial comment—just your basic TV ad family. The second was that the reaction to the ad got so ugly on the comment section on YouTube that it had to be taken down. There was a similar outbreak of online bigotry when a young woman who is the daughter of Indian immigrants was crowned Miss America in the fall of 2013. Obviously we haven't become a "postracial" society; human beings don't seem to be wired that way. But there are fewer out-and-out bigots than there once were. And increasingly, our new racial landscape is bursting with nuance, shadings, subtleties, possibilities, ironies. A few years ago California-based artist Kip Fulbeck put together the Hapa Project, a photographic exhibition that consisted of a series of portraits of multiracial children and adults. Below each portrait was a short personal statement. "My last boyfriend told me he liked me because of my race," wrote one attractive young woman of middle hue and indeterminate race. "So I dumped him."

There's always been a political dimension to identity labels. In 1997, two of the nation's most powerful civil rights groups, the NAACP and the National Council of La Raza, testified in Congress in opposition to the Census Bureau's proposal to allow people to identify with more than one race on the 2000 decennial census. They feared it would reduce the size of traditionally disadvantaged race groups, thereby "diluting benefits to which they are entitled as a protected class under civil rights law," as the NAACP said in its written testimony. A small group called the Association of Multiethnic Americans countered that the census should concern itself first and foremost with accurate racial identification: "We want a choice in the matter of who we are, just like any other community. [We find it] ironic that our people are being asked to correct by virtue of how we define ourselves all of the past injustices of other groups of people." Another small multiracial advocacy group, Project Race, said in its testimony: "Multiracial children who wish to embrace all of their heritage should be allowed to do so. They should not be put in the position of denying one of their parents to satisfy arbitrary government requirements."

THE HISPANIC IDENTITY CONUNDRUM

Those multiracial groups carried the day back in the late 1990s, but even so, racial and ethnic labeling on the census remains today what it has always been: a confusing maze. No group struggles more with this nation's official race categories than the nation's 53 million Hispanics. They are classified by the federal government as an ethnic group, not a racial group. This is a nod to the genetic reality that Hispanics are a mix of races—with bloodlines flowing from Europe, Africa, and the indigenous Native American tribes of North, Central, and South America. But they all have a connection to Spanish language, culture, and heritage—which are standard markers of ethnicity. The designation of Hispanics as an ethnic group was mandated by Congress in 1976 in response to pressure from Hispanic political and civil rights leaders who wanted official data about their community so they could press claims for equal treatment and benefits under the law. This was the first (and so far only) time in US history that an ethnic (as opposed to racial) group had been singled out this way. And it has led to a census form that, for many Hispanics, reads like a riddle.

Race and ethnicity are covered by questions 8 and 9 on the 10-question 2010 census form. Respondents are explicitly instructed to answer BOTH (all caps on the form) questions. Question 8 asks all Americans whether they are Hispanic, and if so, to mark their Hispanic country of origin (Mexico, Cuba, etc.). The question notes that "for this census, Hispanic origins are not races." This is the question that produces the government's official count of Hispanics and—as has been the custom in census-taking since the middle of last century—it is based entirely on self-identification.[7] Question 9 then asks people to state their race, and provides a total of 15 different boxes (including white, black, American Indian, 11 Asian race boxes, and "some other race"—but not including Hispanic). On the 2010 census, about half (53%) of all those who self-identified as Hispanic in question 8 checked the "white" box in question 9, while 3% checked black and 8% checked mixed race or other—and fully 37% checked "some other race."

Those responses stand as a rebuke to the classification system that produced them. If more than a third of our nation's largest minority group finds itself without a race box to check on the census form, it may be time to come up with a different taxonomy.

For Hispanics, the identity riddle doesn't stop there, however. Four decades after the terms "Hispanic" and "Latino" were affixed to them by the federal government, Hispanics themselves haven't fully embraced those labels. Only about one-quarter (24%) of Hispanic adults say they most often identify themselves by

Figure 7.5

→ NOTE: Please answer BOTH Question 8 about Hispanic origin and Question 9 about race. For this census, Hispanic origins are not races.

8. Is Person 1 of Hispanic, Latino, or Spanish origin?
☐ **No**, not of Hispanic, Latino, or Spanish origin
☐ Yes, Mexican, Mexican Am., Chicano
☐ Yes, Puerto Rican
☐ Yes, Cuban
☐ Yes, another Hispanic, Latino, or Spanish origin — *Print origin, for example, Argentinean, Colombian, Dominican, Nicaraguan, Salvadoran, Spaniard, and so on.* ⌐

9. What is Person 1's race? *Mark* ☒ *one or more boxes.*
☐ White
☐ Black, African Am., or Negro
☐ American Indian or Alaska Native — *Print name of enrolled or principal tribe.* ⌐

☐ Asian Indian   ☐ Japanese   ☐ Native Hawaiian
☐ Chinese   ☐ Korean   ☐ Guamanian or Chamorro
☐ Filipino   ☐ Vietnamese   ☐ Samoan
☐ Other Asian — *Print race, for*   ☐ Other Pacific Islander — *Print*
example, Hmong, Laotian, Thai,   *race, for example, Fijian, Tongan,*
Pakistani, Cambodian, and so on. ⌐   *and so on.* ⌐

☐ Some other race — *Print race.* ⌐

either of those pan-ethnic terms, according to a 2011 Pew Research Center survey. About half (51%) say they identify themselves most often by their family's country or place of origin (using such terms as Mexican, Cuban, Puerto Rican, Salvadoran, or Dominican), and 21% say they use the term "American" most often (a share that rises to 40% among those who were born in the US). The terms "Hispanic" and "Latino" are American confections—they get little use in the 20-plus countries where Spanish is the official language. Plus, many Hispanics in this country are frankly doubtful about just how much they have in common with other Hispanics.

In response to another 2011 Pew survey question, about 7 in 10 (69%) Hispanics say that Hispanics in the US have many different cultures; just 29% say they share a common culture. That doesn't mean the labels serve no purpose. They make sense to Hispanic leaders and institutions that want to preserve their power base and to a majority white host culture that, despite its growing ease with racial diversity, still isn't ready to stop putting labels on people it deems to be different.

One of the most interesting demographic, sociological, and political dramas of the coming century will be whether the Hispanic identity marker recedes over time, as it did for the European immigrants. The answer isn't yet clear. Proximity, modern communication technology, and the relative ease of international travel make it much easier for today's Hispanic immigrants and their children to keep their ties to their ancestral countries and language. Plus, the mainstream culture's new embrace of ethnic diversity reduces the incentives for minorities to shed their ethnic identity. On the other hand, if a quarter of Hispanics continue to marry non-Hispanics, these ethnic identity markers are bound to blur over time.

What boxes will the children of these marriages discover on the 2050 census? If history is a guide, they'll be different from the ones in use now. In fact, several changes are already in the works. In 2012, the Census Bureau announced it was contemplating whether to drop the separate Hispanic origin question from its 2020 form and combine it with the race question. If it were to do so, it could then ask a single follow-up question about the national origin of the respondent's family. The net result, according to Kenneth Prewitt, a former director of the US Census Bureau and leading proponent of the change, would be to hold all major racial and ethnic groups harmless in terms of their population counts while at the same eliminating the confusing conflation of race, ethnicity, and national origin.

BLACKS IN OBAMA'S AMERICA

The Census Bureau has already decided to drop the word "Negro" from the 2020 form because its surveys have determined that a dwindling share of blacks—mostly older adults living in the South—still use the term. (Going forward, blacks will still be able to check the box "black" or "African American.") No population group has been subject to more classification changes than this one. The first census, in 1790, distinguished between free white persons and slaves. The term "color" (not "race") first appeared in the 1850 census, with three options: white, black, or mulatto. By 1890, census takers had the option of describing nonwhites as "quadroons" or "octoroons." In 1910, census takers were instructed to write "B" for "black only" and "Mu" for mulatto, a category meant to include "persons who have some proportion or perceptible trace of Negro blood." By 1930, these terms had been dropped, replaced by instructions that said that persons who were a mix of "white and Negro blood" were to be counted by census takers as "Negro" no matter how small the share of Negro blood—an explicit affirmation of the long-standing but unofficial "one-drop rule." By 1970, the race box was no longer to be filled out by the census enumerators based on observations from in-person visits; instead, it was to be done by Americans themselves, checking boxes on forms sent to them in the mail. That remains the practice to this day.

Over the years, as different labels have come into and out of vogue, the real problem for blacks comes not from the words themselves, but from the enduring power of the one-drop formula. When President Obama filled out his census form in 2010, he could have checked black, he could have checked white, or he could have checked *both* black and white. He checked black—a decision that disappointed many mixed-race Americans who'd hoped he would use this official declaration of racial identity to signal that it was time to move beyond the old formula. The president's defenders countered that anyone who looks like him has lived the life of a black person, and that it would be a denial of reality to pretend otherwise. Obama's ambiguous racial identity in a one-drop world is one reason he is such a compelling historical figure. Over the years he has been well served by political instincts that have taught him to be wary of the topic of race, but when it comes up—as with the Reverend Jeremiah Wright controversy in 2008; or the arrest of a prominent black Harvard professor at his home in Cambridge in 2009; or the killing of a black teenager in Florida in 2012 by a white/Hispanic neighborhood watch volunteer—Obama is frequently eloquent. He knows that in post–civil rights America, the only way for a black politician to be a national figure is to talk about race in the language of inclusion, not grievance. Here's what he said in 2008 when his candidacy was briefly threatened by a videotape that surfaced of an anti-white, anti-American tirade delivered by Wright—his pastor, mentor, and friend—from the pulpit of his Chicago church:

> I am the son of a black man from Kenya and a white woman from Kansas. I was raised with the help of a white grandfather who survived a depression to serve in Patton's army during World War II and a white grandmother who worked on a bomber assembly line at Fort Leavenworth while he was overseas. . . . I am married to a black American who carries within her the blood of slaves and slaveowners—an inheritance we pass on to our two precious daughters. I have brothers, sisters, nieces, nephews, uncles, and cousins, of every race and every hue, scattered across three continents, and for as long as I live, I will never forget that in no other country on Earth is my story even possible. It's a story that hasn't made me the most conventional candidate. But it is a story that has seared into my genetic makeup the idea that this nation is more than the sum of its parts—that out of many, we are truly one.

Obama has a complicated relationship with his black constituents. A *Washington Post* article captured a telling moment in 2007 when then-candidate Obama was meeting with a group of black advisers and scholars as he rehearsed for a forthcoming Democratic candidates' debate at predominantly black Howard University.[8] In the article's opening scene, Obama struggles to find the right tone and cadence. "I can't sound like Martin," he finally tells the group. "I can't sound like Jesse." Sometimes his challenge of finding a voice that can straddle the gap between our black and white cultures has produced moments of sweet irony. A few days before his 2009 inauguration, the president-elect stopped by Ben's Chili Bowl, a landmark eatery in Washington, DC's black community, with the usual press gaggle in tow. After paying for his chili dog, Obama was asked by the cashier if he wanted change back from his twenty. "Nah, we straight," he replied.[9] The pool reporter chose to clean up the president-elect's dialect and wrote that he said, "No, we're straight." But a video of the exchange became an Internet hit, especially among blacks who got a kick out of their Harvard-educated president sounding, as one hip-hop commentator put it, "mad cool" with his black street slang.

As president, Obama has faced a quiet but persistent undercurrent of criticism from black leaders who feel he's been too timid about addressing ongoing racial imbalances in the economy and in society at large. Television host and political activist Tavis Smiley complained during the 2012 campaign that "tragically . . . the president feels boxed in by his blackness." Smiley went on: "It has . . . been painful to watch this particular president's calibrated, cautious and sometimes callous treatment of his most loyal constituency. African Americans will have lost ground in the Obama era."[10] Others say the problem isn't that Obama's boxed in by being black—it's that he's not black enough. Typical of the genre: a headline on a column by black *New York Daily News* columnist Stanley Crouch: "What Obama Isn't: Black Like Me." And for others, Obama's mixed-race heritage is fodder for satire. "The first black president!" black comedian Wanda Sykes marveled at a White House Correspondents' Association dinner in 2009, as the president sat a few feet away on the dais. "I'm proud to be able to say that. That's unless you screw up. And then it's going to be, 'What's up with the half-white guy?'"

There's no group in America for whom the election of the nation's first black president has had a more positive impact than African Americans. A nationwide Pew Research survey of blacks conducted in November 2009, a year after Obama's election victory, found that across a wide range of measures—satisfaction with the direction of the country, the state of race relations, the pace of black progress, their personal economic circumstances—black attitudes were significantly more positive than in 2007. On many of these measures, blacks were more upbeat than whites, a reversal of patterns that had prevailed for decades.

This spike in attitudes came in the teeth of an economy that had been in a deep recession for those two years, a downturn that hit blacks especially hard. Nevertheless, twice as many blacks in 2009 (39%) as in 2007 (20%) said that the "situation of black people in this country" was better than it had been five years earlier; this more positive view had taken hold among blacks of all ages and income levels. Asked to look ahead, blacks were also more upbeat. More than half (53%) said that life for blacks in the future will be better than it is now, while just 10% said it will be worse. In 2007, 44% said things would be better for blacks in the future, while 21% said they would be worse.

Figure 7.6

Blacks' Sense of Progress, 1981-2013

% of blacks who say blacks are better/worse off now than five years ago

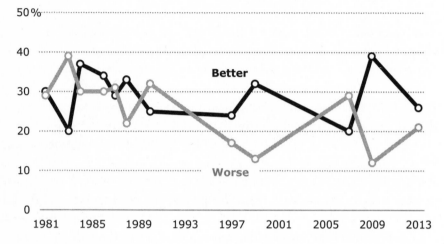

Note: In surveys in 2005 and earlier, blacks include Hispanic blacks. In surveys in 2007 and later, blacks include only non-Hispanic blacks. "Same" response not showed.

Source: Pew Research Center surveys, 1981–2013

Much of this post-election glow would eventually dim. By 2013, when Pew Research asked blacks those same questions in a new survey, the share who said things had gotten better for blacks over the past five years—26%—had fallen most of the way back to its 2007 level, even though this new five-year assessment period encompassed all of Obama's tenure in the White House.

That 2013 survey was taken around the time of the commemoration of the 50th anniversary of Dr. King's famous "I Have a Dream" speech on the steps of the Lincoln Memorial in Washington, DC. It found that just a third of blacks feel there has been a lot of progress toward reaching racial equality over the past half century, while 8 in 10 say much more needs to be done. Whites were more mixed in their assessments. Half said a lot of progress has been made, and 44% said a lot more needs to be done.

Those mixed views on progress toward racial equality were echoed in a Pew Research Center analysis of long-term US government trend data on indicators of well-being and civic engagement, including personal finance, life expectancy, educational attainment, and voter participation. The data looked at equality of outcomes rather than equality of opportunity.

Our analysis found that the economic gulf between blacks and whites that was present half a century ago largely remains. When it comes to household income and household wealth, the gaps between blacks and whites have widened. On measures such as high school completion and life expectancy, they have narrowed. On other measures, including poverty and homeownership rates, the gaps are roughly the same as they were 40 years ago (see appendix Figure 7A.5).

FINANCES. Between 1967 and 2011 the median income of a black household of three rose from about $24,000 to nearly $40,000.[11] Expressed as a share of white income, black households earn about 59% of what white households earn, a small increase from 55% in 1967. But when expressed as dollars, the black-white income gap widened, from about $19,000 in the late 1960s to roughly $27,000 today. The race gap on household wealth has increased from $75,224 in 1984 to $84,960 in 2011.

Other indicators of financial well-being have changed little in recent decades, including homeownership rates and the share of each race that live above the poverty line. The black unemployment rate also has consistently been about double that of whites since the 1950s.

EDUCATION. High school completion rates have converged since the 1960s, and now about 9 in 10 blacks and whites have a high school diploma. The trend in college completion rates tells a more nuanced story. Today white adults 25 and older are significantly more likely than blacks to have completed at least a bachelor's degree (34% versus 21%, a 13 percentage point difference). Fifty years ago, the completion gap between whites and blacks was about 6 percentage points (10% versus 4%). But expressed a different way, the black completion rate as a percentage of the white rate has improved from 42% then to 62% now.

FAMILY FORMATION. The analysis finds growing disparities in key measures of family formation. Marriage rates among whites and blacks have declined in the past 50 years, and the black-white difference has nearly doubled. Today about 55% of whites and 31% of blacks ages 18 and older are married. In 1960, 74% of whites and roughly 6 in 10 blacks (61%) were married. The share of births to unmarried women has risen sharply for both groups; in 2011, more than 7 in 10 births to black women were to unmarried mothers, compared with about 3 in 10 births to white women (72% versus 29%).

INCARCERATION. Black men were more than six times as likely as white men to be incarcerated in federal and state prisons and local jails in 2010, the last year complete data are available. That is an increase from 1960, when black men were five times as likely as whites to be incarcerated.

VOTER TURNOUT. Participation rates for blacks in presidential elections has lagged those of whites for most of the past half century but has been rising since 1996. Buoyed by the historic candidacies of Barack Obama, blacks nearly caught up with whites in 2008 and surpassed them in 2012, when 67% of eligible blacks cast ballots, compared with 64% of eligible whites.

LIFE EXPECTANCY. The gap in life expectancy rates among blacks and whites has narrowed in the past five decades from about seven years to four.

In 2012, when a Pew Research survey asked why many blacks have not advanced in this country, a majority of black respondents (54%) said those

Figure 7.7

Blacks' View of Why Many Blacks Don't Get Ahead

% of blacks who say ...

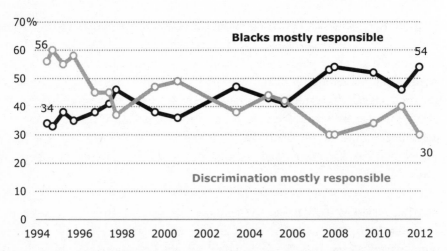

Note: In surveys in 2005 and earlier, blacks include Hispanic blacks. In surveys in 2007 and later, blacks include only non-Hispanic blacks. Question wording: Which of these statements comes closer to your own view—even if neither is exactly right. Racial discrimination is the main reason why many black people can't get ahead these days, OR, Blacks who can't get ahead in this country are mostly responsible for their own condition.

Source: Pew Research Center surveys, 1994–2012.

who cannot get ahead are mainly responsible for their own situation, whereas 3 in 10 (30%) said that racial discrimination is the main reason. Fifteen years before, most blacks held the opposite view. Multiple surveys taken since 1994 show that this shift in blacks' perceptions has occurred in fits and starts over time, and that the change pre-dates Obama's election.

In one of the most intriguing findings of the 2009 survey, most blacks joined with most whites in saying that the two racial groups have grown more alike in the past decade, both in their standards of living and their core values. Seven in 10 whites (70%) and 6 in 10 blacks (60%) said that the values held by blacks and whites have become more similar in the past 10 years. Similarly, a majority of blacks (56%) and nearly two-thirds of whites (65%) said the standard-of-living gap between whites and blacks has narrowed in the past decade.

In fact, most of the racial gaps in key personal finance indicators widened during the 2007–2009 recession and have remained at elevated levels since. But when it comes to race and economics during the Age of Obama, reality is one thing, perception another. In 2013 blacks were still only about half as likely as whites to rate the national economy as poor, and twice as likely to say things will be better in the coming year. They were also more upbeat than whites in their perceptions of the housing market and the job market.

All of these attitudes suggest that Obama's presidency has had a salutary impact on African Americans that's hard to measure but impossible to ignore. Not on their economic circumstances, obviously, but on their sense of belonging. I was a reporter in South Africa for three years in the mid-1990s during the transition from apartheid to democracy. Despite surface similarities, that country's racial dynamics are completely different from ours. No matter what the white settlers had done over the centuries in South Africa, blacks there have always known it was their country, their place—the land of their ancestors. The

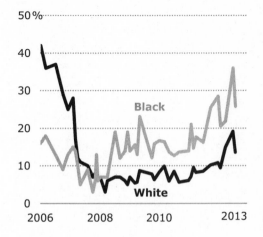

Figure 7.8

Whites, Blacks Assess the National Economy

% saying national economy is excellent/good

Source: Pew Research Center surveys, 2006–2013

same can't be said of blacks in America; their ancestors arrived in chains. For them the color line has been more than an instrument of discrimination, it has been a badge of un-belonging. But when 130 million of their fellow Americans take part in two successive elections that choose Barack Obama as the nation's leader, that badge loses some of its oppressive power. The black-white divide is still America's deepest cleavage, and Obama's presidency hasn't made it go away. But it has made it smaller. To paraphrase Dr. King, the arc of our history is bending toward inclusion.

Whither Marriage?

SIXTY YEARS AGO *Ladies' Home Journal* launched "Can This Marriage Be Saved?," an advice column that has become the longest-running and most widely read standing feature in magazine publishing history. Its "riveting true stories" about marriages in trouble chronicle the everyday stresses that take their toll on the world's most enduring social institution: "He's Always Obsessing About Money"; "The Holidays Make Me Crazy"; "Our Sex Life Is Stale"; "My Stepdaughter Is Ruining Our Marriage"; "We Can't Get Pregnant"; "He Told Our Secrets Online"; "Home Renovations Are Wrecking Us"; and so on. The column is a cornucopia of commonsense advice, but if its mission has been to save marriages, it has been a massive bust. Back when it launched, nearly three-quarters of all adults in the US were married. Now just half are.

Lots of particular marriages fail for lots of particular reasons. But nowadays it's the institution itself that's in big trouble. And the biggest problem isn't that people who try marriage are failing at it. It's that fewer are trying at all.

Marriage's loss of customers has occurred among all age groups, but it's most acute among Millennials. Today just 20% of adults ages 18 to 29 are married, compared with 59% in 1960. During the past half century, the median age at first marriage has risen by about six years for both men and women.

Are today's young adults abandoning marriage or merely delaying it? The weight of history would suggest the latter. In one form or another, marriage has been a social foundation upon which virtually all of the world's cultures and civilizations have been built. Institutions that have endured for thousands of years don't disappear overnight—do they?

Figure 8.1

Marriage Loses Market Share, 1960–2011

% of adults 18 and older, by current marital status

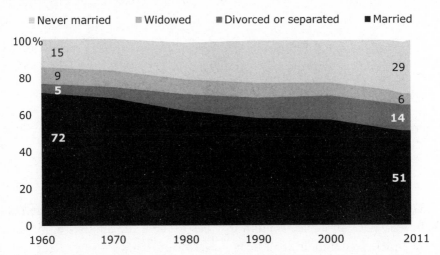

Never married   Widowed   Divorced or separated   Married

Source: Pew Research Center analysis of Decennial Census (1960–2000) and American Community Survey data (2008–2011), IPUMS

Time will tell. For now, it's notable that marriage is in retreat not just in the US but in nearly all developed (and some less developed) countries across the world. The trend is most advanced in Scandinavia, where cohabitation has for all intents and purposes replaced marriage. (But cohabiting unions there are much more durable than those in the US—so much so that a child born to cohabiting parents in Sweden has less of a chance of experiencing his or her parents' breakup than does a child born to *married* parents in the US, according to sociologist Andrew Cherlin.)

In the US, meantime, large swaths of the public—led by Millennials—express doubts about the long-term viability of the institution. In a 2010 Pew Research survey, nearly 4 in 10 (39%) Americans—and 44% of Millennials—agreed that marriage is becoming obsolete. When the same question was posed to voters by *Time* magazine back in 1978, when divorce rates were peaking, just 28% agreed.

This doesn't mean that today's young people don't want to marry. Most still do. If history is a guide, most eventually will. That same 2010 survey also found that 70% of unmarried Millennials say they would like to get married one day. So what's holding them back?

To borrow an old joke about politics: three things—money, money, and I can't remember the third. The retreat from marriage is above all a class-based phenomenon. Back in 1960, there was just a 4 percentage point gap (76% versus 72%) in marriage rates between college graduates and those with a high school diploma or less. By 2011, the gap had ballooned to 17 percentage points (63% versus 46%). The same disparities are found by income and race; over the past half century the greatest declines in marriage rates have been among minorities and those at the lower end of the income scale—categories that overlap (see appendix Figure 8A.1).

It's not that people in these groups lack the motivation to marry. If anything, it's that they place marriage on too high a pedestal. The Pew Research survey found that among the unmarried, there are no differences by education or income in the desire to get married. But the survey also found that the less education and income people have, the more likely they are to say that to be a good marriage prospect, a person must be able to support a family financially. In effect, they create an economic prerequisite for marriage that they themselves can't meet.

Their doubts can be self-fulfilling. Marriage has always been associated with positive economic outcomes—not just because it's an efficient way to allocate and combine labor (yes, two can live more cheaply than one), but because the marital commitment itself tends to promote values and behaviors associated with economic success—constancy, responsibility, persistence, an inclination for pragmatic compromise. On top of that, our tax laws provide lots of benefits to married couples. When people from all walks of life get married in roughly equal shares, marriage spreads these economic and behavioral rewards in roughly equal measure up and down the socioeconomic ladder. But in a world where a disproportionate share of those who tie the knot enter marriage already

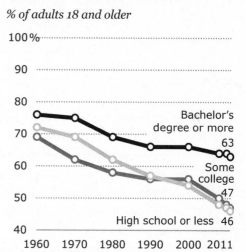

Figure 8.2

Share Married, by Educational Attainment

% of adults 18 and older

Source: Pew Research Center analysis of Decennial Census (1960–2000) and American Community Survey data (2008–2011), IPUMS enjoying the head start of a good education and healthy economic prospects, it's easy to see how the marriage gap and the income gap reinforce each other. That's exactly what has been happening for decades.

Demographers estimate that 8 in 10 adults will eventually marry, but the typical American today spends less of his or her adult life in a marriage than at any time in modern history—and a record 28% of all US households are now headed by a single person. Marriage, in short, has lost its cultural hegemony. It was once the mandated path to adulthood; it's now a lifestyle choice.

The shift is most visible among Millennials, who value marriage somewhat less than the next youngest adult generation, the Gen Xers, did back when they were the age Millennials are now. Just 30% of Millennials say having a success-ful marriage is one of the most important things in life. Back in 1997, 35% of Gen Xers felt that way about marriage. And there's an even bigger disparity between the two generations in their views of parenthood—but that one runs in the opposite direction. Some 52% of Millennials say being a good parent is one of the most important things in life, compared with 42% of Gen Xers who said the same back when they were the age Millennials are now.

Our entertainment culture mirrors and reinforces these changes. In the first several decades of television, the family sitcom ruled the ratings roost. All of the iconic shows—*Ozzie and Harriet, Leave It to Beaver, My Three Sons, Father Knows Best, The Cosby Show,* etc.—revolved around the foibles of every-day life in a tight-knit nuclear family. Dad was both the authority figure and the butt of endless jokes about his clumsiness in matters of the heart and hearth. But the humor was always loving, and it was impossible to miss the meta-message: people, this is how you're supposed to live!

In more recent times, television has done an about-face on marriage. With the exception of the hilariously dysfunctional *Simpsons,* it has been a long time since a happily married nuclear television family grabbed and held the prime-time zeitgeist. Instead television has served up a steady diet of relationship shows, buddy shows, and parenthood shows—*Friends, Seinfeld, Sex and the City, Desperate Housewives, The Good Wife, Two and a Half Men, Parenthood.* When marriage appears at all on the small screen, it's usually as a bridge too far, a cautionary tale, or a full-on calamity.

One need not sentimentalize marriage. The good old Ozzie and Harriet marriages included a lot of relationships that were loveless, or worse. In the days when adults felt overwhelming social pressure to get and stay married, the rate of domestic violence within marriage was an estimated 30% higher than now.[1] And while the great majority of 1950s-era wives never faced that sort of abuse, many felt trapped in other ways. The women's liberation movement drew much of its energy from women who wanted more from life than a wife-as-homemaker marriage.

Half a century later, adults of both genders have their doubts that a person needs to be married to lead a fulfilling life. A 2010 Pew Research survey asked respondents whether they thought it was easier for a married person or a single person to find happiness. About 3 in 10 (29%) said it was easier for married people while just 5% said it was easier for single people. But a sizable majority—62%—said it makes no difference. Even among married people, a majority said marriage has no bearing on one's prospects for happiness.

These findings are notable for a couple of reasons beyond their decidedly lukewarm embrace of the joys of married life. One is a big gender disparity. Some 38% of men say it's easier to find happiness as a married person, compared with just 22% of women—providing some data underpinnings to the folk wisdom and social science that say marriage is a better deal for men than women.

Even more intriguing, however, is that the public appears to be undervaluing the contribution marriage makes to happiness. Pew Research surveys often begin by asking respondents, "Generally, how would you say things are these days in your life—would you say you are very happy, pretty happy, or not too happy?" In the survey profession, this is known as a door-opener question; its main goal is to get respondents comfortable with doing the interview. But because there's quite a cottage industry these days in happiness research, the responses have value in their own right, especially since we can deconstruct the nationwide sample to analyze the various correlates of happiness.

It turns out that happiness and marriage make a great couple. In one recent survey, 36% of married people say they are very happy, while just 22% of unmarried people say the same. These results rarely vary by more than a few percentage points from survey to survey. But they should be kept in perspective. Marriage is correlated with other traits that are also correlated with happiness—such as high income, religiosity, and good health. In other words, the kind of people inclined to be married are the kind of people inclined to be happy.

However, this still leaves open the possibility that marriage in and of itself also helps in life's happiness sweepstakes.

Figure 8.3

Is Marriage Bliss?

% "very happy" by marital status

Source: Pew Research Center survey, Nov. 2012, N=2,511 US adults

One way to test that proposition is through a statistical technique known as regression analysis, which measures the strength of the linkage between a variable of interest (in this case, marriage) and an outcome of interest (in this case, happiness), while holding all other variables constant. Our regression analysis finds that, all else equal, marriage increases one's likelihood of being very happy—by 12%. That might not sound like much. But consider: Gender, race, ethnicity, education and age are among the many characteristics that have no independent statistical impact whatsoever on a person's likelihood of being very happy. Marriage is among a small circle of traits—including good health, high income, and strong religious observance—for which there is an independent impact.

The irony, of course, is that the very public that affirms a link between marriage and happiness doesn't seem to be reading its own memos. Marriage helps make people happier, yet fewer people are marrying. Why?

WHY IS MARRIAGE IN RETREAT?

Most theories about the decline of marriage start with the impact of structural changes to the economy. The most important of these—the movement of women in the workforce—undid the equilibrium of the male breadwinner/female homemaker template for marriage that had prevailed since the industrial era. At the same time, the development of a postindustrial, knowledge-based economy has diminished the job prospects and earning power of less-educated men, creating a "marriage market mismatch" at the lower end of the socioeconomic scale. In the old marriage marketplace, a woman needed a husband for financial security. In the new marriage marketplace, fewer women have that need, and fewer men can cater to it.

Other theories focus on the more intimate realms of marriage. Until not too long ago, marriage was the only socially and morally acceptable gateway to sexual partnerships. The introduction of the birth control pill in the early 1960s helped to pry much of this regulatory authority over sex away from marriage. Adultery remains a taboo, but in an era of "friends with benefits," sex among unmarried or never-married adults carries little if any stigma. This has complicated the case for marriage—and not just because sexual desires can now be respectably accommodated without lifetime commitments, but also because it has increased the demand on marriage to provide something even more precious than sex. More so than ever, people want a spouse to be their lifelong companion, emotional soul mate, partner in the journey toward self-fulfillment. Marriage, in a word, is supposed to be built on love (see appendix Figure 8A.2).

But as social historian Stephanie Coontz has observed, love may be the undoing of marriage.[2] At the very least, it has injected an unstable element into the suddenly fragile heart of an age-old institution. For most of its 5,000-year history, marriage had little to do with love. Across cultures and centuries, it thrived as a way to propagate the species; establish people's place in the social and economic order; acquire in-laws; organize productive activity along gender lines; extract labor from the young; and distribute resources from parents to children. Only in the eighteenth century, with the spread of market economies and the Enlightenment, did love and mutual self-fulfillment start to enter into marital bargain. Today, arguably, they're the dominant part. But love can be fickle and self-fulfillment a high bar. Can an institution built on love be as durable as one built on the stouter stuff of economic self-interest? As a society, we're conducting that experiment right now. So far, the answer appears to be no (see appendix Figure 8A.3).

In the middle of the twentieth century, the anti-Nazi German theologian Dietrich Bonhoeffer sent a congratulatory letter to some newlyweds of his acquaintance. It contained an aphorism about marriage that reflected an old-fashioned view of the institution. "It is not your love that sustains the marriage," he wrote, "but from now on, the marriage that sustains your love." Today one would be hard-pressed to find that sentiment expressed anywhere in Western literature or culture. "If you were to write the same letter to newlyweds now, I don't think they'd have a clue what you were talking about," said David Blankenhorn, founder and president of the Institute for American Values, a nonpartisan think tank whose mission, among others, is to try to restore what he calls the "fractured" institution of marriage.

Other groups have also taken up that challenge, but their contributions

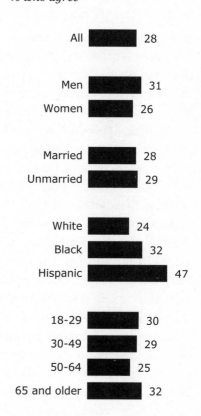

Figure 8.4

Only One True Love?

% who agree

All	28
Men	31
Women	26
Married	28
Unmarried	29
White	24
Black	32
Hispanic	47
18-29	30
30-49	29
50-64	25
65 and older	32

Source: Pew Research Center, Oct. 2010, N=2,691 US adults

so far have been mainly in the realm of diagnosis, not cure. A 2013 research paper, "Knot Yet: The Benefits and Costs of Delayed Marriage," did a wonderful job showing how young adults view marriage as a "capstone" rather than "cornerstone" arrangement—"something they do after they have all their other ducks in a row, rather than a foundation for launching into adulthood and parenthood."[3] Given this new cultural framework for marriage, it's no surprise that it's the high-achieving young adults who are most likely to get hitched. "Marriage has become a status symbol," writes Cherlin, "a highly regarded marker of a successful personal life. . . . Something young adults do after they and their live-in partners have good jobs and a nice apartment."[4] He noted that in 2012, according to a study by *Brides* magazine, 36% of newlyweds paid the entire cost of their wedding receptions, and an additional 26% contributed to the cost.

THE STIGMA OF SINGLE PARENTHOOD

As marriage rates have declined, the reaction of the American public for the most part has been a do-your-own-thing shrug of acceptance. That's not the case, however, for the most important consequence of the decline in marriage—the sharp rise in births outside of marriage. Of all the structural changes on the marriage and family front in recent decades, this one has drawn the most negative reaction by far from the public.

In 2011, 41% of all births in the US were to unmarried mothers, up from just 5% in 1960. Many might assume this has been driven by a surge in teenage births. To the contrary, the teen birthrate (births per 1,000 women ages 15 to 19) in the US today has dropped by more than 60% from its peak in 1957; it is now at the lowest level since the US government started tracking such data in 1940. As recently as 1990, teenage girls accounted for more births in the US than did women ages 35 and older. Now the reverse is true. Teenage mothers today give birth to about 10% of all babies, and 18% of babies born outside of marriage. They may or may not be having more sex than their same-age counterparts of previous generations, but thanks to the widespread use of contraception, they're having fewer kids.

So then, who's having children out of wedlock? Mostly, women in their 20s and 30s. Until not too long ago, marriage and parenthood were linked milestones on the journey to adulthood. And if they happened out of sequence—that is, if a single woman got pregnant—a "shotgun wedding" was the culturally prescribed remedy. This custom now seems quaint. Nowadays an estimated 6 in 10 single mothers have live-in boyfriends when they give birth, about double the rate among unmarried mothers a generation ago. However, these cohabiting unions tend to be of short duration—only about half survive until the child's 5th birthday.

Nonmarital births have also soared in many of the world's other developed countries, for many of the same reasons. But the US is an outlier in its combination of high nonmarital birthrates, high divorce rates, and high turnover in cohabiting relationships. As a result of all these trends, Cherlin says that a teenager in the US has a smaller likelihood than a teenager in any other country in the world of living in a household with both biological parents.

A large body of social science research shows that, on average and controlling for other factors, children have better outcomes in life if raised by both parents than if raised by just one. They are healthier, do better academically, get into less trouble as adolescents, are less likely to drop out of high school or become teenage parents, are less prone to substance abuse or criminal behavior, and are more successful in their jobs and careers.[5]

Policy experts of all ideological stripes accept these findings—and so, as we'll see in a moment, does the public. Yet the topic of single parenthood gets very little public attention these days. It has been politically and racially fraught for decades, ever since Daniel Patrick Moynihan penned the controversial 1965 report "The Negro Family: The Case for National Action." Moynihan, who went on to become UN Ambassador, a US senator from New York, and one of the nation's leading public intellectuals, was at the time a young assistant secretary of labor in the Johnson administration, which was pressing ahead with its ambitious civil rights agenda and its "War on Poverty." Moynihan's thesis was that progress toward racial equality would be held back because so many black children were being raised by single mothers. He argued that such families were a by-product not just of the "tangle of pathologies" in poor communities, but of a matriarchal family culture among blacks that traced its roots to slavery.

Figure 8.5

Share of Births to Unmarried Women, 1960–2011

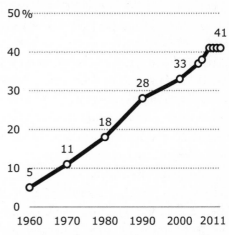

Source: National Center for Health Statistics data

Critics denounced the report for what they deemed its "blame-the-victim" take on poverty and racial inequality; supporters welcomed it as an unvarnished dose of truth. The Johnson administration went ahead and ramped up funding for Aid to Families with Dependent Children, a welfare program that provided cash support to poor single mothers. But the program quickly became a lightning rod for conservatives who said it created incentives for nonmarital motherhood and promoted a culture of dependence. Ronald Reagan, among many others, inveighed against "welfare queens" to good effect on the campaign trail. In 1996 President Bill Clinton joined with a Republican-controlled Congress to kill AFDC and enact a stripped-down replacement, a move that has taken much of the toxicity out of the political debate over welfare policies. Since then, the national conversation about single parenthood has pretty much disappeared.

But single parenthood itself hasn't. Indeed, what's notable about this brief retrospective are the data that attracted Moynihan's notice in 1965. He sounded the alarm because the out-of-wedlock birthrate among blacks had risen to an estimated 25%. Half a century later, the rate is 72%. Among Latinos, the rate is 53%. Among whites, 29% (see appendix Figure 8A.4). What once seemed shocking has become mainstream. Perhaps that's why it draws so little public attention. Or perhaps it's that elites—mindful of the stir the Moynihan report triggered decades ago—find the whole subject to be uncomfortable. "I know of no other set of important findings [about the poor outcomes of children raised by single parents] that are as broadly accepted by social scientists . . . and yet are so resolutely ignored by network news programs, editorial writers for the major newspapers, and politicians of both political parties," wrote conservative scholar Charles Murray in his 2012 book, *Coming Apart*.[6]

The overall verdict from the public about the rise of single parenthood is an emphatic thumbs down. Asked in 2010 whether each of seven demographic changes affecting the composition of families were good or bad for society, 69% said the rise in single women having children was bad, while just 4% said it was good—by far the most negative reading on any of the trends. In 2013, when the question was asked in a slightly different form, 64% said the rising number of children born to unmarried mothers was a big problem for society, 19% said it was a small problem, and 13% said it was not a problem.

However, there are some notable generational differences in these attitudes. Among adults ages 50 and older, 74% say unwed motherhood is a big problem; among adults 18 to 29, just 42% say the same. Along these same lines, a majority of the public (61%) believes that a child is more likely to grow up happy in a home with both a mother and a father, but there are generational differences here too. Silent Generation adults are more likely than Millennials (75% versus 53%) to say this. Also, men are more likely than women (67% versus 54%) to feel this way. And more Hispanics (72%) and blacks (65%) say this than do whites (57%)—more evidence that when it comes to single parenthood, attitudes and behaviors do not always move in sync with one another.

Nonmarital births aren't the only reason more children are being raised by single parents. Divorce has become much more prevalent over the past half century, though rates have declined somewhat in recent decades after peaking in the 1970s and 1980s. Most experts trace the divorce explosion to the same mix of economic and cultural factors that have produced the delayed marriage phenomenon: if marriage is supposed to be mainly about finding love and self-actualization, it's a destination that some share of the married population won't be able to reach.

Divorce is never a happy outcome, but Americans cast a much less disapproving eye on it than they do on nonmarital births. A majority (58%) of the public says that divorce is

Figure 8.6

Trend in Divorce Rate, 1960–2009

Number of divorces per 1,000 population

Source: US Department of Commerce, *Statistical Abstract of the United States: 2012*, published 2011

preferable to maintaining an unhappy marriage, and an even bigger majority—67%—says that if a marriage is very unhappy, the children are better off when the parents get divorced.

Contrary to public perceptions, divorce rates have been declining for several decades. Part of this is simple math: people can't divorce if they don't marry. But rates of divorce have also declined somewhat among married couples. This is likely related to the changing demographics of marriage. Divorce rates have always been highest among couples who marry young and couples at the lower end of the socioeconomic scale. There are fewer of those marriages now. And so as marriage has become more confined to the land of the "haves," divorce has receded.

GRAY DIVORCE

At the same time, however, there has been a sharp rise in "gray divorce"—a Boomer-driven phenomenon exemplified by the breakup in 2010 of the 40-year marriage of former vice president Al Gore and his wife, Tipper. A half century ago, only 2.8% of adults older than age 50 were divorced; by 2011, that share had risen to 15.4%. For the first time in history, more Americans ages 50 and older are divorced than widowed (13.5%).[7]

Family scholar Susan L. Brown has done research showing that divorce has been migrating north on the age pyramid for several decades. Just 1 in 10 people who got divorced in 1990 were ages 50 or older, she reports; now more than 1 in 4 new divorcees are in that age group. Boomers have been at the heart of the divorce explosion throughout all phases of their adult lives. Forty years ago they tended to marry young and divorce young. Now they're more likely than previous generations to divorce later in life (in part because their remarriages are at a relatively high risk of ending in divorce). Given all this, Brown finds that that 1 in 3 Boomers are currently single—which leaves many of them economically and socially vulnerable on the cusp of old age.[8]

But gray divorce may also be a by-product of more positive social trends—for example, advances in the quality of life of older adults and changes in women's roles, opportunities, and expectations. "The extension of the active, healthy life span is a big part of this," said Coontz. "If you are a healthy 65, you can expect another pretty healthy 20 years. So with the kids gone, it seems more burdensome to stay in a bad relationship, or even one that has gone stale." Most divorces among older adults, as among younger adults, are initiated by women, leading Coontz to observe: "Another big factor is that with their increased work experience and greater sense of their own possibilities, [women] are less willing to just 'wait it out.' We expect to find equality, intimacy, friendship, fun and even passion right into what people used to see as the 'twilight years.'"[9]

SAME-SEX MARRIAGE

As marriage is in broad retreat among the general public, it has been embraced by gays and lesbians as the crown jewel of their quest for civil rights and social acceptance. The irony of gays rushing toward marriage while straights seem to be running away hasn't been lost on the commentariat, especially conservatives who see an explicit connection between the opposing trends.

Until not too long ago, the case against same-sex marriage was based at least in part on the notion that it would have the socially undesirable effect of weakening the link between matrimony, procreation, and child rearing. However, as more straight adults are themselves breaking the link, this becomes a much more difficult case to make. "The conservative argument still has serious exponents, but it's now chuckled at in courtrooms, dismissed by intellectuals, mocked in the media and (in a sudden recent rush) abandoned by politicians," wrote *New York Times* columnist Ross Douthat in March 2013, a few days after a pair of same-sex marriage cases were argued before the US Supreme Court.[10]

The near collapse of the elite argument against same-sex marriage is mirrored by an equally dramatic change in the views of the general public. Indeed, it's hard to think of any other social/moral/political issue in modern history that has seen such a large swing in prevailing attitudes in such a short time period. As recently as the 2004 presidential campaign, public sentiment against same-sex marriage was so intense that GOP strategists went out of their way to put the issue on state ballots in key swing states, knowing it would help drive up turnout among social conservatives. Back then, according to Pew Research surveys, just a third of adults supported same-sex marriage. Now half do. There's still a big generation gap on this issue, with 70% of Millennials favoring the legalization of same-sex marriage, compared with just 31% of Silents. George Will among others has stressed the generational replacement component of the shift in public attitudes. "Quite literally the opposition to gay marriage is dying," he noted on ABC's *This Week* in 2012. But along with the demographic dynamics, support has been growing among all age groups.

What has caused the change? Our surveys show that it has little or nothing to do with new attitudes about marriage and everything to do with new attitudes about gays. Among supporters of same-sex marriage in 2013, fully 28% said they were once opponents. Asked why they changed their minds, no one cited changing attitudes about marriage. Instead, the most common response was that familiarity had led to acceptance. Nearly 9 in 10 Americans (87%) now say they know someone who is gay or lesbian, up from 61% in 1993, and about half (49%) say a close friend or family member is gay or lesbian. In a separate 2013 Pew survey of lesbian, gay, bisexual, and transgender (LGBT) adults, more than 9 in 10 said they believe social acceptance of their community has grown in the past decade; they, too, cite "people knowing someone who is LGBT" as the primary driver of change.

Clearly a feedback loop has taken hold: as the social stigma recedes, more gays come out of the closet, and as more gays come out of the closet, the stigma recedes still more. But it hasn't disappeared—not even close. As of 2013, almost half of Americans (45%) said that engaging in homosexual behavior is a sin, a view highly correlated with frequency of religious attendance and other measures of religiosity. And 40% of adults say they would be

Figure 8.7

Growing Support for Same-sex Marriage

Allowing gays and lesbians to marry legally ...

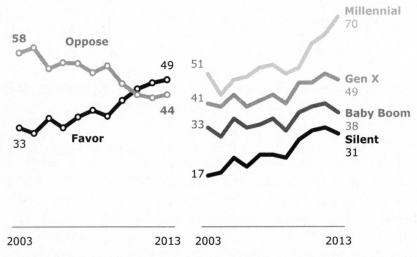

% among all adults

% favor by generation

Source: Aggregated data from surveys conducted by the Pew Research Center for the People & the Press, 2003–2012. 2013 data from Mar. 2013 survey only

upset if they learned they had a gay or lesbian child—down from the 60% who felt this way in 2004, but a sizable minority nonetheless.

Our surveys also toss cold water on the premise that gays are rushing toward marriage while straights are running away. Among LGBT survey respondents, 60% said they are either currently married or would like to marry one day; among the general public, that figure is 76%. Even in its troubled state, marriage hasn't fallen off its pedestal. It remains a life aspiration for the vast majority of Americans—"a status symbol, a highly regarded marker of a successful personal life," in the words of Andrew Cherlin. Indeed, in his majority opinion for the US Supreme Court in the ruling that struck down the Defense of Marriage Act (DOMA), Justice Anthony Kennedy paid homage to the symbolic importance of marriage. He ruled that the federal government's refusal to recognize legal same-sex marriages imposed a "stigma" that "demean(s)" gay couples and "humiliates" their children. DOMA, he wrote, deprives a group of people their Fifth Amendment rights not only because they cannot get access to the many tangible federal benefits that accrue to married couples, but because the law is telling them that their marriages are somehow "less worthy" than those of straight couples.

WHAT'S A FAMILY?

As marriage has receded, family forms have changed. Back when *Ladies' Home Journal* launched its advice column, the preeminent family unit of the mid-twentieth century—mom, dad, and the kids—pretty much had the stage to itself. No longer. Families now come in all shapes, sizes, and constellations: single parent, multigenerational, same sex, different race, step, blended, tangled.

Given the breadth and sweep of these changes, it's reasonable to ask: Just who belongs in the family album these days and who doesn't? As Figure 8.8 shows, a majority considers most of the constellations discussed in this chapter to be a family. Not surprisingly, traditional marriage and parenthood top the list. However, the public is also ready to confer family status on groupings it doesn't always approve of. For example, nearly 9 in 10 say a single parent with a child is a family, and more than 6 in 10 say the same about a same-sex couple

Figure 8.8

Is This a Family?

% saying each grouping is ...

	A Family	Not a family
Married couple w/ children	99	1
Married couple w/o children	88	10
Single parent w/ children	86	12
Unmarried couple w/ children	80	18
Same-sex couple w/ children	63	34
Same-sex couple w/o children	45	52
Unmarried couple w/o children	43	54

Note: Question wording: "As I read you a list of different arrangements, please tell me whether you consider each to be a family or not?"

Source: Pew Research Center survey, Oct. 2010, N=2,691 US adults raising a child. Younger adults are more expansive than older adults with all of these definitions. Thus, the broader boundaries of family would seem to be both culturally and demographically ascendant.

But that doesn't mean all relatives are created equal. In 2010, Pew Research did a survey in which we asked people how obligated they would feel to provide either financial help or caregiving to a relative who had a serious problem. (Each respondent was asked only about the category of relative he or she has, as determined by questions asked earlier in the survey.)

Obviously, these are highly individual matters, but as Figure 8.9 illustrates, some overall patterns emerge. The biblical injunction to honor thy mother and father hasn't been lost on the American public: parents top the list (we didn't ask about young children because we took it as a given that everyone would say they are obligated to help them). From there the rankings descended in a crisp stair-step pattern: grown child, grandparent, sibling, in-law. Steprelatives don't fare as well as biological relatives. But all rank above "your best friend"—which was the lone nonrelative on the list.

All of this suggests that in the face of massive social and demographic change, kinship is still a preeminent element of people's lives. Yes, the institution of marriage is in retreat; yes, the makeup of families is changing; and yes, the public disapproves of the decoupling of marriage and parenthood. But through it all, family remains the center of most people's universe.

Figure 8.9

Ranking the Relatives

% who say they feel "very obligated" to provide needed financial assistance or caregiving to their ...

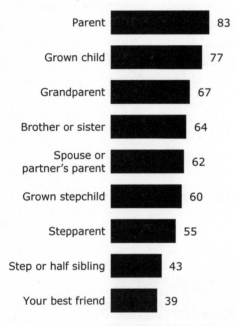

Parent	83
Grown child	77
Grandparent	67
Brother or sister	64
Spouse or partner's parent	62
Grown stepchild	60
Stepparent	55
Step or half sibling	43
Your best friend	39

Note: Each respondent was asked only about relatives he or she has. Question wording: "Suppose someone you know had a serious problem and needed either financial help or caregiving. How obligated would you feel to provide assistance if that person were your [NAME ON LIST]: Would you feel very obligated, somewhat obligated, not too obligated or not at all obligated?"

Source: Pew Research Center survey, Oct. 2010, N=2,691 US adults

Three-quarters of adults say their family is the most important element of their lives. There are very few differences by demographic group. And when asked about the future of the institution of marriage and family in this country, two-thirds say they are optimistic—again, with little variance in responses by age, race, or gender. That same question tested the public's optimism about other key institutions, values, and behaviors that impact the nation's well-being. None rose to the level of family and marriage.

However, the public's upbeat view of the future of marriage finds few takers in the community of scholars and policy advocates who track its faltering fortunes. "I suspect marriage as we have known it is not coming back," writes Isabel V. Sawhill of the Brookings Institution.[11] Social commentator Kay S. Hymowitz concurs, noting that even if a national movement to take up the challenge of restoring marriage were to somehow emerge, "the policy levers are few."[12] At a subdued Brookings symposium in 2013 built around the "Knot Yet" report, Douthat of the *New York Times* struck the closest thing to a hopeful note. He pointed out that over the past several decades, as family instability has grown, many of the dire social consequences that were presumed to be an inevitable by-product—youth crime, high school dropouts, teen pregnancy, etc.—have ameliorated rather than worsened. "[The decline of marriage] may have a negative impact on human flourishing," he said, "but it hasn't dragged us into the kind of abyss that scolds and conservatives usually like to threaten people with." That's not exactly a ringing endorsement of the status quo, but it's a useful reminder of the resilience of the human spirit and human institutions. Looking ahead, as the Boomers grow older and the social safety net grows smaller, that resilience will be put to the test as the nation struggles to figure out how best to care for its elderly at a time when a growing share will have fractured families to which they are only loosely attached.

Nones on the Rise

O N THE EVE OF THE 2004 presidential primaries, David Brooks traced the faith journeys of three of the leading candidates.

"George W. Bush was born into an Episcopal family and raised as a Presbyterian, but he is now a Methodist," Brooks began his *New York Times* column.[1]

"Howard Dean was baptized Catholic, and raised as an Episcopalian. He left the church after it opposed a bike trail he was championing and now he is a Congregationalist, though his kids consider themselves Jewish.

"Wesley Clark's father was Jewish. As a boy he was a Methodist, then decided to become a Baptist. In adulthood he converted to Catholicism, but he recently told Beliefnet.com, 'I'm a Catholic, but I go to a Presbyterian church.'"

In most of the world, such faith-hopping would be unheard of. In America it's practically routine. Some 44% of American adults have a different religious affiliation from the one they were raised in, and an additional 9% left their childhood religion at some point in their lives but have since returned to the fold, according to a massive 2009 Pew Research Center survey on the subject.

Restlessness has been hardwired into America's religious metabolism from the get-go. The *Mayflower* was full of pilgrims who broke from the Church of England in the early 1600s and set sail for a new world so they could practice a devout but nonconformist brand of Christianity. Fire-and-brimstone Puritans like Jonathan Edwards—who sermonized about "Sinners in the Hands of an Angry God"—set the tone for spiritual life in the new colonies. But if America has always been a place for the devout, it has also always been devout in its belief in religious freedom. Our Declaration of Independence pays homage to God as the endower of our unalienable rights; our Constitution forbids the state from establishing a religion and guarantees all Americans the freedom to practice any religion they wish—or none at all. This seemingly incompatible mixture attracted the notice of our most astute early visitor, Alexis de Tocqueville, who marveled that Americans were deeply religious, yet didn't seem to take offense if their neighbors held false versions of the faith.

For much of this country's history, the combination of devoutness and pluralism led to a steady rise in religious institutions of all kinds—schools, universities, hospitals, orphanages, and above all, houses of worship of nearly every conceivable variety, from storefront Pentecostal churches to Roman Catholic cathedrals, Mormon temples, and independent Jewish *havurot*.

According to historical estimates, the share of Americans who were "churched"—who belonged to some congregation—doubled from 17% in 1776 to 34% in 1850 and then climbed steadily after the disruption of the Civil War to 62% in 1980, when it leveled off.[2] Since the 1990s, church membership and self-reported rates of church attendance have either held steady or declined modestly—about 6 in 10 US households still belong to religious congregations and nearly 4 in 10 US adults continue to say they attend religious services once a week or more.

But at the same time, a major new trend has emerged: disaffiliation. Despite the relative stability in church membership, the number of Americans who do

Figure 9.1

The Churching of America

Rates of church membership, 1776–2000

Source: Roger Finke and Rodney Stark, *The Churching of America 1776-2005: Winners and Losers in Our Religious Economy* (Rutgers University Press, 2005)

not identify in surveys with any religion—the "nones"—has been growing at a dramatic pace. As of 2012, one-fifth of the US public—and a third of adults under 30—were religiously unaffiliated, the highest percentages ever in Pew Research Center polling. From 2007 to 2012 alone, the unaffiliated increased from just over 15% to just under 20% of all US adults. Their ranks now include more than 13 million self-described atheists and agnostics (nearly 6% of the US public), as well as nearly 33 million people who say they have no particular religious affiliation (14%).[3]

Not surprisingly, this large and growing group of Americans is less religious than the rest of the public on most conventional measures, including frequency of attendance at religious services and degree of importance they attach to religion in their lives (see appendix Figure 9A.1). But it would be a mistake to think of them as completely secular. A 2012 survey found that roughly two-thirds of the country's 46 million unaffiliated adults believe in God (68%); more than a third classify themselves as "spiritual" but not "religious" (37%); and 1 in 5 (21%) say they pray every day. With few exceptions, though, the unaffiliated say they are *not* looking for a religion that would be right for them. Overwhelmingly, they think that religious organizations are too concerned with money and power, too focused on rules, and too involved in politics.

The growth in the number of religiously unaffiliated Americans is driven largely by generational replacement, the gradual supplanting of older generations by newer ones.[4] Young adults today are more likely than older adults to have no religious affiliation. And today's young adults (ages 18–29) are also much more likely to be unaffiliated than previous generations were when they were young.

In addition, Generation Xers and Baby Boomers have become somewhat more religiously unaffiliated in recent years. In 2012, 21% of Gen Xers and 15% of Baby Boomers described themselves as religiously unaffiliated, up slightly (but by statistically significant margins) from 18% and 12%, respectively, since 2007. The trend lines for the Silent and Greatest Generations are essentially flat.

According to longer trends from the General Social Survey (GSS), the percentage of Americans who were raised without any religious affiliation has been rising gradually, from about 3% in the early 1970s to about 8% in the past decade. However, the overwhelming majority of today's adult "nones" were brought up in some religious tradition. The 2012 Pew Research survey found that about three-quarters of unaffiliated adults were raised with an affiliation (74%).

TRENDS IN RELIGIOUS COMMITMENT

Despite these trends, the US remains a highly religious country—particularly compared with other advanced industrial democracies—and some measures of religious commitment in America have held remarkably steady over the years. For instance, the number of Americans who currently say religion is very important in their lives is little changed since 2007 and remains considerably higher than in Britain, France, Germany, or Spain.[5] And over the longer term, Pew Research surveys find no change in the percentage of Americans who say that prayer is an important part of their daily life. It was 76% in 2012, exactly the same as 25 years earlier, in 1987.

Figure 9.2

Religious Affiliation, by Age

% saying they are ...

Source: Aggregated data from surveys conducted by the Pew Research Center for the People & the Press, Jan.-Jul. 2012

But on some other measures, such as attendance at worship services, there is evidence of a gradual decline in religious commitment. Numerous studies indicate that people tend to report going to church more often than they really do, so these numbers are perhaps best understood not as measuring how many Americans actually are in the pews each week, but as gauging whether Americans *think of themselves* as regular attenders. At the high end of the spectrum, there is relative stability: 37% of US adults reported in Pew surveys in 2012 that they go to religious services at least once a week, about the same as in 2003 (39%). But at the low end, there is a small but statistically significant change: in 2003, 25% of US adults indicated they seldom or never attend religious services; by 2012, that number had ticked up 4 points, to 29%.

Similarly, the percentage of Americans who say they never doubt the existence of God has fallen modestly but noticeably over the past 25 years. In 1987, 88% of adults said they never doubt the existence of God. As of 2012, this figure was down to 80%.

In addition, the percentage of Americans who say the Bible should be taken literally has fallen in Gallup polls from an average of about 38% of

Figure 9.3

Importance of Religion   Morality and Belief in God*

% saying "very important"   *% saying, in order to be moral, it is ...*

				Not necessary to believe in God	Necessary to believe in God
United States	████████ 50				
Spain	███ 22		United States	46	53
Germany	███ 21		Germany	66	33
Britain	██ 17		Britain	78	20
France	██ 13		Spain	80	19
			France	85	15

*Question: "Which one of these comes closest to your opinion, number 1 or number 2?...#1 – It is not necessary to believe in God in order to be moral and have good values or #2 – It is necessary to believe in God in order to be moral and have good values"

Source: Pew Research Center survey, Mar.–May 2011, N= 27,130 adults in 23 countries

the public in the late 1970s and early 1980s to an average of 31% since.[6] And based on analysis of GSS data, Mark Chaves of Duke University has found that Americans born in recent decades are much less likely than their elders to report having attended religious services weekly at age 12. Young adults are also less likely than older adults to report that when they were growing up, their parents attended religious services regularly.

Chaves recently summarized trends in American religion by noting that "there is much continuity, and there is some decline, but no traditional religious belief or practice has increased in recent decades."[7]

RELIGIOSITY AND DISAFFILIATION

How can church membership, self-reported attendance at religious services, and other key measures of religiosity in America be holding fairly steady or declining only modestly while disaffiliation is rising dramatically? The answer is that the growth of the unaffiliated is mostly among people who are *already at the low end* of the religiosity spectrum (see appendix Figure 9A.2). In the past many of them might have retained a connection to a religious tradition, even if it was only nominal. Now they identify as "nones."

In 2007, 38% of people who said they seldom or never attend religious services described themselves as religiously unaffiliated. In 2012, 49% of infrequent attenders eschewed any religious affiliation. By comparison, the percentage describing themselves as unaffiliated has been flat among those who attend religious services once a week or more often.

THE RISE OF THE UNAFFILIATED

What accounts for the rise of the "nones"? There are four leading theories:

1: Political Backlash

Several leading scholars contend that Americans—and younger adults, in particular—have turned away from organized religion because they perceive it as deeply entangled with conservative politics and do not want to have any association with it. University of California, Berkeley, sociologists Michael Hout and Claude S. Fischer first suggested in 2002 that "part of the increase in 'nones' can be viewed as a symbolic statement against the Religious Right."[8] In their recent book, *American Grace: How Religion Divides and Unites Us,* Robert Putnam of Harvard University and David Campbell of Notre Dame marshal evidence from various surveys that supports this thesis. From the 1970s through the 1990s, they argue, "religiosity and conservative politics became increasingly aligned, and abortion and gay rights became emblematic of the emergent culture wars." The result, they write, was that many young Americans came to view religion as "judgmental, homophobic, hypocritical, and too political." It should be noted, however, that the percentage of religiously unaffiliated people has risen among Republican voters as well as among Democratic voters (though the increase is greater among Democrats).

2: Delays in Marriage

Some sociologists, including Robert Wuthnow of Princeton University, attribute the overall decline in church attendance since the 1970s to broader social and demographic trends, such as the postponement of marriage and parenthood by growing numbers of young adults.[9] Aggregated data from Pew Research Center polls are broadly consistent with this theory. They show that among adults under 30, the married are more likely than the unmarried to have a religious affiliation. But an analysis of religious affiliation patterns by generation suggests that Americans do *not* generally become more affiliated as they move through the life cycle from young adulthood to middle age and retirement.[10] Rather, the percentage of people in each generation who are religiously affiliated has remained stable, or decreased slightly, as that generation has aged.

3: Broad Social Disengagement

Yet another theory loosely links the rise of the unaffiliated to what some observers contend has been a general decline in "social capital"—a tendency among Americans to live more separate lives and engage in fewer communal activities, famously summed up by sociologist Robert Putnam as "bowling alone."[11] In this view, the growth of the religious "nones" is just one manifestation of much broader social disengagement.

Various Pew Research Center surveys offer support for this hypothesis. Young adults, the age group that is least likely to be affiliated with a religion, are also the group least trusting of their fellow human beings. On the other side of the same coin, a survey by the Pew Research Center's Internet & American Life Project found that the 40% of Americans who describe themselves as "active" in religious organizations—a higher bar of commitment than affiliation with a religious group—are more likely than other Americans to be involved in all types of volunteer and community groups, from sports leagues to arts groups, hobby clubs, and alumni associations.

And a 2012 Pew Research Center survey found that religiously unaffiliated Americans are less inclined than Americans as a whole to feel that it is very important to belong to "a community of people who share your values and beliefs" (28% of the unaffiliated say this is very important to them, compared with 49% of the general public).

4: Secularization

Finally, the rise of the unaffiliated in the US also has helped to breathe new life into theories that link economic development with secularization around the globe. Back in the 1960s, when secularization theories first achieved high visibility, they were sometimes accompanied by predictions that religion would wither away in the US by the twenty-first century.[12] The theories social scientists propound today are more subtle—contending, for example, that societies in which people feel constant threats to their health and well-being are more religious, while religious beliefs and practices tend to be less strong in places where there is more "existential security."[13] In this view, gradual secularization is to be expected in a generally healthy, wealthy, orderly society.

Pew Research Center surveys have asked people in many countries about the importance of religion in their lives, how often they pray, and whether they think it is necessary to believe in God to be a moral person. Throughout much of the world, there is a negative correlation between these measures of religiosity and a country's national wealth: publics in countries with a high gross domestic product (per capita) tend to be less religious, while publics in countries with a low GDP tend to be more religious. Americans, of course, are a major exception to the rule, because the US has both high GDP per capita and high levels of religious commitment.[14] Nonetheless, some theorists view the rise of the unaffiliated as a sign that secularization is advancing in America.[15]

MYTHS ABOUT THE UNAFFILIATED

While the root causes of disaffiliation are still open to debate, Pew Research Center surveys can lay to rest some common misperceptions and establish some baseline truths about the "nones."

First, disaffiliation has taken place across a wide variety of demographic groups, including both men and women, college graduates and those without a college degree, people earning $75,000 or more and those making less than $30,000 annually, and residents of all geographic regions of the country. This phenomenon isn't confined—as some have mistakenly suggested—to college campuses, the east and west coasts, or the affluent. It is true, however, that the recent change has been concentrated in one racial group: whites. One-fifth of (non-Hispanic) whites now describe themselves as religiously unaffiliated, up 5 percentage points since 2007. By contrast, the share of blacks and Hispanics who are religiously unaffiliated has not changed by a statistically significant margin in recent years (see appendix Figure 9A.3).

Second, the unaffiliated are far from uniformly secular (see appendix Figure 9A.4). One-third say religion is at least somewhat important in their lives. Two-thirds believe in God (though fewer than half say they are absolutely certain of God's existence). And although a substantial minority of the unaffiliated consider themselves neither religious nor spiritual (42%), a majority describe themselves either as religious (18%) or as spiritual but not religious (37%).

Nor are the "nones" uniformly hostile toward organized religion. They are much more likely than the public overall to say that churches and other religious organizations are too concerned with money and power, too focused on rules, and too involved in politics. But at the same time, a majority of the unaffiliated clearly think that religious institutions can be a force for good in society. Three-quarters say religious organizations bring people together and help strengthen community bonds (78%) and a similar number (77%) say they play an important role in helping the poor and needy (see appendix Figure 9A.5).

Like most of the US public, a solid majority of the unaffiliated think religion as a whole is losing its influence on American life. But they are less inclined than the general public to view this as a bad thing—only 26% say it is, compared with half of the public at large. And atheists and agnostics overwhelmingly view religion's declining influence as a *good* thing for society (see appendix Figure 9A.6).

Another common misperception is that religiously unaffiliated Americans are "seekers" who haven't yet found the right church for them. In fact, very few are in the market. Leaving aside atheists or agnostics, just 10% of those who describe their current religion as "nothing in particular" say they are looking for a religion that is right for them; 88% say they are not.

Nor are the ranks of the unaffiliated predominantly composed of practitioners of New Age spirituality or alternative forms of religion. Generally speaking, the unaffiliated are no more likely than members of the public as a whole to have such beliefs and practices (see appendix Figure 9A.7).

POLITICAL COUNTERWEIGHT TO WHITE EVANGELICALS

When it comes to politics, the religiously unaffiliated have a distinct identity. They are heavily Democratic in their partisanship and liberal in their political ideology. More than 6 in 10 (63%) describe themselves as Democrats or say they lean toward the Democratic Party (compared with 48% of all registered voters), while just 26% identify with the GOP. And there are roughly twice as many self-described liberals (38%) as conservatives (20%) among the religiously unaffiliated. Among voters overall, this balance is reversed.

Figure 9.4

Partisanship and Ideology

% among registered voters

	All registered voters	Unaffiliated
Party identification	%	%
Dem/lean Dem	48	63
Rep/lean Rep	43	26
Independent/ other –no lean	9	11
Ideology		
Conservative	39	20
Moderate	36	38
Liberal	21	38

Source: Aggregated data from surveys conducted by the Pew Research Center for the People & the Press, Jan.–Jul. 2012

The liberalism of the unaffiliated extends to social as well as political issues. Nearly three-quarters (72%) of religiously unaffiliated Americans say abortion should be legal in most or all cases, compared with 53% of the public overall. And 73% of the religiously unaffiliated express support for same-sex marriage, compared with about half of the public at large. But the portion of the unaffiliated who say they would prefer a smaller government providing fewer services to a larger government providing more services (50%) is similar to the share of the general public (52%) who take the same view (see appendix Figure 9A.8).

In recent elections, the religiously unaffiliated have become among the most reliably Democratic segments of the electorate. In 2008 fully three-quarters of the religiously unaffiliated voted for Barack Obama over John McCain, and they were as strongly Democratic in their vote choice as white evangelicals were Republican. Obama's margin of victory among the religiously unaffiliated was 52 points; McCain's margin of victory among white evangelical voters was 47 points.

Moreover, the religiously unaffiliated constitute a growing share of the Democratic electoral base. Back in 2007 there were about as many religiously unaffiliated Democratic and Democratic-leaning registered voters as there were white mainline and white Catholic Democratic voters. And the religiously unaffiliated were only slightly more numerous among Democratic and Democratic-leaning registered voters than were black Protestants (17% versus 14%).

Today the religiously unaffiliated are significantly more numerous than any of these groups within the Democratic coalition (24% unaffiliated, 16% black Protestant, 14% white mainline Protestant, 13% white Catholic). By contrast, Republican and Republican-leaning registered voters are only slightly more likely to be religiously unaffiliated today than in 2007 (11% versus 9%).

Figure 9.5

Presidential Vote of the Religiously Unaffiliated, 2000–2012

% voting for each candidate

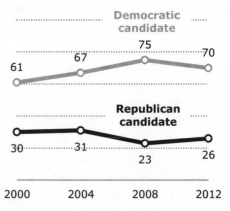

Source: Exit polls conducted by the National Election Pool, 2000, 2004, 2008 and 2012

PROTESTANTS IN DECLINE

The growth in the ranks of the unaffiliated is not the only big change in America's religious landscape in recent years. There has been an equally large shrinkage in the Protestant share of the population—from 53% in 2007 to 48% in 2012. The decline has been concentrated among white Protestants, both evangelical and mainline. Currently 19% of US adults identify themselves as white, born-again, or evangelical Protestants, down slightly from 21% in 2007. And 15% of adults describe themselves as white Protestants but say they are not born-again or evangelical Christians, down from 18% in 2007.[16] There has been no change in minority Protestants' share of the population over the past five years, and the Catholic share has remained relatively stable. Pluralism also is increasing, as the percentage of Americans who identify with non-Christian religions, including Buddhism and Hinduism, continues to tick up, albeit from a very low base (see appendix Figure 9A.9).

Figure 9.6

Who Achieves Eternal Life?

% among respondents who are affiliated with a particular religion

My religion is the one, true faith leading to eternal life	29
Many religions can lead to eternal life	65
Don't know/Refused	6

What Determines Eternal Life?

% of adults saying ...

One's belief	30
One's actions	29
Combination of actions/beliefs	10
Other	10
Don't believe in eternal life	7
Don't know/Refused	14

Source: Pew Research Center survey, Jul.–Aug. 2008, N=2,905 U adults. For more information, see Pew Research Center's Religion & Public Life Project, "Many Americans Say Other Faiths Can Lead to Eternal Life," Dec. 18, 2008

DISAFFILIATION AND PLURALISM IN THE AMERICAN CONTEXT

One way to reconcile the three seemingly incompatible strands of American religion today—continued devoutness despite rising pluralism and increasing disaffiliation—is to keep in mind that even religious Americans typically take a nonexclusivist view of the path to salvation. According to a 2008 Pew Research survey, 65% of *religiously affiliated* adults say many religions can lead to eternal life, while just 29% say theirs is the one true faith leading to eternal life.

That poll also found that roughly equal numbers of Americans say that whether a person achieves eternal life is determined by the person's beliefs (30%) as say it depends on a person's actions (29%). An additional 1 in 10 Americans say the key to obtaining eternal life lies in a combination of belief and actions. The remaining one-third of the public says that something else is the key to eternal life, or that they don't know what leads to eternal life, or that they don't believe in eternal life.

Who Can Go to Heaven?

The view among religious believers that there are many paths to salvation isn't limited to Christians of one denomination accepting Christians of a different denomination. It's more expansive.

Among non-Protestants who say that many religions can lead to eternal life, roughly three-quarters (74%) say that Protestantism can lead to eternal life. A similar proportion of non-Catholics who believe that many religions lead to eternal life (73%) say that Catholicism leads to salvation.

The numbers are only slightly lower for Judaism, with the overwhelming majority (69%) of non-Jews who say many religions can lead to salvation saying that Judaism can bring eternal life. A slight majority of non-Muslims (52%) also say Islam can lead to eternal life, and a similar number (53%) of non-Hindus say the same of Hinduism.

Taken as a whole, these responses reveal that most American Christians, including evangelicals, have more than just other Christian denominations in mind when they say there are many paths to salvation. For example, among white mainline Protestants (85%), black Protestants (81%) and white Catholics (88%), more than 8 in 10 of those who say many religions can lead to eternal life include at least one non-Christian religion.

Significant numbers of white evangelical Protestants also believe various non-Christian religions can lead to eternal life, though these figures tend to be lower than those seen among other religious groups. Nearly three-quarters (72%) of evangelicals who say many religions can lead to salvation name at least one non-Christian faith that can do so. White evangelicals who say that many faiths can lead to salvation are just as likely as other groups to cite Catholicism. However, evangelicals are less likely than other groups to say that non-Christian faiths can lead to eternal life. About two-thirds of evangelicals (64%) who see multiple paths to salvation say that Judaism, for example, can bring eternal life, lower than the 73% among mainline Protestants and the 77% among white Catholics who say this. And only about one-third of evangelicals who say there are multiple paths to salvation say that Islam (35%) or Hinduism

(33%) can lead to eternal life, with 26% saying that atheists can achieve eternal life (see appendix Figure 9A.10).

CHURN

All of these surveys portray an American religious marketplace in its familiar state of churn. The decline of affiliation is a relatively new phenomenon, but the restless search for a true path is as old as the Pilgrims. And so is Americans' live-and-let-live attitude toward people with different faiths. Those who worry that America is heading toward a European future of institutionalized secularism and empty cathedrals would do well to reflect on the resilience that religion in the US draws from this genius for tolerance and reinvention. Americans have never launched crusades or inquisitions; we've never gone to war over God. And so we haven't felt the need to suppress religion out of fear of its destructive furies. At the same time, our organized religions have always understood they need to adapt to survive. The fact that "nones" are on the rise indicates that religious institutions have some work to do. In modern times, American religion has become "more personalized and individualistic, less doctrinal and devotional, more practical and purposeful," in the words of sociologist Alan Wolfe.[17] Those are the market-driven impulses behind the evangelical mega-churches that now dot the American landscape, often offering an I'm-OK-You're-OK-Jesus-Loves-You theology of affirmation and self-help. Their message is a far cry from "Sinners in the Hands of an Angry God." They aren't for the whole American flock; nothing ever is. But they're animated by a restlessness that's uniquely American, and that keeps religion more vibrant here than perhaps in any other advanced country on earth.

Living Digital

NATALIE MARKS'S DIGITAL COMING-OUT moment came when she was in sixth grade.[1] It was 2000; she was 11 years old and had just heard about online chat rooms from a classmate. So one day after school she went over to her best friend Leigh's house, where the two of them navigated the beeping and buzzing of the dial-up modems of that long-ago era, created AOL user names, and started chatting up the world.

If her parents had known what Natalie was up to, they would have been worried sick that their little girl chose an online handle that was a bit saucy and unmistakably female. They would have been borderline apoplectic if they had known that, from her earliest postings, Natalie encouraged strangers of unknowable age, sex, and location to believe that she was interested in meeting them in person. "I didn't have many friends at school, and it was a fun way to act older and have weird personalities," she recalled. "I'd try to imagine myself as a 23-year-old and talk to people in that voice. I actually never told anyone exactly where I lived and I usually played pranks on the ones who got too aggressive. I'd write, 'meet me at this mall,' but I'd never show up. I was kind of a bully about that and I was different from the way I really acted at school."

Natalie is a digital native—a member of the first generation in history for whom digital technology platforms are the essential mediators of social life and information acquisition. Her parents and grandparents use many of the same gadgets and social networks she uses—and do so with increasing ease and frequency. But Natalie and her fellow Millennials are different. Their relationship with digital technology is unique precisely because it's *not* something they've had to adapt to. It's all they've ever known. It has played a fundamental role in shaping the nature of their friendships, the structure of their social networks, the way they learn, their provision and acceptance of social support, the way they interact with groups and institutions, their posture toward the wider world, and the way they allocate their time. During the course of Natalie's adolescence, thanks to the likes of Google and Facebook, she migrated from a digital universe where the Web didn't have a clue who she really was to one where it seems to know everything about her—and everyone else. What kind of adults will these digital natives become? We'll speculate on that at the end of this chapter. First let's follow the trail of Natalie's technology biography.

Once she entered middle school, Natalie's social circumstances changed radically. She developed lots of friends and her online life switched from chat rooms to instant messaging (IM). She was on AOL Instant Messenger constantly, with multiple screens open. Each contained a different conversation and each contained the seeds of five-star drama. The last thing she and her friends did at school each day was to figure out which pals to IM after the short trip home from school. "The transition from 8th period class to continuing the gossip at home was effortless," she recalled. "Our conversations never, ever ended, and it was 'mean girl' kinds of stuff. You'd have your phone to your ear and your hands on the keyboard and you'd repeat to everyone else the secret that had just been told you on the phone. And then you'd watch everybody trash everybody else."

Sometimes Natalie was the tormenter; sometimes the tormented. A common strategy among her peers was to lure someone into saying something catty and intimate, then to cut and paste the exchange into another IM conversation, or—better yet—to print it out and show it around school. "You had no privacy and you were constantly in arguments about the things you said or that were said about you," she said. Cliques were identified by her classmates' profiles. The ever-changing profiles, with their evolving keyword clues and announced alliances and feuds, often identified the newest social faction that the tribal school groups had assembled. Those left out or not in-the-know usually were outraged. "Away messages were the play-by-play of people's lives," said Natalie. "Kids were annoying in how much detail they shared. 'Going to take a shower now.' And they used away messages to break up with someone or ask someone out. Every day brought screaming and crying battles over some IM away message issue. I lost tons of friends doing those things, but I wasn't often bored. Basically, we had a lot to say about nothing."

An equal share of distress accompanied the school-wide habit of sharing IM account passwords. It was a sign of "true love" when students did that and it almost invariably led to heartbreak when the relationship soured and the scorned party—usually—decided to make the scorner suffer for causing the breakup. At times, third parties learned the password through these networks. Natalie was burned when an unknown someone pretended to be her and posted lies about her sex life. "I was mortified and had no way to disprove the rumors," she said.

The most spectacular social debacle at her school occurred when an upper-class girl filmed a bedroom episode with her boyfriend and sent it to him, thinking it would stay private between them. But he forwarded it to some friends, and eventually it found its way to members of the town's school board. His motives were not clear. Some classmates thought it was a prank that was supposed to be funny. Others thought he did it for revenge—or to spice up their relationship. Still others thought it was an accident. Whatever the case, the girl "vanished from the face of the earth," Natalie recalled. "Everyone in the school saw it within 24 hours of his e-mail. She was gone—and untraceable." This episode came before youthful "sexters"—people who share risqué photos via cell phones—started to get arrested on accusations they were trafficking in child pornography when they shared such photos.

With less melodrama, Internet use also became the dominant venue for homework for Natalie and her classmates. "The meaning of the word 'research' was 'type keywords into Google,' and neither teachers nor parents could force us to crack open a reference book," she said. Students turned to the Internet first to do the legwork for major research projects. Most used online Spark-Notes to complete class assignments. It was a free online service akin to Cliffs Notes, which at the time was a fee-based service. (By 2013, Cliffsnotes.com was ad-supported and free.) Teachers soon enough caught on and used the increasingly sophisticated search engines of the early 2000s to grab blocks of text from student papers and see that they were copied word for word from SparkNotes and other "term paper" services. The younger teachers were the first to catch on and train the older teachers.

THE TEACHERS' TAKE

To find out what teachers make of the digital revolution and its impact on education, the Pew Research Center teamed up with the College Board and the National Writing Project in 2012 to survey 2,462 middle and high school teachers about the research habits of their students.[2] This wasn't a nationally representative sample; all respondents had either taught Advanced Placement courses or participated in a summer institute sponsored by the National Writing Project. Overall, 77% said the impact of digital technologies had been mostly positive. Yet when asked whether they agreed or disagreed with specific assertions about how the Internet is impacting students' research, their views were decidedly mixed.

On the plus side, virtually all (99%) AP and NWP teachers agreed that the Internet enables students to access a wider range of resources than would otherwise be available, and 65% also agreed that the Internet makes today's students more self-sufficient researchers.

At the same time, however, 76% of teachers surveyed "strongly agreed" with the assertion that Internet search engines have conditioned students to expect to be able to find information quickly and easily. Large majorities also agreed that the amount of information available online today is overwhelming to most students (83%) and that today's digital technologies discourage students from using a wide range of sources when conducting research (71%). Fewer teachers, but still a majority of this sample (60%), agreed with the assertion that today's technologies make it harder for students to find credible sources of information.

Some of the teachers who took part in focus group sessions reported that for their students, "doing research" has shifted from a relatively slow process of intellectual curiosity and discovery to a fast-paced, short-term exercise aimed at locating just enough information to complete an assignment. Here, in descending order, are the sources teachers in our survey said students are "very likely" to use in a typical research assignment:

- Google or other online search engine (94%)
- Wikipedia or other online encyclopedia (75%)
- YouTube or other social media sites (52%)
- Their peers (42%)
- SparkNotes, Cliff Notes, or other study guides (41%)
- News sites of major news organizations (25%)
- Print or electronic textbooks (18%)
- Online databases such as EBSCO, JSTOR, or Grolier (17%)
- A research librarian at their school or public library (16%)
- Printed books other than textbooks (12%)
- Student-oriented search engines such as Sweet Search (10%)

What kind of employees and adults will these students become? The consensus view, expressed by a diverse group of 1,021 technology stakeholders, scholars, and experts interviewed as part of a different Pew Research survey in 2011, is that today's teens and young will be nimble, quick-acting multitaskers who treat the Internet as their external brain and who approach problems in a different way from their elders.[3] But the respondents were evenly divided as to whether their hyperconnectivity and always-on lifestyles will prove to be a net positive or negative. For each expert who said that Millennials' use of digital technologies would empower them to learn more than previous generations and become more adept at finding answers to deep questions, a different expert worried that this generation will exhibit a thirst for instant gratification and quick fixes, a loss of patience, and a lack of deep-thinking ability due to what one referred to as "fast-twitch wiring."

CELL PHONES AND SOCIAL NETWORKS

By the middle of Natalie's high school career in the mid-2000s, cell phones and social networking sites such as Facebook became integral parts of students' lives. Each produced changes in Millennials' behavior. In Natalie's world, the story arc for arrival of cell phones in a household usually went like this: Parents would buy their teen a cell phone in the name of safety and logistical convenience. They were comforted they could talk to their child wherever she was and that it made life easier to be able to coordinate transportation, meal planning, and errand running on the fly. But within a few months, a darker side would emerge. There would be a major family blow-up as teens discovered texting and parents discovered how many hundreds of dollars they had to pay for the extra thousands of texts when the teen exceeded the limits on the data plan for the family phone. In Natalie's case, a "texting shock" bill of $200 one month triggered her parents' rage. Her phone was confiscated. She was grounded. Negotiations ensued. Limits were set. An all-you-can-eat data plan was eventually purchased. "That kept the peace," she said.

Then texting became the norm for her and her peers. By mid-2009, research by the Pew Internet Project had found that when it came to contact outside school with their friends, teens treated texting as their primary form of daily communication. It surpassed voice calling, face-to-face contact, e-mail, and instant messaging[4]—and the trend line has continued to move in an upward arc ever since.

Why? Natalie explains: Texting is private and covert, even when you're in a crowd. Texting is efficient when basic information is exchanged. "Why waste time talking?" she asks. Texting is "less rude"—or, as communications scholars would say, it's asynchronous. You can send your messages when you want and check your messages on your timetable, rather than being interrupted by a phone call or annoying someone else. Yet, it also has the advantage of being immediate. The query-reply transaction can be completed in seconds.

The rise of mobile connectivity tracked with the explosion of social media in 2005–2009. Some Millennials had been interested in blogging in the early

2000s, but their embrace of social media was much more widespread once social networking services emerged. Friendster (launched in 2002), MySpace (launched in 2003), and Facebook (launched in colleges in 2003, in high schools in 2005, and among the general public in 2006) brought waves of Millennials into the world of building technological social networks and sharing content with the friends in those networks (see appendix Figure 10A.1). Their parents and grandparents lagged in their adoption of the sites, but became fairly avid users over time. The differences between the generations now are more qualitative than quantitative. But Millennials continue to be the early adopters of the social media universe, which by 2013 meant they were the first to register a noticeable dose of Facebook fatigue. In a Pew Research survey and set of focus groups conducted that year among 12- to 17-year-olds, a staggering 94% reported using Facebook, but many expressed waning enthusiasm for the platform. The culprits: too much drama; too much oversharing of the minutiae of life; and too many adults on the site. Some teenagers also reported being stressed by the need to constantly tend to their online reputation, but nearly all said they had to be on the site so as not to miss out.

Figure 10.1

Texting

Among cellphone owners, the % who send or receive text messages

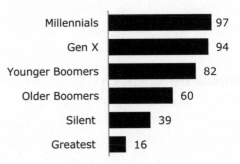

Source: Pew Research Center survey, Apr.–May 2013, N=2,076 US adult cell phone owners

Natalie was a bit behind her classmates in starting on Facebook, but she reports that she became "addicted" as she prepared for college. She was accepted at a prestigious southern university and like many of her classmates joined a Facebook group of incoming freshmen to the school. The school offered a personality test to the Facebook group and Natalie joined the many classmates who took it, posted her results in her profile, and began chatting on the site with others about their test results. There was one girl whose personality type seemed a good match with Natalie's and whose narrative answers in the test struck Natalie as "cool." The girl and Natalie launched an epic discussion thread during the early summer and decided to room together because they hit it off so well. "Big mistake," Natalie remembers. "She was a completely different person online than offline. I got totally fooled. And we hated each other."

They parted ways after a tense year together, but that did not diminish Natalie's enthusiasm for Facebook. She quickly amassed several thousand "friends" and spent a great deal of time on the site almost every day because it answered perhaps the central question of any young person's life: What are my friends doing and saying now? "It was a never-stop bull session with enough news and comedy and tragedy to be worth sticking around." (see appendix Figure 10A.2).

As time passed, Natalie developed a better sense of how different kinds of people acted on Facebook and which of them were likely to be long-term friends. She became a quick-skimmer of her news feed, pausing to read only a few of the most interesting items. She tried to write her own updates more thoughtfully, crafting them as items she would want to read or watch if they had been posted by one of her friends. "I got tired of knowing too much and trying too hard to keep up," she said.

As Natalie neared her graduation, she became hypervigilant about her reputation. She deleted hundreds of pictures of her at parties or tailgates and even vacations. She carefully checked all the references to her and occasionally got into fights with people who would not take down a post that she felt reflected poorly on her. She knew that people were judging her based on how she was represented on Facebook and she wanted to present well.

Still, a Facebook search for her as this chapter was being written showed that she has a pretty public status. And the featured picture has her in a pink wig. "This type of picture isn't something I would have chosen while job hunting, but now that I've been at my job for 10 months, and I'm pretty positive they like me, I feel it's OK for me to be myself," she said. "I'm Facebook friends with some of my coworkers who are in their 40s and 50s but they know that I'm a little weird and I feel close enough with them in real life that I don't mind them seeing what I'm like outside of work. I've already proven that I work hard, so it's OK for them to see that I play hard too."

WORKING IN A CONNECTED WORLD

After graduating from college in 2011, Natalie returned to her home in the Northeast for a few months but felt the tug to return to her southern college town. She found her first job there through the Craigslist classifieds working for a dance troupe doing marketing, especially via social media. Both Natalie and her prospective employer checked each other out on Facebook before Natalie showed up at the employer's home in a not-so-nice part of town. They also did enough Googling ahead of time to have a decent sense of each other. "She [the employer] looked legit and she told me that I didn't come off as too weird in my profile," Natalie said. "That's the basis of moving ahead in relation-ships these days." So, they advanced to the face-to-face meeting and got along well enough that Natalie was offered the post on the spot.

That job was only part-time, so Natalie kept looking and was alerted (via a Facebook friend) that a very hot Internet company was hiring. The job inter-view was a group interview in a local bar and it featured several group activi-ties to test the "social intelligence" and sociability of the participants. She got the job and became a "glorified brand ambassador" at the firm's events around the city for clients. She met a lot of people that way and, soon enough, one of them offered her a job at the big professional sports team in town working on game days. Then another friend from her short-lived job with the Internet startup helped her connect to an events planning job for a local racetrack.

Natalie's search for employment obviously isn't the prescribed route into a career in law, medicine, science, engineering, or other professions, but most twenty-somethings, like her, find themselves hunting for jobs rather than careers. "The job-searching scene is a blur of friends and connections and tips and false leads," she said. "It's gossip over drinks, quick little text messages, occasional trips to jobs websites, scans of [Facebook] news feeds, anything that might produce useful material." She noted that the process, much like the information exchanges on other subjects, takes place in multiple kinds of channels (face-to-face, phone, electronic) on multiple screens using multiple apps. It has the feel of dipping into and out of streams of information, rather than a comprehensive review of a centralized, single source of information. Media companies and those with goods, services, and ideas to promote are eager to know which channels matter most to this hyperconnected generation. Millennials insist that is the wrong way to think about how they acquire and share created information. Asking Millennials whether Facebook matters to them more than texting or whether apps on their smart phones are more use-ful than searches on their computers only prompts puzzled looks. "It's all of the above," Natalie said. (See appendix Figure 10A.3.)

NETWORKED INDIVIDUALS
USING NETWORKED INFORMATION

Millennials like Natalie function in networks. Their elders do, too. But the avid embrace of technology by Millennials has particularly affected how they use those networks and how those networks shape their lives. A new "social oper-ating system" has been emerging for several generations but has accelerated in recent decades due to widespread broadband adoption, ubiquitous mobile connectivity, and the rise of technological social networks.[5] Sociologist Barry

Wellman coined the term "networked individualism" to describe the way loose-knit networks of people—especially Millennials—are overtaking more tight-knit groups and large hierarchical bureaucracies as the most prevalent relationship structure. The defining features of networked Millennials are:

THEY ENJOY MORE PERSONAL FREEDOM BUT NEED TO EXPEND MORE PERSONAL EFFORT TO MEET THEIR NEEDS. In the world of networked individuals, it is the person who is the focus: not the family, not the work unit, not the neighborhood, and not the social group. Many meet their social, emotional, and economic needs by tapping into loosely knit networks of diverse associates rather than relying on tight connections to a relatively small number of core associates. This means that networked individuals can have a variety of social ties to count on but are less likely to have one surefire "home" group of protectors and observers.

Often individuals rely on many specialized relationships to meet their needs. For example, a typical social network might have some members who are good at meeting local, logistical needs (pet sitting, watering the plants), while others are especially useful when medical needs arise. Yet others (often sisters) provide emotional support. Still others are the ones whose political opinions carry more weight, while others give financial advice, provide restaurant recommendations, or suggest music and books to enjoy.

This social operating system gives people new ways to solve problems and meet social needs through wider and more diverse networks and use of new media, as Natalie did in finding jobs. It offers more freedom to individuals than people experienced in the past, because now they have more room to maneuver and more capacity to act on their own.

At the same time, life as networked individuals requires that people develop new strategies and skills for handling problems. People like Natalie must devote more time and energy to the art of networking. They need to expend effort and sometimes money to maintain their ties near and far; choose whether to phone, visit, or electronically connect with others; remember which members of their network are useful for what sorts of things (including just hanging out); and forge useful alliances among network members who might not have known each other previously. In short, networked individualism is both socially liberating and socially taxing. Paradoxically, the technology that promises to connect us also threatens to overload us with extra work.

THE NEW MEDIA ARE THE NEW NEIGHBORHOOD. More than two-thirds of American adults and more than 80% of Millennials create content through social networking sites, other social media, and their various rankings, ratings, commenting, and remixing applications. In an environment where most are "publishers" and "broadcasters" and where powerful search technologies make it easy to find such content, people can easily locate and connect with others who share their tastes, lifestyles, political beliefs, spiritual practices, health conditions, hobbies, or professional quests. The act of creating on new media is often a social—and often networking—activity, in which people work together or engage in short- and long-term dialogues.

People still value their neighbors, because living nearby remains important for everyday socializing and for dealing with emergencies large and small. Yet, neighbors are only about 10% of people's significant ties.[6] As a result, people's social routines are different from those of their parents or grandparents. Although people see their coworkers and neighbors often, most of their important contacts are with people who live elsewhere in the city, region, nation—and abroad. The Internet, either mobile or wired, is especially valuable for those kinds of connections.

Networked technology has also changed the social point of contact from the household (and work group) to the individual. Each person also creates her own Internet, tailored to her needs. Each person builds and maintains her own network and maintains it through her own address book and individually controlled e-mail address(es), screen name(s), social and technological filters, and mobile phone number.

NETWORKING WORKS BEST WITH LOTS OF INFORMATION DISCLOSURE. ONE CONSEQUENCE IS LESS PRIVACY. A moral and practical imperative of successful networking is to follow the Golden Rule—if you expect people to share their information with you, you need to share yours with them. Similarly, the acquisition of social capital depends on the expenditure of social capital. As Natalie put it, "I want to be findable and I want to make my share of [content] contributions. To me, that's how things get done." People cannot build networks without describing who they are, what talents or skills they possess, what they know, and what their needs are. There is also some pressure for deliberate, considered disclosure in social media when people cannot fall back on close, long-term friends who perpetually stand ready to help them. Finally, there is encouragement to be connected. People cannot easily ask for help from their networks without using digital tools and they cannot be available to help others if they are off the grid.

The cost of more transparency and connectedness will be additional transparency and connectedness, whether people like it or not. This level of personal transparency produces a loss of privacy and the perhaps unwanted commercialization of personal information that others can capture. As former Google CEO Eric Schmidt boasted, "We know where you are. We know where you have been. We can more or less know what you're thinking about."

THE REVOLUTION'S REACH

It's not just the social life of Millennials that has been shaped by the digital revolution. Other domains of their life, learning, work, and leisure have been affected as well. A brief rundown:

TIME USE AND MEDIA CONSUMPTION. The Kaiser Family Foundation reported several times in the 2000s on the media consumption of Natalie's cohort, which it called Generation M^2 (the "M" stood for "media").[7] In 2009, it found that those ages 8–18 were exposed to 10 hours and 45 minutes of media of all kinds during a typical day and spent 29% of that time multitasking with several kinds of information in front of them at the same time.[8] Technology analyst Linda Stone calls this a state of "continuous partial attention" and Millennials are in this state more often than their elders.[9]

There is conflicting evidence about whether this is harmful, specifically in the sense of whether people perform tasks well and completely when they are dividing their attention among various input sources. But this certainly reflects the reality Natalie described as she discussed the way she dips into different media and social information streams at various points during her day. Some wags have suggested that this instinct to try to monitor things constantly is the result of FOMO—"fear of missing out." Natalie doesn't object to that characterization, but says she also multitasks because it sometimes feels efficient and urgent to try to juggle a variety of things at the same time.

"I'm constantly staring at my phone and so are my friends even when we're all together," Natalie said. "We're all extremely addicted and even though I don't want to be, I'm not doing anything to change it because ultimately I like feeling like I'm in touch and know what's going on at all times. I'm always checking the usual apps—Facebook and [photo-sharing service] Instagram— even if someone is trying to have a conversation with me. I see other people do it to me. I'll be telling a story and they're nodding along with one word semi-responses but I know that half of my story has been lost because their attention is mostly focused on whatever they're texting about or reading on the screen. It's irritating but I know I do it, too."

Long-running studies by the Pew Research Center have shown sweeping changes in news consumption patterns since the mid-1990s. Most are tied to technology and there are notable differences by generation.[10] Millennials now are less likely to get news on a given day than their Gen X predecessors were in the mid-1990s at their same age. Compared with all their elders, Millennials who do get news are more likely to use the Internet, their cell phones, mobile apps, and tablet computers. They are more likely to say they get news from social networking sites. They are less likely to get news from newspapers, TV either in broadcast or cable stations, radio, or magazines. They are more likely to say that comedy cable shows are a source of news. "I do not miss *The Daily Show* [with Jon Stewart] and *The Colbert Report*, if I can help it," Natalie said. "I get all of my pop-culture from PerezHilton.com (my guilty pleasure) and general information from *Huffington Post*. I'm also constantly kept up-to-date from just signing into Facebook. If something is 'trending,' then my entire news feed will be filled with links to articles or YouTube videos."

In addition, Millennials are more likely to say they graze for news at various times of the day, rather than consume it at set time periods. Natalie says she feels a responsibility as a citizen to stay up with news, but that doesn't mean she engages in active searches. "My feeling is that if I'm constantly checking things, the most interesting stuff or most important news will cross my path, rather than me thinking it's my responsibility to be an active searcher for it," she said. But she acknowledges that her news consumption strategy is better at harvesting cat videos and Kardashian sightings than updates on poverty or global warming, which is one reason that Millennials (like their same-age counterparts in the past) are much less well informed than their elders about public affairs.

Other Pew Research studies show Millennials are more likely than older Americans to participate in news by sharing links, contributing comments, and posting their own material.[11] They are more likely than their elders to judge news operations—especially Web-based offerings—based on the willingness of a news organization to allow comments and contributions from users and to be transparent about its operations. Millennials are more likely to say search engines and social media steer them to local news and information on a variety of topics, including most dimensions of civic news such as local government, political news, and educational news.[12]

PATTERNS OF INFLUENCE AND DECISION MAKING. In an environment of information overabundance, social networks have become a tool that helps people figure out how to drink from the proverbial fire hose. A mantra for many is, "If news is important, it will find its way to me." For Millennials, this is a primary reason to check their social networking spaces with some regularity. Half of Millennial users of social networking sites check them multiple times a day, compared with fewer than a third of Boomers who do so. In addition, people often turn to their social networks to help them evaluate the new information they encounter. For example, Millennials are the most likely generation to use online social spaces to discuss and share health information and stories, though they still rely on doctors and other health providers when they need to make health decisions.[13] Also, about 3 in 10 social networking Millennials say they have gotten more involved in a political cause after discussing it or reading about it in social networking spaces, compared with about 1 in 4 social networking Boomers.[14] But on the flip side of the same coin: Millennials are also twice as likely as Boomers to say they have become less active in a cause after reading what their friends said about it on social networking sites.

As more and more people become content creators, it is increasingly common for Millennials to assume that when they discover something, they will share it with their broad network. This is part of the ongoing process of building and maintaining a vibrant social network; reciprocal sharing is the way Millennials build their social capital and reputations. "When I discover a story that I think is hilarious or a new song, I want everyone to know about it so we can talk about it and laugh or sing along with them," Natalie said.

There are several other ways that the technological environment especially affects Millennials' decision making. One is crowdsourcing. Millennials overperform when it comes to creating and reading user reviews and comments online as they make up their minds about where to eat and drink, what movies and musical acts to see, and what Web content to access. They are also ripe targets for the algorithms that many popular websites use to organize their content. Search engines are particularly potent gatekeepers and arrangers of information for Millennials; social networking sites follow close behind. Not only does this apply to the main content of the site, but it also applies to the advertisements that surround that content—more and more of which is sorted by the websites' understanding of what matters to users, based on their previous use of the site and other material that is collected about them and added to their data-based profiles.

NETWORKING LITERACY. The most successful Millennials thrive because they have a set of new literacies that amount to mastery of networking and troves of information—social and otherwise—that stream into their lives.[15] Networking literacy starts with *graphic literacy* that recognizes that life is experienced as communications, media, and data on screens. They can interpret this material and feel comfortable contributing to it. Successful networking also requires *navigation literacy,* a sense of Internet geography that allows them to maneuver through multiple information channels and formats. They understand the changes that have occurred as information has become networked—by links, by continual editing, by algorithmic authority. Beyond that, Millennials have *context and connections literacy* that helps them weave together the information and chatter that is flowing into their lives at a quickening pace. Even if the tidbits they gather are disaggregated from any larger context, they have the wherewithal—often with help from the network helpers—to puzzle through the material they collect.

Millennials also have mastery over their own attention, a kind of *focus literacy*: that is, the capacity to minimize distractions and complete what they need to do. Natalie speaks of how she has learned through trial and error when it is essential to be connected and when to disengage. "There are times to need to be quiet to recharge and figure things out," is how she puts it. Yet, despite their focus, they also have *multitasking literacy*: the ability to do several things (almost) at once. With multiple inputs from family, friends, work, and institutions—and multiple in-person, Internet, and mobile sources provide these inputs—thriving networkers such as Natalie have gained the ability to attend to them without lots of fuss.

The age of information overload also requires *skepticism literacy*. Internet veteran Howard Rheingold says people need a fine-tuned sense of "crap detection" to evaluate what they encounter online. This means weeding out the media and people who have outdated, biased, incomplete and agenda-driven, or just dead wrong ideas to promote.

IDENTITY AND ETHICS. The technology-mediated environment has created new conditions under which Millennials form and reform their identities and ponder what it means to be a moral actor. Media scholar danah boyd argues that many people—and most Millennials—live in "networked publics" organized around networked information that has four properties:

- It is *persistent*: People's online creations and material about them is automatically recorded and archived.
- It is *replicable:* People's content can easily be duplicated and passed along to others.
- It is *scalable:* Content about people can be visible in all kinds of public and networked places.
- It is *searchable:* Content in networked publics can be easily found and displayed through search engines.[16]

She argues that this new kind of individualized publishing power and communication capacity has led Millennials into a new world where (1) invisible audiences can observe what people are saying and doing; and (2) the barriers between public and private are porous.

> These four properties structure network publics and the interactions that take place in them. Many of these properties are not unique to networked publics—oral histories made stories persistent, the printing press replicated content with ease, broadcast media scaled the visibility of live acts, and librarians have long invested in approaches to searching for information. Yet in networked publics, these properties are a part of the environment by default and are interconnected in new ways. Furthermore, because they play a role in all mediated interactions and because networked publics play a significant role in the lives of many teens, teens who participate in social network sites must account for these properties during everyday acts and interactions.[17]

Millennials are the generation most affected by these changes because they grew up knowing no other platform for social commerce. Like all teens and young adults since the beginning of time, they're constantly trying to figure out their identity, social status, group affiliations, and passions. The only reality they've known is one in which the boundaries are blurred between private and public, work and play, present and absent, and home and school. Inevitably, they'll be the ones setting the social mores of the new digital age. When is it rude to look away from someone to check out the latest text message on your smart phone? When is it appropriate to pass along a communication or keep it closely held? When should you share your real name or make one up? When to lurk and when to engage? When to declare a relationship or abandon it? All of those norms are still works in progress, but it's the Millennials who'll be making up the rules.

WHAT'S NEXT?

The Pew Research Center's Internet Project periodically tries to gaze into the future by teaming with researchers at the Imagining the Internet Center at Elon University on opt-in online surveys of technology experts and scholars. We typically ask them to weigh in on the probability that one of two opposite scenarios will unfold—a technique known as assessing a "tension pair." In 2011, after a spate of magazine articles raised the "Is Google Making Us Stupid?" question, we asked about the following two scenarios. The first posited:

- In 2020 the brains of multitasking teens and young adults are "wired" differently from those over age 35 and overall it yields helpful results. They do not suffer notable cognitive shortcomings as they multitask and cycle quickly through personal- and work-related tasks. Rather, they are learning more and they are more adept at finding answers to deep questions, in part because they can search effectively and access collective intelligence via the Internet. In sum, the changes in learning behavior and cognition among the young generally produce positive outcomes.

Some 55% of the 1,021 respondents agreed with that statement, while 42% agreed with the opposite statement, which posited:

- In 2020 the brains of multitasking teens and young adults are "wired" differently from those over age 35 and overall it yields baleful results. They do not retain information; they spend most of their energy sharing short social messages, being entertained, and being distracted away from deep engagement with people and knowledge. They lack deep-thinking capabilities; they lack face-to-face social skills; they depend in unhealthy ways on the Internet and mobile devices to function. In sum, the changes in behavior and cognition among the young are generally negative outcomes.

Many who chose the upbeat scenario made it clear that it was more their hope than their best guess, and a number said the most likely outcome is a combination of both. So the real result here is probably closer to 50/50. By the way, to encourage a spirited discussion, respondents were given no middle-ground choice, nor were they offered another alternative altogether—that young people's brains would *not* be wired differently. Some of the respondents made that argument, positing that people's patterns of thinking will likely change but that their mechanisms of brain function won't.

Survey participants did offer strong, consistent predictions about the most desired life skills for young people in 2020. Among those they listed were: public problem-solving through cooperative work; the ability to search effectively for information online and to be able to discern the quality and veracity of the information one finds and then communicate these findings well; synthesizing (being able to bring together details from many sources); being strategically future-minded; the ability to concentrate; and the ability to distinguish between the "noise" and the message in the ever-growing sea of information.

Futurist John Smart, president and founder of the Acceleration Studies Foundation, recalled an insight of economist Simon Kuznets about the evolution of technology effects known as the Kuznets curve: "First-generation tech usually causes 'net negative' social effects; second-generation 'net neutral' effects; by the third generation of tech—once the tech is smart enough, and we've got the interface right, and it begins to reinforce the best behaviors—we finally get to 'net positive' effects," he noted. "We'll be early into conversational interface and agent technologies by 2020, so kids will begin to be seriously intelligently augmented by the Internet. There will be many persistent drawbacks however. The biggest problem from a personal-development perspective will be motivating people to work to be more self-actualized, productive, and civic than their parents were. They'll be more willing than ever to relax and remain distracted by entertainments amid accelerating technical productivity."

"As machine intelligence advances," Smart continued, "the first response of humans is to offload their intelligence and motivation to the machines. That's a dehumanizing, first-generation response. Only the later, third-generation educational systems will correct for this."

Barry Chudakov, a Florida-based consultant and a research fellow in the McLuhan Program in Culture and Technology at the University of Toronto, wrote that by 2020,

> Technology will be so seamlessly integrated into our lives that it will effectively disappear. The line between self and technology is thin today; by then it will effectively vanish. We will think with, think into, and think through our smart tools but their presence and reach into our lives will be less visible. Youth will assume their minds and intentions are extended by technology, while tracking technologies will seek further incursions into behavioral monitoring and choice manipulation. Children will assume this is the way the world works. The cognitive challenge children and youth will face (as we are beginning to face now) is integrity, the state of being whole and undivided. There will be a premium on the skill of maintaining presence, of mindfulness, of awareness in the face of persistent and pervasive tool extensions and incursions into our lives. Is this my intention, or is the tool inciting me to feel and think this way? That question, more than multitasking or brain atrophy due to accessing collective intelligence via the Internet, will be the challenge of the future.

No one knows what the future holds, but it's clear that Natalie's information ecosystem and social platforms are vastly different from those of her forebears. The ever-changing digital landscape is likely to keep those generation gaps quite wide for the foreseeable future. It may even change the very nature of what it means to be human and to grow old.

11

Getting Old

AMERICANS ARE GETTING OLD and, before too long, they may be getting *very* old. A Methuselah drug awaits its inventor, but scientists at major universities and research institutions are hard at work. Some believe it may be only a matter of decades before someone in a lab coat makes a breakthrough that leads to an entirely new aging paradigm, one that replaces the generally accepted limits of human longevity with wondrous new possibilities. Merely imagining such a prospect raises mind-bending questions. Will radically extended life spans be the path to nirvana or dystopia? Will the extra years be available only to those who can afford them? What becomes of family bonds, medical costs, retirement finances, and social safety nets when America is awash with 120-year-old great-great-grandmas?

Aging and dying have always fascinated, haunted, and ultimately defined human beings. But the boundaries between the two have shifted dramatically over the centuries. For most of human history, life was "nasty, brutish and short," in the memorable synopsis of Thomas Hobbes, the seventeenth-century British philosopher. A newborn in the Roman Empire could expect to live to be about 25. As recently as 1900, the typical American lived to be just 47, with averages yanked down by the appallingly high share of newborns and infants who succumbed to infectious diseases. Even in ancient times, however, living into old age, while rare, was not unheard of. The Bible speaks of people living to be "three score and ten" (70 years) or even "four score" (80 years). And early American history is full of famous people who led famously long lives. When they died within hours of each other on the Fourth of July, 1826, Thomas Jefferson was 83 and John Adams was 90.

In the modern era, life expectancy at birth in the US has been increasing by about a year every six years.[1] The typical American baby born today can expect to live an average of 78.7 years, up from 75.4 years two decades ago—steady progress but not as rapid as the rise in many other developed countries, leading the US to slip from 20th to 27th in the rankings for life expectancy among the world's 34 OECD countries. During the same two-decade period, the number of centenarians in the US grew by about 50%, to more than 50,000. By the middle of this century, according to Census Bureau forecasts, close to a half million people in the US will be at least 100 years old. (The oldest person on record—Frenchwoman Jeanne Calment—lived to be 122.[2])

Even today, scientists don't know exactly why people age and die. They understand many of the mechanisms that lead the body to break down and stop working over time, but the underlying causes of aging are still a mystery. One popular theory holds that humans are essentially programmed to die after they are no longer needed to raise the children they produce. According to this theory, evolution has ensured that people are strong and vigorous during their fertile years, so they can have and rear offspring, but this bodily vigor subsides after people's reproductive and parenting years are over.[3]

Despite the unknowns about human longevity, a host of companies these days are offering a variety of treatments, from human growth hormones (HGH) to testosterone, aimed at helping people to slow down the aging process. Drugs such as resveratrol and rapamycin and experiments with new genetic combinations have the allure of a magic bullet: take a pill or flip a genetic switch and live an extra 20, 30, or even 40 healthy years. These therapies have largely been shunned by the mainstream medical community and, so far, they have not been scientifically shown to increase a person's life span in any meaningful way.

Some in the anti-aging movement believe that real gains will not be made by ingesting one compound but through a combination of medical therapies. Aubrey de Grey, a former Cambridge University researcher and now the chief science officer at an anti-aging think tank in Mountain View, California, called the Strategies for Engineered Negligible Senescence (SENS) Foundation, says aging will be conquered through a variety of "rejuvenation biotechnologies" that will repair and maintain the body indefinitely, much in the way a good mechanic can keep a vintage car running indefinitely. Under this scenario, various treatments including stem cell and gene therapies would be applied at the cellular level to halt the damage to the body caused by aging. "I'd say we have a 50/50 chance of bringing aging under what I'd call a decisive level of medical control within the next 25 years or so," de Grey said in 2010.[4]

Other experts believe that aging ultimately will be conquered by engineers and computer scientists rather than biomedical researchers. Ray Kurzweil, an American computer scientist and inventor whose work has led to the development of everything from checkout scanners at supermarkets to text-reading machines for the blind, says that what might seem outlandish today eventually will become possible because technological change is exponential rather than linear. "The reason information technology grows exponentially is that we use the latest technology to create the next," he said in a recent interview. "So each new generation of technology grows exponentially in capability and the speed of that process accelerates over time."[5]

Soon, Kurzweil predicts, it will be possible to place powerful machines in the human body that replace or improve existing biological systems. Machines, from pacemakers to cochlear implants, already play a huge role in medicine, and you don't need to be a science fiction writer or a professional futurist to see that the role of technology in medicine will continue to grow. But Kurzweil and other scientists say that greater computing power combined with extreme miniaturization (nanotechnology) will allow scientists to put microscopic machines in the body—at first to protect and maintain people's organs and ultimately to effectively replace them. In essence, Kurzweil says, scientists will "reverse engineer" bodily systems so that they can be replaced with much more reliable machines. He doesn't stop at this "bionic man" scenario. Eventually, he claims, human beings will achieve immortality by fully merging with machines. Kurzweil predicts that scientists will one day find a way to reverse engineer the brain and download human consciousness into it. Blood, bone, skin, and organs (what he and others call "wetware") will no longer be necessary.[6]

A Baby Boomer who turns 66 in 2014, Kurzweil makes it clear he has a very personal stake not just in the development of these new technologies, but in how quickly they come on stream. He believes that if he hangs on for another 15 years, he'll have a shot at immortality. "I'm right on the cusp," he told a *Wall Street Journal* reporter in 2013, then added some words of encouragement to his fellow Boomers: "I think some of us will make it through." As for the concern that only the wealthy will have access to such technologies, he noted with a dismissive shrug that people not too long ago said the same about cell phones.[7]

If the public policy questions raised by radical life extension are dizzying, the social and ethical questions are even more complex. Would it change the way we view marriage and children? Would it alter our sense of what it means to be human? Leon Kass, who chaired the President's Council on Bioethics under President George W. Bush, has observed that one of the "virtues of mortality" is that it instills a desire to make each day count. Knowledge that one will soon die "is the condition . . . for treasuring and appreciating all that life brings," he says.[8] Along these same lines, Stanley Hauerwas, a theologian at the Duke University School of Divinity, says that without death, love as we know it would cease to exist because it is the finite nature of life that prompts people to wholly commit themselves to others. "Death . . . creates an economy that makes love possible," he says. "If you lived forever there would not be the necessity of loving this one not that one. You could love them all." But others see the possibility of significantly longer life spans as a blessing—one that people will embrace, just as they have with all previous social and technological advances. De Grey says that people fear much longer life spans only because they have talked themselves into believing that death is natural, and even good. He calls this a "pro-aging trance," which he says was "a sensible way of coping with the inevitability of aging" when it was inevitable. But now that aging and dying might not be inevitable, this mind-set "becomes part of the problem."[9]

PUBLIC ATTITUDES

It's only been in the past few years that the issue of radical life extension has begun to attract the notice of the mainstream press; before that it had been pretty much consigned to the realm of scientists, futurists, and ethicists. The May 2013 cover of *National Geographic* featured a picture of a newborn with the attention-grabbing caption: "This Baby Will Live to Be 120." In September 2013, a *Time* cover asked: "Can Google Solve Death?" Still, most of the American public is either unfamiliar or uncomfortable with the subject. In the spring of 2013, a majority (54%) of respondents to a Pew Research survey said they'd heard nothing about radical life extension. When prompted, respondents voiced ambivalence. Our survey asked, "If new medical treatments slow the aging process and allow the average person to live decades longer, to at least 120 years old, do you think that would be a good thing or a bad thing for society?" Respondents were closely divided; about half (51%) said bad while 41% said good. Follow-up questions produced more uncertainty. When asked if they themselves would want such medical treatments, a majority (56%) said they would not. But when asked if they thought most people would want such treatments, two-thirds (68%) said yes, most others would.

Men are more likely than women to say they want such treatments for themselves; blacks and Hispanics more likely than whites; and the young more likely than the old—but all of these demographic differences are relatively modest (see appendix Figure 11A.1). There's a much bigger gap in personally desiring treatments between those who think that extending longevity will be good for society

(71% in this camp said they would want the treatment for themselves) and think it would be bad (just 13% said they would want the treatments).

The public is skeptical that that such medical advances are coming anytime soon; only a quarter think these therapies will be available in 2050. In comparison, many more believe that by midcentury, scientists will be able to bring back extinct species by cloning (50%), there will be a cure for most forms of cancer (69%), and artificial arms and legs will perform better than natural ones (71%).

Even though 4 in 10 Americans say life-extending therapies would be good for society, large majorities fear negative impacts of one kind or another. For example, while about 8 in 10 say "everyone should be able to get these treatments if they want them," two-thirds say that only wealthy people would have access to treatments. Two-thirds also say they believe that "longer life expectancies would strain our natural resources" and that "medical scientists would offer the treatment before they fully understood how it affects people's health."

Figure 11.1

Do You Want to Live to be 120 Years Old?

% saying (they/most people) would or would not want medical treatments that slow the aging process and allow the average person to live to at least 120 years

Note: Half of survey respondents were asked about their personal option and half were asked about "most people"

Source: Pew Research Center survey, Mar.–Apr. 2013, N=4,006 US adults

And about 6 in 10 (58%) say that "these treatments would be fundamentally unnatural." Opinion is divided over whether the economy would be more productive because people could work longer: 44% say it would and 53% say no (see appendix Figure 11A.2). Views on many of these questions are related to beliefs about the overall effect of radical life extension treatments on society. For example, among those who think the economy would be more productive with longer life spans, 70% think new medical treatments to radically extend life would be a good thing for society, while just 25% say it would be a bad thing.

GETTING OLDER, FEELING YOUNGER

Aging is life's great mystery. Whether or not radical life extension comes to pass, virtually everyone wonders what it will be like to grow old. When the Pew Research Center did a national survey on the subject among adults of all ages, we found a striking dissonance: Getting old isn't nearly as bad as people think it will be. Nor is it quite as good.

On aspects of everyday life ranging from mental acuity to physical dexterity to sexual activity to financial security, the survey showed a sizable gap between the expectations that young and middle-age adults have about old age and the actual experiences reported by older Americans themselves.

These disparities came into sharpest focus when respondents were asked about a series of negative benchmarks often associated with aging, such as illness, memory loss, an inability to drive, an end to sexual activity, a struggle with loneliness and depression, and difficulty paying bills. In every instance, older adults report experiencing them at lower levels (often far lower) than younger adults report expecting to encounter them when they grow old.

At the same time, however, older adults report experiencing fewer of the benefits of aging that younger adults expect to enjoy when they grow old, such as spending more time with their family, traveling more for pleasure, having more time for hobbies, doing volunteer work, or starting a second career.

These generation gaps in perception also extend to the most basic question of all about old age: When does it begin? Survey respondents ages 18 to 29 believe that the average person becomes old at age 60. Middle-age respondents put the threshold closer to 70, and respondents ages 65 and above say that the average person does not become old until turning 74.

Other potential markers of old age—such as forgetfulness, retirement, becoming sexually inactive, experiencing bladder control problems, getting gray hair, having grandchildren—are the subjects of similar perceptual gaps. For example, nearly two-thirds of adults ages 18 to 29 believe that when someone "frequently forgets familiar names," that person is old. Less than half of all adults ages 30 and older agree (see appendix Figure 11A.3).

However, a handful of potential markers—failing health, an inability to live independently, an inability to drive, difficulty with stairs—engender agreement across all generations about the degree to which they serve as an indicator of old age.

The survey findings would seem to confirm the old saw that you're never too old to feel young. In fact, it shows that *the older people get, the younger they feel*—relatively speaking. Among 18- to 29-year-olds, about half say they feel their age, while about a quarter say they feel older than their age and another quarter say they feel younger. By contrast, among adults 65 and older, fully 60% say they feel younger than their age, compared with 32% who say they feel exactly their age and just 3% who say they feel older than their age.

Moreover, the gap in years between actual age and "felt age" widens as people grow older. Nearly half of all survey respondents ages 50 and older say they feel at least 10 years younger than their chronological age. Among respondents ages 65 to 74, a third say they feel 10 to 19 years younger than their age, and 1 in 6 say they feel at least 20 years younger than their actual age.

In sync with this upbeat way of counting their felt age, older adults also have a count-my-blessings attitude when asked to look back over the full arc of their lives. Nearly half (45%) of adults ages 75 and older say their life has turned out better than they expected, while just 5% say it has turned out worse (the remainder say things have turned out the way they expected or have no opinion). All other age groups also tilt positive, but considerably less so, when asked to assess their lives so far against their own expectations.

Figure 11.2

Markers of Old Age

% saying that a person is old when he or she ...

Turns 85	79
Can't live independently	76
Can't drive a car	66
Turns 75	62
Frequently forgets familiar names	51
Finds health is failing	47
Has trouble walking up stairs	45
Has bladder control problems	42
Is no longer sexually active	33
Turns 65	32
Retires from work	23
Has grandchildren	15
Has gray hair	13

Source: Pew Research Center survey, Feb.–Mar 2009, N=2,969

THE DOWNSIDE OF GETTING OLD

Of course, there are burdens that come with old age. About 1 in 4 adults ages 65 and older report experiencing memory loss. About 1 in 5 say they have a serious illness, are not sexually active, or often feel sad or depressed. About 1 in 6 report they are lonely or have trouble paying bills. One in 7 cannot drive. One in 10 say they feel they aren't needed or are a burden to others.

But when it comes to these and other potential problems related to old age, the share of younger and middle-age adults who report expecting to encounter

Figure 11.3

The Gap Between How Old We Are and How Old We Feel

Averages for actual age vs. felt age, by age group of respondent

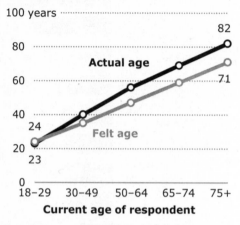

Note: Responses of "Don't know/Refused" not included in averages.

Source: Pew Research Center survey, Feb.–Mar 2009, N=2,969

them is much higher than the share of older adults who report actually experiencing them.

These problems are not shared equally by all groups of older adults. Those with low incomes are more likely than those with high incomes to face these challenges. The only exception to this pattern has to do with sexual inactivity; the likelihood of older adults reporting a problem in this realm of life is not correlated with income.

Not surprisingly, troubles associated with aging accelerate as adults advance into their 80s and beyond. For example, about 4 in 10 respondents (41%) ages 85 and older say they are experiencing some memory loss, compared with 27% of those ages 75–84 and 20% of those ages 65–74. Similarly, 30% of those ages 85 and older say they often feel sad or depressed, compared with less than 20% of those who are 65–84. And a quarter of adults ages 85 and older say they no longer drive, compared with 17% of those ages 75–84 and 10% of those who are 65–74.

But even in the face of these challenges, the vast majority of the "old old" in our survey appear to have made peace with their circumstances. Only a miniscule share of adults ages 85 and older—1%—say their lives have turned out worse than they expected. It no doubt helps that adults in their late 80s are as likely as those in their 60s and 70s to say they are experiencing many of the good things associated with aging—be it time with family, less stress, more respect, or more financial security.

THE UPSIDE OF GETTING OLD

When asked about a wide range of potential benefits of old age, 7 in 10 respondents ages 65 and older say they are enjoying more time with their family. About two-thirds cite more time for hobbies, more financial security, and not

Figure 11.4

The Challenges of Growing Older

It's not as bad as younger adults think

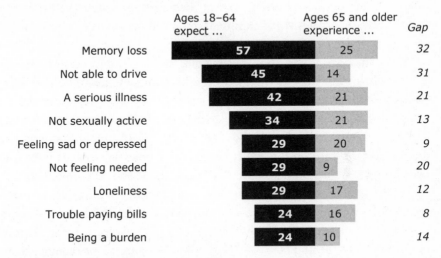

	Ages 18–64 expect ...	Ages 65 and older experience ...	Gap
Memory loss	57	25	32
Not able to drive	45	14	31
A serious illness	42	21	21
Not sexually active	34	21	13
Feeling sad or depressed	29	20	9
Not feeling needed	29	9	20
Loneliness	29	17	12
Trouble paying bills	24	16	8
Being a burden	24	10	14

The Benefits of Growing Older

Reality doesn't measure up to expectations

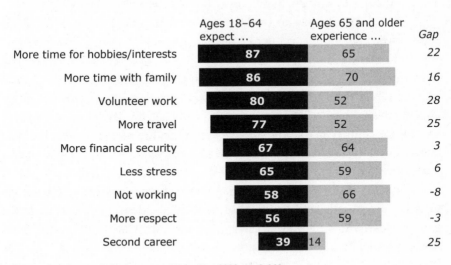

	Ages 18–64 expect ...	Ages 65 and older experience ...	Gap
More time for hobbies/interests	87	65	22
More time with family	86	70	16
Volunteer work	80	52	28
More travel	77	52	25
More financial security	67	64	3
Less stress	65	59	6
Not working	58	66	-8
More respect	56	59	-3
Second career	39	14	25

Source: Pew Research Center survey, Feb.–Mar 2009, N=2,969

having to work. About 6 in 10 say they get more respect and feel less stress than when they were younger. Just over half cite more time to travel and to do volunteer work. As Figure 11.4 illustrates, older adults may not be experiencing these "upsides" at quite the levels that most younger adults expect to enjoy them once they grow old, but their responses nonetheless indicate that the phrase "golden years" is something more than a syrupy greeting card sentiment.

Of all the good things about getting old, the best by far, according to older adults, is being able to spend more time with family members. In response to an open-ended question, 28% of those ages 65 and older say that what they value most about being older is the chance to spend more time with family, and an additional 25% say that above all, they value time with their grandchildren. A distant third on this list is having more financial security, which was cited by 14% of older adults as what they value most about getting older.

When, exactly, does old age begin? The aggregated wisdom of our survey respondents is at age 68. But that average masks a wide, age-driven variance in responses. More than half of adults under 30 say the average person becomes old even before turning 60. Just 6% of adults who are 65 or older agree (see appendix Figure 11A.4). Moreover, gender as well as age influences attitudes on this subject. Women, on average, say a person becomes old at age 70. Men, on average, put the number at 66.

Even if the public has decreed that the average person becomes old at age 68, you won't get too far trying to convince people that age that the threshold applies to them. Among respondents ages 65–74, just 21% say they feel old. Even among those 75 and older, just 35% say they feel old.

The survey found that the average age that people aspired to live to was 89. One in 5 would like to live into their 90s, while just 8% say they would like to surpass the century mark. The public's verdict on the most desirable life span appears to have ratcheted down a bit in recent years. A 2002 AARP survey found that the average desired life span was 92.

The same factors that predict happiness among younger adults—good health, good friends, and financial security—by and large predict happiness among older adults. However, there are a few age-related differences. Most notably, once all other key demographic variables are held constant, although being married is a predictor of happiness among younger adults, it is not so among older adults (perhaps because a significant share of the latter group is made up of widows or widowers, many of whom presumably have "banked" some of the key marriage-related correlates of happiness, such as financial security and a strong family life).

Aging is more than a human drama. It's also a societal drama. Between now and midcentury, even absent any breakthroughs in life extension, the graying of the world's population will put enormous stress on economies, families, and governments in the US and around the world.

12

Empty Cradle, Gray World

ANYONE REMEMBER THE JAPANESE MIRACLE? A genera-
tion ago the phrase ricocheted around the world wherever political and
economic elites gathered. As the US struggled with recessions, inflation, and
energy crises, Japan was busy building the world's best cars and coolest electronic gadgets. It boasted a soaring GDP, productive workforce, efficient factories, clean streets, and virtually no crime. Its banks had become the world's
biggest. Its corporations were scooping up iconic chunks of America, from
Rockefeller Center to Columbia Pictures to Pebble Beach to 7-Eleven, leading
one US congressman to worry that "the United States is rapidly becoming a
colony of Japan." In 1979 Harvard sociology professor Ezra Vogel published
Japan as Number 1: Lessons for America, in which he described how an insu-
lar island nation had risen phoenix-like from the self-inflicted catastrophe of
World War II by reengineering its political, economic, and social institutions.
The book was an international bestseller.

Japan is still a global economic powerhouse, but the triumphalism of that
bygone era has been replaced by a declinism nearly as pervasive. Not only
did its economy never become number one, it's now no longer number two:
in 2010 Japan relinquished that spot to its once and future nemesis, China.[1]
Its GDP per capita, which had closed to within 87% of the US level in 1991,
has since retreated to 72%. Its Nikkei average stands at less than half of its
1989 peak; its land prices are at 1975 levels; its government debt has ballooned above 200% of GDP, more than double that of most other advanced
nations. What went wrong? Lots of things: speculative bubbles, unproductive

investments, crony capitalism, weak governance. But one factor exacerbates all others: demographics.

Japan has the oldest population in the world, and as scores of other countries are about to discover for themselves, aging societies have trouble maintaining their economic vitality. The active share of the population needs to support the inactive share, and older folks simply don't have the energy, imagination, entrepreneurship, and drive that younger ones do. Going forward, the age pyramid in the Land of the Rising Sun will only grow more top-heavy. Japan's median age is 45 today. By 2050 it will be 53. By 2060, 37% of its population will be 65 or older. No country in history has ever had to cope with that old a population. The challenges go well beyond economic growth; they go to the very fabric of the nation's social, family, and political life. The Japanese have a word, *kodokushi*, to describe the phenomenon of older, often childless adults who die lonely deaths, sometimes at their own hand. It is a growing problem. As of 2010, some 4.6 million elderly Japanese lived alone, and the share who died at home grew by 61% between 2003 and 2010, according to Japan's bureau of social welfare and public health. In early 2013, Japan's finance minister, Tara Aso, 72, caused a stir when he suggested at a meeting of a national council on social security reforms that the elderly "hurry up and die" to ease the strain on the nation's finances.[2] He later said his remarks were inappropriate, but over the years he has also talked about "doddering pensioners" and "tube people." In any case, Japan's government continues to chip away at the social safety net for seniors.

Longevity, however, isn't the main cause of Japan's demographic winter. The real problem is too few births. If present trends were to continue—which they won't—Japan would eventually un-breed itself into extinction. Today its population is 127 million. By 2100, if you believe the United Nations projection, it will be down to 84 million, and if you believe the Japanese government's own worst-case projections, it could fall as low as 47 million. "I am the last Japan optimist," muses Jesper Koll, an American economist who has lived in Tokyo since the Miracle era. "[People here] say, 'Oh, in 600 years there will be 480 Japanese left.'"[3] Japan's fertility rate—1.4 per woman—is among the lowest in the world and far below the 2.1 level that most developed societies must maintain to keep from depopulating over time.

How did this happen? Many Japanese tell some version of the following story: After the real estate and stock market bubbles burst in 1990, the Japanese essentially lost some of their faith in themselves and their collective future. The ensuing decades of economic stagnation, coming so hard after the go-go decades, which came so quickly after the war years, have rattled this proud, ancient, and still somewhat xenophobic society to such a degree that many of its young have turned inward. In an age of declining expectations, Japan's Millennials are setting their life compasses on individual fulfillment—getting what they can for themselves. They're delaying marriage and childbearing, or abandoning it altogether. There's even some suggestion that they're losing their appetite for sex. According to one recent survey, one-third of young men ages 16 to 19 express no interest in sex, a puzzling sentiment reportedly shared by 60% of young women that age.[4] It hasn't helped that Japan's day care centers are too expensive for most families. In 2013 the *New York Times* ran a feature story about a pregnant Tokyo woman who had toured 44 day care centers in a desperate search to find an affordable one that met her standards. Such expeditions have their own name—*hokatsu*—and as a source of stress are said to be on par with the notorious job searches of newly minted Japanese college graduates.[5]

Japan's baby bust is the most acute in the world, but similar dynamics are taking hold on every continent. The demographic term of art is "sub-replacement-level fertility." It first emerged in Scandinavia in the 1970s and is now common throughout Europe, Russia, East Asia, and some South American, Caribbean, and Middle Eastern countries. It's most prevalent in the wealthy countries of "old Europe"—Germany, France, Italy, and Spain—as well as in the Asian Tigers of Japan's neighborhood: China, South Korea, Singapore, Hong Kong, and Taiwan. But this not merely a phenomenon among the affluent. More than 20 Muslim countries have had fertility declines of at least 50% since the late 1970s, with the sharpest drops in Iran, Oman, the United Arab Emirates, Algeria, Bangladesh, Tunisia, and Libya. The typical Iranian woman had nearly 7 children as recently as the late 1970s; now she has 1.9. Halfway around the world, Mexico has seen its fertility rates plunge by a similar order of magnitude over roughly the same time period. In fact, Mexican women now have a lower fertility rate than Mexican-American immigrants. According to UN projections, some 49 countries are now producing so few children that they will see their populations decline between now and 2050; about a third are "developing" economies and two-thirds are more affluent economies.

All of this marks an unprecedented turning point in human history. Until a few centuries ago, the prevailing demographic paradigm consisted of high birthrates, high infant mortality, and relatively short life expectancy. In modern times, advances in sanitation, nutrition, medicine, and public health dramatically reduced infant mortality and increased longevity. This produced a huge demographic and economic dividend for the world, at least initially. More children surviving into adulthood meant more producers and consumers—more units of economic activity. Starting around 1900, the world's population expanded more rapidly than ever before, growing fourfold in the twentieth century alone, to about 7 billion today. Standards of living also rose dramatically, especially in the developed world. But not everyone saw these trends as a cause for celebration. In 1968, just as the oldest of America's Baby Boomers was entering the workforce, sociologist Paul Ehrlich published *The Population Bomb*, which began on this attention-grabbing note: "The battle to feed all of humanity is over. In the 1970s hundreds of millions of people will starve to death in spite of any crash programs embarked upon now. At this late date nothing can prevent a substantial increase in the world death rate." Ehrlich, who was channeling the apocalyptic visions conjured up two centuries earlier by British scholar Thomas Malthus, called for a wide range of population control measures to mitigate the looming disasters of overpopulation. His book, like Vogel's, became an international bestseller.

How times change. Today's demographic doomsday scenarios tend to revolve around too few, not too many. Yes, there are still "explosionists" concerned that an overpopulated planet will deplete the earth's resources, but they now share the stage with "implosionists" troubled by a world of too few young supporting too many old. These compositional shifts in the global age pyramid are the result of what has been dubbed the "second demographic transition." The old paradigm of high birthrates, high infant mortality, and short life expectancy has been replaced by a new paradigm of low birthrates, low infant mortality, and long life expectancy. For the most part, these changes weren't driven by public policy edict. Rather, they're a natural adaptation to improvements in medical science and public health. In olden days, people felt they needed to have lots of kids to ensure that some would survive to take care of them in their old age. Now they feel safe having fewer. Other social changes—secularization, urbanization, the women's revolution, modern media—contributed to the trend. In advanced societies, the less religious tend to have, on average, about half a child less than do the religiously observant; as religiosity has declined around the world, so has childbearing. Urbanization has raised the cost and reduced the economic rewards of child-rearing; not many family farms need tending in Shanghai, London, or Mexico City. Meantime, the movement of women into the workforce has upped the opportunity cost of baby-making; nowadays, if a woman chooses to be a stay-at-home mom, it typically means she's forgoing income. Then there are the norms set by a media-saturated popular culture. In Brazil, where television began being introduced sequentially into the provinces a few generations ago, researchers found a correlation between the arrival of television and the decline of birthrates, prompting demographer Phillip Longman to observe: "Discuss among yourselves whether this was because of what's on Brazilian television—mostly soap operas depicting rich people living the high life—or simply because a television was now on at night in many more bedrooms."[6]

When birthrates tumble, there's a short-term economic dividend for society. Children are expensive—not just for their parents but for the governments that underwrite the cost of their education and health care. Over time, however, the cost-benefit equation shifts. Small cohorts of children grow up to become small cohorts of workers—at which point there aren't enough of them to keep the economy humming. During the 20th and now 21st centuries, different countries around the world have experienced these phases at different times, but the sequence and trajectory are the same. And the pattern is now sufficiently universal that the world is on the cusp of a milestone that would have astonished explosionists from Malthus to Ehrlich: the growth in the population of children is about to grind to a halt. Between now and midcentury, according to UN estimates, the number of children under age 15 will grow by just 10%. In this same period, the global population of seniors (ages 65 and older) will nearly triple as today's middle-age bulge matures and as medical science extends the human life span. Graying populations create financial stress for social insurance systems. They have a tendency to trigger unproductive changes in public investments, such as the reallocation of resources from the needs of children to the needs of seniors. And of course, they exert financial pressures on the elderly themselves, as well as their families.

In all of these trends, the US is an outlier. The fertility rate here is among the highest in the wealthy world (just under 2 per woman), so our median age won't rise nearly as fast. Ours is 37 now; by 2050, it is projected to be 41. The global median age, by contrast, is expected to climb from 29 in 2010 to 36 in 2050.[7] The overall US population is projected to increase at a faster rate than average, thanks to births and immigration. By 2050, it is expected to be about 400 million, up from today's 315 million. The world's population is projected to rise from about 7 billion now to 9.6 billion by the middle of the century, before leveling off at around 10 or 11 billion in 2100 (though projections that far into the future should be treated with caution).

The vast bulk of the global growth will come in the poor countries of Africa and Asia, while most of today's economic powers will, like Japan, see their populations shrink or flatline. Germany, for example, has not had a single year since 1972 in which births exceeded deaths. Even with an ongoing stream of immigration from Turkey and other neighbors, it will see a significant population decline by midcentury. Meantime in China, where the official government estimate is that the one-child policy has prevented 400 million births over the past 30 years, there are growing worries about a graying population, a shrinking labor force, a skewed gender ratio (118 baby boys for every 100 baby girls, the most lopsided ratio of any country in the world), and a radically attenuated kinship structure.[8] China's population is projected to remain flat through midcentury. In recent years the government has begun to relax the one-child policy, and some believe it will eventually be scrapped altogether. When the policy was first put into effect in the 1970s, the conventional wisdom was that it represented an enlightened form of state-enforced family planning (at best) or a necessary evil (at worst). Now, roughly half a billion abortions and sterilizations later, it has become the target of bitter resentment throughout much of China, in part because it's viewed as an affront to a basic human right, in part because it has been applied unevenly, and in part because it has created a generation of "little emperors" who've grown up without brothers and sisters and whose children will grow up without cousins, aunts, uncles, nephews, or nieces. A recent paper by Chinese demographers attacked the policy with unusual fervor:

> The One-Child Policy will be added to other deadly errors in recent Chinese history, including the famine in 1959–61 . . . and the Cultural Revolution of the late 1960s and early 1970s. While those grave mistakes both cost tens of millions of lives, the harms done were relatively short-lived and were corrected quickly afterward. The One-Child Policy, in contrast, will surpass them in impact by creating a society with a seriously undermined family and kin structure, and a whole generation of future elderly and their children whose well-being will be seriously jeopardized.[9]

No other country has gone to China's extremes to limit births. None has felt the need. In most countries, the decline has come without official prodding. One way to think about population decline is that it is a price societies pay for modernity and prosperity. However, it's a bit more complicated than that. As already noted, some of the steepest birthrate declines have come in poor or developing countries, including many in the Muslim world. Meantime, in Western Europe and other industrialized countries, there's now a positive correlation between female labor force participation and high birthrates, a trend reversal that first appeared about two decades ago. Relatively high-fertility countries like Sweden, Norway, Iceland, and Denmark now have more women employed than do low-fertility countries like Italy, Spain, Greece, and Germany. This may be related to the Calvinist work ethic of Northern Europe, or to their robust network of day care and other social support systems for children, or to the economic woes of Southern Europe. Pick your hypothesis. Meantime, in the US the sharpest declines in fertility since the onset of the Great Recession have been among women on the lower rungs of the socioeconomic ladder (in particular, immigrants and women with only a high school degree or less). Today women with a college degree in the US are more likely to give birth than those with a high school diploma or less, and women in their 30s are giving birth at a higher rate than women under the age of 20. On this demographic front as on so many others, the US finds itself in better shape than any of its major economic and geopolitical competitors.

DEPENDENCY RATIOS

The principal economic implication of an aging population is that it potentially reduces the share of the population that is in the prime of its working life. This can slow overall economic growth, absent a compensating rise in productivity. At the same time, the share of the population that depends on those at work may increase. The "dependent" population includes most seniors who, in addition to their savings, depend on family transfers, private pensions, and social insurance. Children, of course, are principally dependent on their parents.

The potential burden on the working-age population to provide for the dependent population is measured by the dependency ratio, which can be expressed by three different metrics. The old-age dependency ratio is defined as the ratio of the population ages 65 and older to the working-age population (ages 15 to 64). The child dependency ratio is the ratio of population younger than age 15 to the working-age population. Finally, the total dependency ratio is the ratio of the overall population of dependents (those younger than 15 or older than 64) to the working-age population.[10]

The old-age dependency ratio in the US is projected to nearly double, from 19.5 in 2010 to 35.5 in 2050. That will mostly be due to the aging of the Baby Boomer generation. However, because the child and middle-age populations in the US are expected to increase at about the same pace, the child dependency ratio in the US will be about the same in 2050 (30.1) as in 2010 (29.6). Thus, future increases in the total dependency ratio in the US—from 49 in 2010 to 65.6 in 2050—are driven entirely by aging.

The increase in the old-age dependency ratio in the US is not a new phenomenon. The ratio previously rose from 12.8 in 1950 to 19.5 in 2010. However, the child dependency ratio fell sharply in the past, from 41.7 in 1950 to 29.6 in 2010. That was the consequence of tumbling birthrates in the wake of a Baby Boom–fueled bulge in the middle of the US age distribution. Thus, despite an overall aging of the population, the total dependency ratio in the US had fallen from 54.5 in 1950 to 49.0 in 2010.

Old-age dependency ratios in the world overall are lower than in the US but they are rising faster, projected to more than double from 11.7 in 2010 to

Figure 12.1

Dependency Ratios in the United States

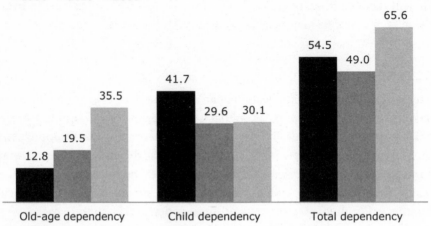

Old-age dependency Child dependency Total dependency

Global Dependency Ratios

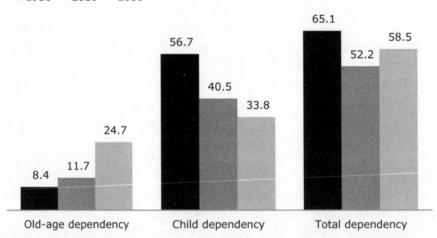

Old-age dependency Child dependency Total dependency

Note: The old-age dependency ratio is the population age 65 and over divided by population age 15–64. The child dependency ratio is the population age 0–14 divided by population age 15–64. The total dependency ratio is the population age 65 and over plus population age 0–14, divided by population age 15–64.

Source: United Nations, Department of Economic and Social Affairs, *World Population Prospects: The 2012 Revision*, June 2013

24.7 in 2050. However, global increases in old-age dependency are balanced by steep declines in the child dependency ratio, from 40.5 in 2010 to a more US-like level of 33.8 in 2050. This means that the total dependency ratio in the world is expected to increase from 52.2 in 2010 to 58.5 in 2050, a much smaller increase than in the US.

Old-age dependency ratios are also expected to rise in all major regions of the world—Asia and Oceania, Africa, the Americas, and Europe. In all regions but Africa the old-age dependency ratio will at least double from 2010 to 2050. As old-age dependency ratios increase, there are expected to be countervailing decreases in the child dependency ratios in all regions except Europe, with the sharpest decline in Africa.

In Asia and Oceania and the Americas, the expected reductions in child dependency are not sufficiently large to make up for the growing numbers of seniors. The result is an increase in total dependency from 2010 to 2050—from 47.7 to 54.8 in Asia and Oceania and from 51.7 to 61.0 in the Americas. Europe, where only the population of seniors is growing, is projected to experience the sharpest increase in the total dependency ratio, from 46.5 to 73.2. In other words, in 2050, there will be about 73 dependents for every 100 people in the prime of their working years in Europe, almost a 1 to 1 ratio.

Africa is the only region where dependency ratios are projected to decline. With the prime working-age population growing rapidly, the total dependency ratio in Africa is expected to decrease from 80.4 in 2010 to 61.5 in 2050. Thus, by 2050, there will be almost 20 fewer dependents per 100 working-age people in Africa. That is a potentially a very favorable demographic tailwind for economic growth in Africa (see appendix Figure 12A.1).

THE G7 AND THE BRICS

This section analyzes demographic projections for two prominent blocs of countries—the G7 and the BRICS—which together account for roughly two-thirds of the global economy. The G7 includes the US, UK, Germany, France, Italy, Japan, and Canada. These seven countries accounted for 38% of global output in 2012, half of which originated from the US alone. BRICS refers to five of the world's major emerging economies: Brazil, Russia, India, China, and South Africa. These five countries accounted for 27% of world output in 2012, with China alone responsible for more than half of that contribution.[11]

The G7 and BRICS also include the three most populous countries in the world—China, India, and the US. Collectively, the G7 countries were home to 743 million people in 2010, or 11% of the world population. The BRICS carried much greater heft, being home to nearly 3 billion people in 2010, or 43%

of the global population. This section reports on the demographic future for six of the G7 countries—the original G6—and the five BRICS.[12]

Most G6 and BRICS countries face significant demographic headwinds between 2010 and 2050. Their populations are projected to grow at below-average rates or to decline, several will age to unprecedented levels, and most will experience large increases in their dependency ratios. Within this general landscape, the US in the G6 and India and South Africa within the BRICS will experience the most favorable demographic outcomes.

Population Change

Only the US and India are expected to see notable gains in population from 2010 to 2050. The growth in India (34%) will be slightly less than the global increase of 38%. The US will lag behind a bit, its population increasing by 28% from 2010 to 2050. Other countries will either grow at about half the global pace (UK, France, Brazil, and South Africa) or actually shrink in size (Japan, Germany, Italy, and Russia). These trends point to the US increasing its demographic influence and its relative economic power within the G6 and India doing the same within the BRICS (see appendix Figure 12A.2).

Median Age

The G6 countries are among the oldest countries in the world today. Three of them—Japan, Germany, and Italy—are projected to reach median ages of 50 or higher by 2050. The US is the youngest country in this group and will retain that distinction in 2050, aging up modestly from 37 in 2010 to 41 in 2050.

The BRICS, with the exception of Russia, are currently among the younger countries in the world. As of 2010, the median age in India and South Africa is only 26 and 25, respectively, and Brazil, too, is quite young with a median age of 29. However, these countries are projected to age rapidly. By 2050, median ages are expected to have risen to 37 in India, 34 in South Africa, and 44 in Brazil. Among the BRICS, only India and South Africa will be younger than the G6 economies in 2050. Brazil, Russia, and China will look more like "old" Europe (see appendix Figure 12A.3).

Dependency Ratios

The total dependency ratio is projected to increase significantly in all G6 countries. The most notable case is Japan, where the ratio is expected to climb to 96, meaning Japan will have almost as many dependents as those in the workforce in 2050. Russia and China are also projected to experience sharp increases in the total dependency ratio—from 39 to 60 in Russia and from 36 to 63 in China. By contrast, the ratio is expected to decrease in India and South Africa, signaling a greater potential for economic growth as a result of the so-called demographic dividend. Even so, the old-age dependency ratio is projected to double in both countries.

Within the G6, the US is projected to see an increase in the old-age dependency ratio, from 19 in 2010 to 36 in 2050. Japan and Italy are expected to double the old-age dependency ratio to 72 and 62, respectively, and Germany will see its ratio increase to 60. By this measure, these three countries will greatly outdistance their G6 counterparts (see appendix Figure 12A.4).

PUBLIC ATTITUDES ABOUT AGING POPULATIONS

Depending on the country, there are vastly different views about the gravity of the challenges posed by aging populations; for example, 87% of the public in Japan say it is a major problem for their country, while just 23% of Egyptians say the same. As appendix Figure 12A.5 illustrates, Americans are near the bottom of the pack, with just 26% saying that aging is a major problem in this country.

Respondents in 21 countries were also asked who should bear the greatest responsibility for people's economic well-being in their old age—their families, the government, or themselves? Once again, the Americans stand out. Nearly half (46%) say people themselves should be mainly responsible, second only to the 53% of South Koreans who feel the same way. The Germans (41%) and Brits (39%) aren't far behind, but beyond those four, in the vast majority of countries surveyed, only a small sliver felt that people themselves should be mainly responsible. This is a question that evokes the creed of self-reliance. Who should care for me when I'm old and creaky? In effect, the Americans say: I'll do it myself. The Russians, Italians, and Israelis nominate their government, and the Pakistanis and Brazilians volunteer their families.

Not all Americans are rugged individualists, however. About a quarter of the survey respondents in this country said the government should be primarily responsible, while a fifth said the job should fall mainly to the families of the elderly. But here, too, American public opinion is an outlier. In other countries, many more said this is a government rather than a family responsibility, typically by ratios of 2 to 1 or more. Americans rank second-to-last (behind only Pakistanis) in the share who think the responsibility lies mainly with government (see appendix Figure 12A.6).

Notably, the American penchant for self-reliance doesn't translate into a particularly robust belief that everything will be just fine for them in their golden years. When the survey asked people around the world how confident they are that they'll have an adequate standard of living in their old age, US respondents finished a bit above the middle of the pack, with more than 6 in 10 saying they are very (24%) or somewhat (39%) confident.

The Chinese and Brazilians are the most confident, followed by the publics of the three African countries that were part of the survey—Nigeria, South Africa, and Kenya. Given that none of those countries has a robust public pension program or a high standard of living, the confidence would appear to be based on family and cultural factors rather than simple economics.

At the other end of the spectrum, the countries where people are the least confident they'll have a good standard of living in their retirement are Russia, Italy, and Japan. That is hardly a surprise, given their looming demographic winter (see appendix Figure 12A.7).

IS DEMOGRAPHY DESTINY?

How closely linked are a country's demographic and economic destinies? Obviously, when a country's workforce grows relative to its youth and elderly populations, the stage can be set for rapid economic growth. But these outcomes aren't inevitable. Countries that reap the benefits of the so-called demographic dividend tend to have complementary factors at play, such as good governance, high saving rates, investments in schooling and public health, policies promoting gender equity, and openness to trade and foreign investments.[13] Thus, many of the countries on the cusp of the demographic dividend—India, Pakistan, Egypt, Nigeria, and Kenya—can't automatically assume that economic benefits will flow. India, for example, ranks very low on indicators of nutrition, health, and education for its youth population and has regressed in recent years. And as Egypt's leaders have discovered, having a young, well-educated but unemployed labor force can be a recipe for unrest, even revolution.

By the same token, it's not inevitable that the aging of a country's population portends gloom for its economic prospects. As labor will become scarcer and more expensive, employers can try to raise productivity through capital deepening or innovation. Japan, for example, has become a global leader in the fast-developing field of robotics (including robots that learn how to care for the elderly). It's also possible to boost the size of a workforce through immigration, though that will require some cultural adjustments in societies, such as Japan's, that have a history of closing themselves off to foreigners. And workers themselves may choose to work longer in aging countries, especially since life expectancy and health outcomes are improving at older ages. In the US, for example, labor force participation among those 65 and older has risen from a low of 10.8% in 1985 to 18.5% in 2012, according to the Bureau of Labor Statistics.

Among all of the world's countries, Japan has the most experience trying to figure out how to maintain its vitality while going gray. After 30 years and counting, the returns aren't very encouraging. It's true that the Japanese economy and public mood brightened somewhat in 2013 with the return to power of Prime Minister Shinzo Abe, a hard-line nationalist who has pushed through a popular pro-growth economic agenda that's been dubbed Abenomics. Nonetheless, the country's demographic challenges persist. In 2012 the *New York Times* ran a fascinating story about the clash of generations in Onagawa, a community wiped out by the infamous 2011 tsunami that also destroyed one of the country's nuclear power plants.[14] Like hundreds of other small communities throughout rural Japan, this one had been losing population and growing older for decades—long before the natural disaster hit. In the wake of the tsunami, the question before the town council was how and where to rebuild. The mayor proposed a reconstruction plan that would consolidate its 15 tiny fishing villages into a central location in the hope of saving money and giving the area a more sustainable future. Younger residents supported the plan, but they were vastly outnumbered by their elders, who wanted to live out their remaining years in their small ancestral villages. The mayor was summarily ousted. His successor is rebuilding all 15 villages, including one that has 22 residents. This is not an isolated case. For decades the Japanese government has been pouring resources into big rural infrastructure projects to try to stem the economic decline. It has been a boon for the politically connected construction industry, but the hinterlands haven't come back. Now they're filled with deserted train stations, empty resorts, bridges to nowhere, and schoolhouses built for thousands that serve dozens.[15] All of this has left the government with a huge overhang of debt that the Japanese will be paying off for generations. There may not be many children in Japan's schoolhouses these days, but as they grow up, they'll have plenty of bills to pay.

The Reckoning

IDA MAY FULLER, A NEVER-MARRIED legal secretary from Brattle-boro, Vermont, was the first person in the United States to retire on Social Security. Her initial monthly check, bearing the auspicious number 00-000-001, arrived in the mail on January 31, 1940, shortly after her 65th birthday. It was for $22.54. Being of sturdy New England farm stock, Ida proceeded to live for 35 more years. The checks just kept coming. By the time she died at age 100, she'd drawn $22,888.92 from Social Security.

Doesn't sound like much? Well, consider this: Ida had only started to pay Social Security taxes in 1937, the year the program began. Her total contribution during those three years amounted to a princely $24.75. Her employer kicked in another $24.75. Which means that Ida received a nearly five hundred–fold return on those combined contributions, courtesy of younger generations of workers and taxpayers who supported the system during her retirement years.

If you're inclined to think of Social Security as a giant government-run Ponzi scheme, Ida's good fortune is a good place to start your story.[1] Her windfall was one-of-a-kind, but all beneficiaries of her generation got far more out of the system than they paid in. Over time, as the ratio of workers to retirees has grown less favorable, successive generations have done less well. Still, all of the Silents are enjoying positive returns from their taxes and virtually all Boomers will come out ahead, too. But absent changes to the system, most Gen Xers and virtually all Millennials will get back less in benefits than they contribute in taxes.[2] This will be the case despite the fact that annual spending on Social Security and its sidekick, Medicare, is on track to consume ever larger shares of the federal budget—50% of all non-interest spending in 2030, up from 28% in 1980.[3]

Every single day between now and then, 10,000 more Baby Boomers will turn 65. During the years this pig-in-a-python generation was fully in the workforce, the tax revenues that flowed into Social Security and Medicare not only covered these programs' obligations to older folks who were already retired, they also built up a big surplus that would help pre-fund the Boomers' own retirement. But in 2010, around the time the oldest of the Boomers began to retire, annual revenues into the system began to fall below annual payouts. This new upside-down arithmetic will persist for as far as the eye can see. Social Security and Medicare will be able to stay afloat for a while by drawing down on the reserves. Eventually, however, the well will run dry. According to Social Security's trustees, the Medicare trust fund will be empty by 2026 and the main Social Security trust fund will be insolvent by 2033.[4] At that point, the trustees say, the policy options are all unpalatable. Either retirees will be hit with a benefits cut of 23%, or workers will have to absorb a massive payroll tax increase of that size, or the two will have to share the pain.

At its core, this is a problem of generational equity. The young today are paying taxes to support a level of benefits for the old that they themselves have no prospect of receiving when *they* become old. Meantime, as a rising share of their tax dollars goes to fund the social safety net for the old, government spending on other priorities, especially on investments that would improve the economic prospects of the young, is being crowded out. Some sort of rebalancing is plainly in order, and every day that elected officials put off the reckoning is a day that generational inequities increase. "Substantial further delay risks further concentrating the burdens of correcting the shortfall on younger workers who already stand to be treated less favorably," wrote the Social Security system's two public trustees, Democrat Robert D. Reischauer and Republican Charles P. Blahous III, in their 2013 annual report.[5]

Before we consider how to take on this challenge, let's spend some time unpacking Social Security. No other government program in history has lifted so many out of poverty or become so integral to so many family budgets— and yet is so poorly understood. This is not an accident. It's the legacy of the political genius who created it, Franklin Delano Roosevelt. When he pushed the Social Security Act through Congress in 1935 as one of the centerpieces of his New Deal, the US and world were still drowning in the Great Depression. Millions of Americans were homeless, tens of millions had lost their life savings, unemployment hovered around 25%, and poverty was endemic, especially among the elderly. Several decades before, a number of European countries had created the first generation of rudimentary publicly financed national retirement systems—Germany in 1889; England in 1908. Until the onset of the Depression, there hadn't been much appetite for such programs in the US, and Roosevelt understood why: self-reliant Americans scorned them as welfare. However, in the depths of the economic calamity of the 1930s, he saw both need and opportunity. He surmised the country was ready to build a public social safety net for the elderly, provided it was properly designed. To him, that meant one thing above all. It had to be a contributory system; workers would pay wage taxes that would be held by the government and eventually returned to them in the form of a pension. "We put those payroll contributions there to give the contributors a legal, moral and political right to collect their pensions," Roosevelt said. Because of them, he boasted: "No damn politician can ever scrap my Social Security program!"

But right from the get-go, Social Security was never a pure contributory system. Despite the president's misgivings, and sometimes over his objections,[6] FDR's own cabinet worked with Congress (liberals as well as conservatives) to fashion it into something much more akin to a "pay-as-you-go" generational transfer program, in which today's workers are taxed to pay the benefits of today's retirees. What they wound up concocting was a complex hybrid. Beneficiaries receive payments based in part on what they've put in, but in part on other formulas designed to serve a range of social purposes. The taxes are regressive (they land most heavily on those in lower income brackets) while the benefits are progressive (those in lower brackets get the best rate of return), a politically ingenious balancing act that simultaneously disguises and protects its overall redistributionist impact. Other features favor certain categories of recipients. For example, the benefits are far more generous to one-earner married couples than to two-earner couples or single adults. And like all defined pension systems, its best deals go to recipients who, like Ida, are clever enough to live to a ripe old age. It also doubles as a life insurance policy and triples as a disability insurance policy. Of Social Security's roughly 57 million beneficiaries (as of mid-2013), 41 million are retirees and their dependents, an additional 10 million are the disabled and their dependents, and 7 million more are early retirees or survivors of deceased workers.

This all makes for a pretty opaque program, its complexities best understood by those well versed in the actuarial arts. As a layman, I would summarize Social Security's balance sheet as follows: it redistributes wealth in a measured way from young to old, from rich to poor, from the healthy to the infirm, and from everyone to the long-lived. Columnist Robert Samuelson calls it "a huge welfare program grafted onto the rhetoric and psychology of a contributory pension," while Nobel laureate Milton Friedman, less charitably, inveighed against the contributions paradigm as a "myth" that Roosevelt and his political progeny sold to a gullible public using "the worst devices of Madison Avenue."[7]

Over the years, the Friedman broadside has been echoed by successive generations of conservative politicians, from Ronald Reagan to George W. Bush to Paul Ryan, who've periodically tried to rally the public behind privatization proposals. Their efforts have never gotten off the ground, even though they poll well among the young. It turns out that Roosevelt may have been disingenuous about the financing of Social Security, but he was spot-on about the politics. To this day Social Security remains the "most sacred of sacred cows," in Friedman's lament. Countless millions of Americans still think of it the way my mother (a child of the Roosevelt era) did: the government takes a bit of money out of your paycheck each week, puts it into a drawer with your name on it, then gives it back to you when you retire, with interest. This accounting fiction is reinforced by every pay stub every wage earner receives; each one meticulously notes how much Social Security and Medicare tax (also referred as the FICA tax, for Federal Insurance Contributions Act) has been deducted. So: You make your contribution and you earn your retirement benefit. What could be more fair?

Unfortunately, there are plenty of fairness issues, and they've grown more acute as the program itself has aged. As already noted, if one evaluates the system through a generational return-on-investment lens, Social Security has been all downhill since Ida's day. Back when the program first started, 42 workers were making contributions for every retiree drawing benefits. That allowed for windfalls galore, especially for recipients in that first generation, who were eligible for lifetime benefits in retirement even if, like Ida, they had paid just a few years' worth of taxes. But the ratio of workers to retirees has fallen precipitously over the decades. It is currently a bit under 3 to 1 and is slated to drop below 2 to 1 by 2035. To compensate, the Social Security tax (employee plus employer) has been raised time and again, from 2% in Ida's day to 12.4% now. And the cap on wages subject to this tax has gone up even more—from $3,000 then to $113,700 now.

If one were to look just at the income returns on Social Security taxes alone (and take Medicare out of the equation), many of today's 65-year-olds won't get back in lifetime benefits what they and their employers paid in taxes, and negative rates of return will become even more pervasive for tomorrow's retirees, according to an analysis by the Urban Institute's C. Eugene Steuerle.[8] "The bottom line is that the older you are, the more likely that your Social Security benefits exceeded your contributions," says Blahous, a former adviser to President George W. Bush. "The younger you are, the more certain it is that your tax burden will exceed what you ever get out."[9]

But that's not the whole picture. When you widen the return-on-investment lens to take in Medicare as well as Social Security, the payout analysis shifts back to positive territory for nearly all of today's retirees. A 65-year-old single woman retiring in 2014 with median lifetime earnings can expect to get $544,000 in combined benefits from Social Security and Medicare if she lives out her actuarially allotted 20 years in average health. During her working years, she and her employer will have put in about $407,000 in taxes.[10] Current and future taxpayers will cover the remaining $137,000. In short, she's ahead of the game. So are most others her age, though the size of the windfall varies dramatically, depending on a person's demographics, economics, and health. For example, the returns wouldn't be quite as attractive if she were a single man at the median. Because of his shorter life span, he'll get back roughly $60,000 less in benefits. On the other hand, if she were a spouse in a one-earner married couple, the couple would have paid the same $407,000 in taxes, but would get about $910,000 in benefits, thanks to the generous formula for spousal coverage. And if she and her spouse were, say, a mix of higher earner and median earner two-earner couple, they would have paid much more into the system (about $1,055,000 by the Urban Institute's estimate) and also gotten back more in benefits (about $1,146,000)—a tidy sum, but not the windfall returns enjoyed by lower income workers or single-wage-earner couples.

As those examples make clear, payout formulas serve a variety of social purposes. But if they're positive for virtually all current retirees, that leaves today's and tomorrow's taxpayers with a huge and escalating tab. The main driver of the rising costs has been Medicare, which was added to the Social Security system in 1965 by Lyndon Johnson, FDR's political heir, at a time when health costs were impoverishing millions of older adults. The program helps pay for the medical care of nearly everyone ages 65 and older. Its tax rate is much lower than Social Security's (1.45% apiece for employers and employees on all wages; an additional 0.9% on employers for wages above $200,000). Without increases to this tax base, the Medicare Trust Fund, starting in 2026, will be unable to fully cover promised benefits. Partly that's because of population aging and increased longevity, but it's also because the program provides a guaranteed benefit—health care—whose costs have been rising for decades at a budget-busting pace.[11] Many economists fault Medicare itself for having contributed to these outsized increases. Its fee-for-service payment structure, they argue, creates incentives for doctors and hospitals to keep providing services, sometimes beyond medical need.[12] As is well known, the US is in its own stratosphere when it comes to health costs. We currently spend 17.6% of our gross domestic product on medical care, roughly double the median share spent by the world's other economically advanced countries.

Medicare and its cousin, Medicaid (the health entitlement program for the poor), have for decades been the fastest-growing major programs in the federal budget. Medicare rose from 4% of federal spending in 1970 to 16% in 2011 and, absent policy changes, is on track to reach 19% in 2035. Medicaid is projected to consume 10% of the federal budget in 2035, up from 1% in 1970 and 8% in 2011.[13] By the time all the Boomers retire, half of the entire federal budget will go to Social Security, Medicare, and the non-child portion of Medicaid. Much of the rest will go to paying interest on the national debt and maintaining the national defense, which leaves little in the coffers for investments in future economic growth. Fifty years ago, the government spent $3 on public investments that spur economic activity for every $1 it spent on entitlements. Today that ratio has flipped, and within a decade the government will be putting $5 into entitlements for every $1 that goes to roads, education, scientific research, and the like, according to an analysis by Third Way, a centrist public policy think tank.[14]

At this stage of our story, the Ponzi metaphor starts to sound, if anything, too kind. So let's spend a little time rallying to Social Security and Medicare's defense before confronting the generational equity issues they pose. There's a reason both programs are so popular: they're wildly successful. Social Security lifts more than 20 million people out of poverty, two-thirds of them elderly, the rest children, dependents, and the disabled. Without it, nearly half of America's seniors would be living in poverty; with it, only about 1 in 10 seniors are poor. It provides 37% of the annual income for all Americans over age 65 and 80% of the income for seniors in the bottom half of the income distribution. Moreover, for the vast majority of retirees, Social Security is their only source of income that's not subject to investment risk, market fluctuations, or erosion by inflation—making it a psychological as well as financial safety valve. Medicare, too, has greatly improved the peace of mind of older Americans; without it, the rising cost of health care would be an even more crushing burden than it already is. And despite the perverse incentives created by its fee-for-service reimbursement system, the program in recent years has begun doing a better job of leveraging its vast market power to negotiate lower prices from health care providers.[15]

These two programs, in short, are in a league of their own when it comes to improving the quality of life of seniors. And because of that, they also improve the quality of life of everyone who loves and depends on seniors— which means virtually everyone. The fact that they've done so without being viewed as welfare is a testament to the enduring popular appeal of FDR's paradigm for Social Security as a contributions-based program. In 2012, in response to an op-ed column in the New York Times that proposed that Social

Security benefits be means-tested, Haskel Levi of Oakland, California, wrote a letter to the editor that went to the nub of the matter. "Entitlements without means-testing unites us into one country," he wrote. "Means-testing divides us into rich and poor, each resenting the other."[16] Levi is not alone in worrying that if you whittle away at the universality of the program, you risk bringing down the whole edifice. The old aphorism gets it right: means-testing makes for mean politics.

As both programs come under demographic stress, it's going to take a president with FDR's feel for the psyche of the public and the power of the bully pulpit to preserve them for future generations. The politics will be extremely difficult. There are deep partisan differences in Congress on this issue, with Democrats preferring to target tax hikes and/or benefit cuts on the well-to-do, and Republicans favoring a broad-based benefits cut. About the only thing that leaders of the two parties share is a mutual fear of seniors, the nation's most habitual voters, whose ranks keep growing and whose power to punish politicians who even think of tampering with Social Security or Medicare benefits is the stuff of political legend. But at the end of the day, the equities and the politics will work only if everyone is cajoled into taking a hit (except the neediest, who are the reason to have a safety net in the first place). A few months into his second term, President Obama took a small step in the direction of a comprehensive share-the-pain solution by rolling out a centrist blueprint for entitlement reform that married a slowdown in cost-of-living increases for retirees with an increase in taxes for the wealthy and corporations. Predictably, it provoked howls of protest from leaders in both parties, and Obama hasn't put any political muscle into it. But as the math becomes unsustainable, he or a successor will have to finish the job.

GENERATIONAL EQUITY

When that day comes, Social Security's twenty-first-century saviors will do well to frame the fix around the imperatives of generational equity, a principle with a rich history in American political thought. Aside from the Declaration of Independence, the most famous passage in Thomas Jefferson's writings is the one in which he declares that "the earth belongs to the living, and not the dead," and that therefore no generation has a moral right to bind successor generations with debt. He goes on to say that the natural life span of a generation is 19 years and proposes that all laws—even the constitution itself—should expire "naturally" at the end of that period. This is arguably the most radical of Jefferson's ideas, but he was in some esteemed company. A few years earlier, Thomas Paine, a leading theorist of the Revolutionary era, had written that "it is the summit of human vanity, and shows a covetousness of power beyond the grave, to be dictating to the world to come." Paine believed a generation lasted for 30 years, not Jefferson's 19, but proposed the same remedy: no laws adopted in a democracy should have legal force beyond 30 years. Both Paine and Jefferson lived in a world where kings ruled by divine right. Both were champions of the then-radical notion that the people, not the monarchs, were sovereign. But having recoiled at the excesses of kings, both were keen to put constraints on the excesses of the public, including the bills that one generation might be tempted to leave for the next. As Jefferson put it, laws that had built-in expiration dates would "put the lenders, and the borrowers also, on their guard . . . [and] it would bridle the spirit of war."

His proposal was never put into effect, in part because it suffers from something of a logical fallacy. The public isn't composed of a single same-aged generational cohort whose members will all pass away in 19 (or 30) years; it's made up of people of all ages and life spans. Also, as Jefferson himself acknowledged, not all debts assumed by one generation represent a burden on future generations. Some enhance the future. So he provided for exceptions: "Debts may be incurred for purposes which interest the unborn, as well as the living: such debts are for repelling a conquest, the evils of which descend through many generations," Jefferson wrote. "Debts may even be incurred principally for the benefit of posterity. The term of 19 years might not be sufficient for discharging the debts in either of these cases."

Through the centuries, how has America measured up on this Jeffersonian test of intergenerational equity? The record is mixed. As Figure 13.1 illustrates, national debt as a share of GDP has tended to spike during periods of economic crisis or war, then retreat during periods of normalcy. The troublesome thing about the recent spike (as well as the long-term trend, which tilts upward after smoothing for peaks and valleys) is that today's debt is near the historic World War II level despite the absence of a triggering event of that magnitude. Debt, of course, is not the only measure of the burdens and benefits that each generation leaves for its successors. But applying a broader set of metrics only makes the current picture more problematic. A 2013 cross-national study by a prominent European research institute found that the US ranked worst among 29 advanced countries in the degree to which it imposes unfair burdens on future generations.[17] The study looked at measures such as public debt per child, the ratio of childhood poverty to elderly poverty, and the elderly skew in social spending. An American might quibble with some of the study's inputs and weighting variables, but the story it tells is consistent with what policy analysts of all ideological stripes in the US have been saying for decades: we're robbing the future to pay for the present.

Figure 13.1

US Federal Debt as Share of GDP, 1790–2012

Note: Debt held by the public includes marketable (e.g. Treasury notes) and nonmarketable securities (e.g. savings bonds) issued by the US Treasury to finance government activities and owned by the public. Gross debt is debt held by the public plus securities held by federal trust funds and other government accounts.

Source: Bureau of the Public Debt (http://www.treasurydirect.gov/govt/reports/pd/histdebt/histdebt.htm), Office of Management and Budget (http://www.whitehouse.gov/omb/budget/Historicals), Bureau of Economic Analysis (http://www.bea.gov/national/index.htm#gdp), and http://www.measuringworth.com/usgdp/

GENERATIONAL INTERDEPENDENCE WITHIN FAMILIES

Come the day when the safety net is downsized, how will the public cope? We can draw some lessons from recent history. Consider all the economic hardships that Americans have endured in recent years: the housing market crash, the persistently high unemployment, the rise in wealth and income inequality, the stagnation in standard-of-living growth. In the face of all this, the public safety net has been a key line of defense, but it hasn't operated in a vacuum. Increasingly, Americans have also turned to what Margaret Mead called "the only faithful human institution": their families. One particularly vivid example: During the worst of the 2007–2009 recession, the number of Americans living in multigenerational family households grew by about 10%, from 46.5 million to a record 51.4 million. Many of those households functioned as an unofficial antipoverty program. People living in them had a lower poverty rate than those who didn't, even though they also had lower incomes, according to a 2011 Pew Research analysis.[18] Multigenerational households come in multiple varieties—Boomerangers waiting for the economic clouds to lift so they can launch themselves into adulthood; grandmothers on nanny duty so their children can earn paychecks that will support the grandkids; middle-age adults who've taken up residence with elderly parents after they've lost a home or job. Robert Frost was more prescient than he knew when he wrote a century ago that "home is where, when you have to go there, they have to take you in."

Of course families, especially poor ones, cannot fully replace the safety net. The scale of the task is simply beyond them. But it's worth remembering that families are humanity's original safety net, and in many ways better suited than governments for the job. Means-testing in the hands of government will always be fraught, pitting group against group. Means-testing within the confines of a family is taken as a given. Without anyone having to spell out the rules, regulations or eligibility thresholds, support flows organically in the direction of need.[19]

For most of human history, this has meant parents caring for children when they're young, and children caring for parents when they're old. But in the modern era, the creation of a government safety net for the old has led most families to reverse the intergenerational flow of support at the latter stages of the life cycle. Now, more older parents support grown children than the other way around. Families remain a bulwark of intergenerational support, but they've adapted to new demographic and economic realities.

The most comprehensive effort in recent times to measure the magnitude and direction of these flows is the Health and Retirement Survey (HRS), funded by the National Institute on Aging and the Social Security

Administration. It has found that among parents ages 51 to 64, between two-thirds and three-quarters (depending on marital status) have given some form of money, time, or residential support to their grown children, while fewer than half reported *receiving* substantial transfers from those same children.[20] These patterns persist even as parents grow older. Among parents ages 65–79, more than half have given help in the form of money, care, or co-residence to a child in the past two years, while between 25% and 37% have received any form of assistance from a child during the same period. In a different study, Michael Hurd and his colleagues at the RAND Center for the Study of Aging estimated that the total amount of money (excluding bequests) that the typical parents ages 53 and older will give to their children throughout the remainder of the parents' lives is about $50,000.[21] Grandparents get into the act, too. A 2012 survey by the insurance company Metlife found that more than 6 in 10 (62%) grandparents ages 45 and older have given grandchildren money over the past 5 years and a 2009 Metlife survey indicated that the median amount these grandparents gave was about $3,000.[22]

In addition to these *inter vivos* transfers (those that occur while the giver is still alive), there's a much larger flow that comes in the form of inheritances. Scholars Edward Wolff and Maury Gittleman estimate that roughly 80% of all wealth that's passed down from elderly parents to adult children arrives when the giver has passed away. Boomers are now entering their peak inheritance years; many are in line to receive sizable sums from parents who are part of the wealthiest cohort of elderly adults in history. A Metlife study estimated that two-thirds of Boomers will ultimately receive some type of monetary inheritance. The size of inheritances is highly uneven, but researchers estimate that at the median, they will account for up to 40% of the wealth of the adults in the typical recipient household near the end of their lives.[23]

Turning from transfers of money to those of time and caregiving, here, too, the flow is more downstream than upstream. In any given year, a relatively small share (about 5%) of middle-age children provides substantial care for a parent or parent-in-law—in the form of help with eating, dressing, keeping the household books, or doing household chores.[24] By contrast, an estimated 40% of grandparents provide at least 100 hours of care to a grandchild annually, according to the HRS survey. And a growing share of grandchildren—10%—are actually living with a grandparent.

While families typically direct money and care toward need, they are human institutions, subject to the foibles and frailties of our glorious species. In other words, sometimes these transfers go horribly wrong. In *Someday All This Will Be Yours,* historian Hendrik Hartog explored the legal dramas and emotional traumas unleashed when elderly parents try to use the promise of inheritance to keep adult children in tow as caregivers.[25] If either party reneges on the deal, or if jealous siblings or aggrieved spouses take exception to the terms, all hell can break loose. Hartog dug up the records of probate court cases from the late nineteenth century and compared them with the same genre of litigation in the modern era. He concluded that while Social Security and Medicare may have changed some of the contours of the intergenerational bargain within families, they haven't repealed human nature or rescinded the complexities of the parent-child relationship at the latter stages of the life cycle.

And if human nature isn't unpredictable enough, there's another wild card in the deck—the changes in the structure of the family itself. "Relationships in aging families have become more fluid and less predictable, as reduced fertility and increased rates of divorce, remarriage and stepfamily formation have altered the micro-context in which intergenerational, spousal, and sibling relationships function," write family scholars Merril Silverstein and Roseann Giarrusso.[26] They note that intergenerational exchanges within families have always been driven by a complex mix of altruism and reciprocity, love and guilt, obligation and resentment. These intra-family exchanges are influenced, too, by a variety of demographic factors—daughters, for example, tend to be more attentive to elderly parents than are sons; elderly blacks and Hispanics tend to compensate for low incomes by providing more downstream support in time and housing. Now, on top of these complications, come the sweeping social, economic, and demographic changes that have shaken the family tree to its roots and that threaten to leave older adults with fewer strong bonds to their younger family members.

THE NEXT COMPACT

Going forward, it's unrealistic to expect families to take on more of the challenge of caring for the elderly; it's quite possible they'll do less. That puts the question that has animated this book squarely in the laps of public policy-makers: how best to honor our commitments to the old without bankrupting the young and starving the future? The most promising answer, in my view, lies with a Jeffersonian approach based on the proposition that *no generation should be asked to provide a level of support for older folks beyond what its members can expect to receive when they grow old themselves.* Or to put it more simply: *every generation should pay its own way.* That ideal puts generational equity where it belongs, at the heart of the effort to modernize Social Security and Medicare. It will infuse some urgency into the issue, because with each passing day, the fixes get harder and the generational skew further out of balance. Liberals would have to ask themselves how they can justify taxing the hard-pressed young to maintain benefits for the well-to-do old. Conservatives would need to confront the folly of not investing in the nation's future work-force and economic vitality. Leaders from all parts of the ideological spectrum would be able to borrow the most appealing idea in Roosevelt's original sales pitch—you get back what you put in—but apply it to generations rather than individuals.

All of this is easier said than done. Roosevelt had the advantage of sell-ing the public on a benefit. The system's saviors will need to sell a retrench-ment. Every group except the neediest will have to take a hit—young and old, taxpayers and beneficiaries. The cuts to current retirees could be modest (for example, a slowdown in annual cost-of-living adjustments for all, or targeted reductions aimed at the well-to-do) but anything that hurts seniors makes for scary politics. They are deemed to be untouchable not just because elected offi-cials fear them but because their children and grandchildren love them—and benefit from their economic well-being. As the survey findings presented in Chapter 4 make clear, cutting benefits to retirees is the public's least favorite way to reform the system. America's growing racial and ethnic diversity adds to the challenge. In any society, but especially an increasingly heterogeneous one, people are more willing to sacrifice for their own children than for other people's children. That explains why the family is the most resilient safety net.

But this cause is by no means hopeless. The changes explored through-out this book—political, demographic, economic, attitudinal—align in ways that will eventually compel a fix, and perhaps sooner than seems imaginable in today's politically gridlocked Washington, DC. For one thing, the changing demographics of the electorate could create some surprising new alliances on this issue. In years past, the generational equity argument was the near exclu-sive preserve of small-government conservatives. Now, however, the groups that stand to gain the most from any generational equity-based formula for reform are the young and minorities—the country's most liberal voters. Can fiscal hawks and social policy progressives find common ground on modern-izing the safety net? They can if they pursue their overlapping interests.

The absence of any public appetite for generational warfare is another reason for optimism. Despite their many differences, young and old in America aren't spoiling for a fight on this issue. They like each other too much. Their fates are too intertwined. No one needs to explain to them that Grandma's well-being and Junior's are braided together. They know. And they view this interdependence in moral as well as practical terms. If a fam-ily or government doesn't provide a safety net for older adults who would otherwise spend their golden years in poverty, the public believes these enti-ties have failed a moral test.

But, with Jefferson, Americans of all ages and ideologies also believe it is wrong for a society to burden its children with excessive debt and diminished opportunity. They know that every American alive today is the beneficiary of all the generations that came before—the ones that fought the wars, built the infrastructure, conducted the scientific and medical research, educated the children, promoted the entrepreneurship, and nurtured the values that have made this such an exceptional country. They would like to pass the torch in similar style.

Moreover, there's a broader consensus on how to tackle this challenge than is apparent from the dreary cycle of brinksmanship and kick-the-can that recurs whenever today's leaders in Washington, DC, are forced by the budget calendar to take up the hard politics of deficit, debt, spending, taxes, and entitlements. Indeed, if bipartisan blue-ribbon panels or mainstream editorial and opinion writers were magically empowered to resolve the problem, one suspects the elusive "grand bargain" on entitlements and taxes would have already been struck. And generational equity would be a key element of the fix. What these thought leaders *can* do is frame the challenge in generational terms; this has been happening with growing frequency. For example, in the depths of the manufactured government shutdown crisis of 2013, a Thomas Freidman column in the *New York Times* was headlined "Sorry, Kids. We Ate it All." It told the story of an unlikely duo of prominent Baby Boomers—Stanley Druckenmiller, a billionaire hedge fund manager and philanthropist, and Geoffrey Canada, the legendary Harlem-based social activist and educator—who have been touring college campuses and urging students to get more involved in the political process so they can demand a more equitable share of government outlays. To critics who say they're fomenting a generation war, Friedman quotes Druckenmiller's sharp response: "No, that war already happened, and the kids lost. We're just trying to recover some scraps for them."[27] As noted, the war metaphor isn't likely to play well with any generation. But the equity argument should play well with all of them. Among the organizations that understand this is the AARP, the massive and muscular lobby group for adults over the age of 50. It is committed to protecting the interests of today's retirees, but in the past year its leaders have begun sending public signals that adjustments need to be made to Social Security and Medicare to preserve those programs for tomorrow's retirees (and the AARP's future members).[28] Across all realms of society—business, labor, educators, nonprofits, and elected officials from both parties—this consensus is deepening.

At the end of the day, though, this is a challenge that can only be overcome with presidential leadership. What's needed is someone who can use the bully pulpit to educate the public about the inequities in the status quo. Someone who can make the case that the pain of cuts today will be more than offset by the gain in prosperity tomorrow. Someone who can explain that FDR's great innovation of the twentieth century—the radical improvement of old age in America—can work for the rising generations in a new century only if the safety net is modernized. The demographics have changed. The old math doesn't work anymore.

ACKNOWLEDGMENTS

As the author of a book built on a bedrock of data, I owe my first thanks to the colleagues at the Pew Research Center who created so much of that data. We work in a highly collaborative setting. Some of these coworkers conceived and carried out the original research, others wrote up the findings, others disseminated it in various formats and media. I'm lucky to count them as friends as well as collaborators. My gratitude to:

Jodie Allen, Richard Auxier, James Bell, Anna Brown, Andrea Caumont, Leah Christian, D'Vera Cohn, Alan Cooperman, Drew DeSilver, Michael Dimock, Carroll Doherty, Bruce Drake, Susannah Fox, Richard Fry, Cary Funk, Ana Gonzalez-Barrera, Sara Goo, Elizabeth Gross, Mark Jurkowitz, Michael Keegan, Scott Keeter, Jocelyn Kiley, Donald Kimelman, Rakesh Kochhar, Andrew Kohut, Vidya Krishnamurthy, Amanda Lenhart, Gretchen Livingston, Mark Lopez, Luis Lugo, Mary Madden, David Masci, Amy Mitchell, Rich Morin, Seth Motel, Alan Murray, Russ Oates, Kim Parker, Jeffrey Passel, Eileen Patten, Michael Piccorossi, Kristen Purcell, Lee Rainie, Molly Rohal, Tom Rosenstiel, Jessica Schillinger, Aaron Smith, Greg Smith, Sandy Stencel, Bruce Stokes, Roberto Suro, Wendy Wang, Richard Wike, and Diana Yoo.

A number of them made special contributions to the book that warrant special note. Chapter 10, Living Digital, was written by Lee Rainie. As founder and director of the Pew Research Center's Internet & American Life Project, Lee was responsible for most of the research presented in that chapter; he also interviewed Natalie Marks (a pseudonym), the young woman whose digital coming-of-age story gives the chapter its narrative arc. Chapter 11, Getting Old, draws on portions of a fine 2013 essay about the scientific and ethical dimensions of radical life extension written by David Masci for the Pew Research Center's Religion & Public Life Project. In Chapter 12, Empty Cradle, Gray World, the section that looks at cross-national trends in median age, population size, and dependency ratios is based on the work of Rakesh Kochhar, the center's senior economist. Chapter 9, Nones On the Rise, draws heavily on a report of the same name published by our religion project; Alan Cooperman and Greg Smith worked on the original report and helped me adapt it for the book. Eileen Patten has been indispensable in her role as editorial assistant on this book project, keeping tabs on charts, tables, text, and footnotes while also holding down her day job as a research analyst with the center's Social & Demographic Trends Project. Diana Yoo, the center's art director, helped adapt the charts and tables to book format. I'm grateful to them all.

The terrain covered by this book has been explored by a wide array of scholars, academics, and journalists, many who have far more subject area expertise than I do. Their names appear throughout the book in citations, quotes, and footnotes. Their work has sharpened my thinking as I've looked for meaning in the data. I'm grateful for their intellectual stimulation.

I owe a thank you to the center's parent organization, the Pew Charitable Trusts, including President and CEO Rebecca W. Rimel and members of the board, for their generous support over the years. And to the Pew Research Center's board, led by Donald Kimelman, a friend of more than 30 years. I'm especially grateful to Peter Bernstein, a Pew Research board member who served as the agent for this book. Thanks as well to the entire team at PublicAffairs, especially Clive Priddle, the publisher, who edited the manuscript with a sharp pencil and unerring eye.

Finally, a few words about the two people to whom the book is dedicated.

Andy Kohut, the founding director of the Pew Research Center, is a man of enormous intellectual passion, integrity, curiosity, and entrepreneurship. He figured out decades ago that if you brought social scientists and journalists into the same sandbox and gave them the right tools, values, and mission, you could create a new kind of institution—a "fact tank"—that helps people understand the world around them. Andy and I didn't begin our professional association until I was in my mid-50s, but if anyone were to ask me to name the best teacher I ever had, it would be him.

And lastly Stefanie, forever Stefanie. She and I met at age 3 and married at 21. Now we're on the doorstep of old age (how can that be?) with a family that spans four generations, from our 1-year-old granddaughter to her 90-year-old parents. Stef is the hub of this loving family—nanny to the youngest, caregiver to the oldest, touchstone of the whole flock. Better than anyone else I know, she embodies what it means for the generations within a family to live interdependently and in harmony. Thanks for everything, my darling.

APPENDIX

NOTES ON TERMINOLOGY

Here are definitions and explanations of terms used throughout this book:

Race and ethnicity. Blacks, whites, Asians, and other racial groups include only non-Hispanics. Hispanics are of any race. The terms "Latino" and "Hispanic" are used interchangeably.

Nativity. "Native born" refers to persons who are US citizens at birth, including those born in the US, Puerto Rico, or other US territories and those born abroad to at least one whom US citizen. "Foreign born" refers to persons born outside of the US, Puerto Rico, or other US territories to parents, neither of whom was a US citizen.

Immigrant generation. "First generation" refers to foreign-born people. The terms "foreign born," "first generation," and "immigrant" are used interchangeably. "Second generation" refers to people born in the US, with at least one first-generation parent. "Third and higher generation" refers to people born in the US, with both parents born in the US. This is sometimes shortened to "third generation."

Generation. The Greatest Generation refers to those born before 1928; the Silent Generation refers to those born from 1928 to 1945; the Baby Boom Generation refers to those born from 1946 to 1964; Generation X refers to those born from 1965 to 1980; and the Millennial Generation refers to those adults born after 1980. The youngest members of the Millennial Generation are still in their teens. No chronological end point for their generation has yet been fixed, nor has the zeitgeist coined a term for their successor generation.

Educational attainment. "College graduates" refers to those with a bachelor's degree or more. "Some college" includes those with associate's degrees.

High school graduates include those with a regular high school diploma or its equivalent, such as a GED.

Additional Notes

- In most figures related to public opinion survey findings, the shares of respondents who said "Don't know" or refused to answer the question are not shown. In some figures, additional voluntary response categories with small shares, such as "Depends" or "Other," may be missing.
- Figures may not add up to 100% because of these missing responses or because of rounding.
- All net figures and change columns are computed prior to rounding.

ADDITIONAL CHARTS AND TABLES

These provide detail and context for the material presented in the book.

Figure 3A.1

The Generation Gap

% saying that young and older people are different in...

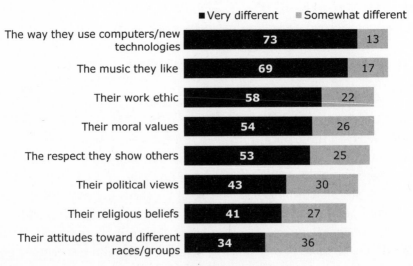

Source: Pew Research Center survey, Jul.–Aug. 2009, N=1,815 US residents ages 16 and older

Figure 3A.2

Silents Not So Positive about New Face of America

% saying each is a "change for the better"

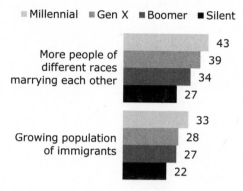

Source: Pew Research Center survey, Oct. 2012, N=2,008 US adults

Figure 3A.3

Social Conservatism Index

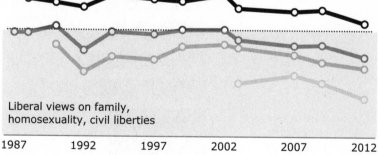

Note: Five-item scale of social attitudes

Source: Pew Research Center surveys, 1987–2012

Figure 3A.4

Business Attitudes Index

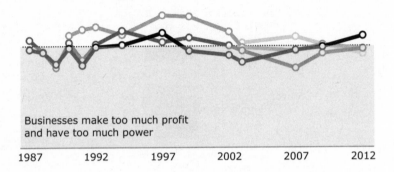

Note: Three-item scale of attitudes about business

Source: Pew Research Center surveys, 1987–2012

Figure 3A.5

National Security Index

Note: Three-item scale of attitudes about national security

Source: Pew Research Center surveys, 1987–2012

Figure 3A.6

The Best Way to Ensure Peace Is Through Military Strength

% who agree

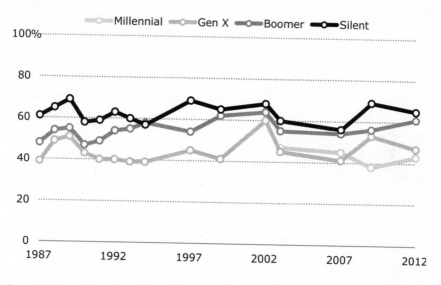

Source: Pew Research Center surveys, 1987–2012

Figure 4A.1

Generations Agree: Entitlement Programs Have Been Good for Country, Face Financial Trouble

		Total	Millennial	Gen X	Boomer	Silent
Social Security		%	%	%	%	%
Over the years, it has been...	Good for the country	87	81	88	88	91
	Bad for the country	11	16	10	10	6
Current financial condition	Excellent/Good	18	20	10	18	26
	Only fair/Poor	77	74	86	79	67
Medicare						
Over the years, it has been...	Good for the country	88	87	89	85	92
	Bad for the country	10	10	10	13	6
Current financial condition	Excellent/Good	18	24	11	16	24
	Only fair/Poor	74	69	79	78	66

Source: Pew Research Center surveys June 15–19, 2011 (N=1,502) and June 16–19, 2011 (N=1,003)

Figure 4A.2

Younger Generations Support Privatization Proposals

% who *favor*	Millennial	Gen X	Boomer	Silent	Mill.–Silent diff.
	%	%	%	%	%
Changing Social Security to let younger workers put SS taxes in private accounts	86	69	58	52	34
Changing Medicare so people can use benefits toward purchasing private health insurance	74	60	61	48	26

Silents Support Raising Retirement Age

% who *favor*	Millennial	Gen X	Boomer	Silent	Mill.–Silent diff.
	%	%	%	%	%
Gradually raising the Social Security retirement age	40	30	39	51	-11
Gradually raising the Medicare eligibility age	35	35	38	50	-15

No Generational Divide over Means Testing

% who *favor*	Millennial	Gen X	Boomer	Silent	Mill.–Silent diff.
	%	%	%	%	%
Reducing Social Security benefits for higher income seniors	51	57	56	50	1
Reducing Medicare benefits for higher income seniors	54	55	57	56	-2

Source: Pew Research Center survey, Sept.–Oct. 2011, N=2,410

Figure 4A.3

Maintaining Benefits Trumps Deficit Reduction

% who favor ...

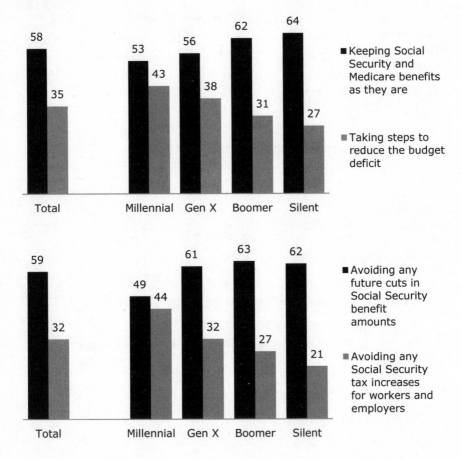

Source: Pew Research Center survey, Sept.–Oct. 2011, N=2,410

Figure 4A.4

More Concern Over Keeping Current Benefits Than Burdening Young People

How concerned are you that ... (%)

In the future there may not be enough money to provide Social Security and Medicare benefits at their current levels

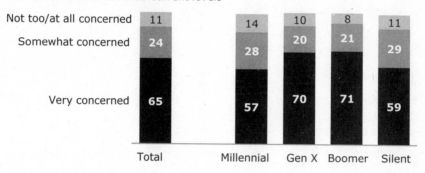

Keeping Social Security and Medicare benefits at their current levels may put too much of a financial burden on younger generations

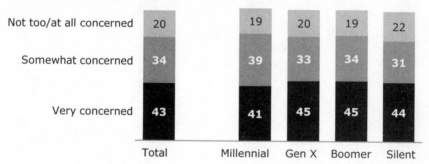

Source: Pew Research Center survey, Sept. 2011, N=2,003

Figure 4A.5

Young and Old Agree: Government Does Too Little for Seniors, Too Much for the Wealthy

	Millennial	Gen X	Boomer	Silent	Mill.– Silent diff.
	%	%	%	%	%
Government doesn't do enough for ...					
Children	57	64	59	44	13
The poor	62	54	57	53	9
The middle class	56	59	62	50	6
Older people	55	64	64	52	3
Government does too much for ...					
The wealthy	62	66	68	63	-1

Source: Pew Research Center survey, Sept.–Oct. 2011, N=2,410

Figure 4A.6

Whose Job Is It to Look Out for Older People?

Who should be _mainly_ responsible for ensuring retired adults have at least a minimum standard of living?	Total	Millennial	Gen X	Boomer	Silent
	%	%	%	%	%
Government	43	44	47	43	36
Individuals and families	40	42	34	39	44
Both equally (Vol.)	14	13	16	14	14
Other/Don't know	3	2	2	3	6
	100	100	100	100	100

If individuals/families mainly responsible ...

	Total	Millennial	Gen X	Boomer	Silent
If people or families cannot do this, gov't should be responsible	30	33	26	29	30
Gov't should still not be responsible	9	8	7	9	12
Other/Don't know	1	1	1	2	2
	40	42	34	40	44
NET: Government is mainly responsible, jointly responsible, or responsible if families cannot do so themselves	87	90	89	86	80

Source: Pew Research Center survey, Sept.–Oct. 2011, N=2,410

Figure 5A.1

Share of Population Employed, by Age, 1967–2012*

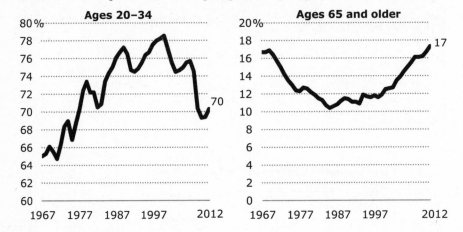

*Note differences in scales along the y-axis.

Source: Pew Research Center analysis of Bureau of Labor Statistics data

Figure 6A.1

Three Great Waves of Immigration to the US

Era and country	Total	%
Modern Era (1965–present)	**44,495,000**	**100**
Mexico	12,416,000	28
China*	2,479,000	6
India	2,077,000	5
Philippines	1,990,000	4
Korea	1,391,000	3
Vietnam	1,291,000	3
Former USSR	1,272,000	3
El Salvador	1,101,000	2
Cuba	1,090,000	2
Dominican Republic	912,000	2
Region totals — Latin America	22,111,000	50
Region totals — South/East Asia	11,811,000	27
Region totals — Europe, total	5,373,000	12
Region totals — Canada**	880,000	2
Region totals — Africa/Middle East	3,211,000	7
Region totals — All other	1,110,000	2
Southern/Eastern Europe Wave (1890–1919)	**18,244,000**	**100**
Italy	3,764,000	21
Austria-Hungary	3,690,000	20
Russia & Poland	3,166,000	17
United Kingdom	1,170,000	6
Germany	1,082,000	6
Ireland***	917,000	5
Region totals — Europe, total	16,134,000	88
Region totals — North/West Europe	4,757,000	26
Region totals — South/East Europe	11,377,000	62
Region totals — Canada	835,000	5
Region totals — Latin America	551,000	3
Region totals — South/East Asia	315,000	2
Region totals — Africa/Middle East	332,000	2
Region totals — Other/Not specified	77,000	<0.5
Northern Europe Wave (1840–1889)	**14,314,000**	**100**
Germany	4,282,000	30
Ireland***	3,209,000	22
United Kingdom	2,586,000	18
Norway-Sweden	883,000	6
Region totals — Europe, total	12,757,000	89
Region totals — North/West Europe	11,700,000	82
Region totals — South/East Europe	1,058,000	7
Region totals — Canada	1,034,000	7
Region totals — Latin America	101,000	1
Region totals — South/East Asia	293,000	2
Region totals — Africa/Middle East	5,000	<0.5
Region totals — Other/Not specified	124,000	1

Notes: Population figures rounded to the nearest thousand. Data for 1965–2011 include legal and unauthorized immigrants. Data for 1840–1919 include only legal admissions. *Includes Hong Kong, Taiwan, and Macao. **Includes other North America. ***Includes Northern Ireland. Persons from Puerto Rico not included.

Source: For 1965–present, Pew Hispanic Center tabulations of 1980, 1990, and 2000 Censuses and 2005–2011 American Community Surveys (with 2010-based weights), IPUMS; for 1840–1919, Table 2 from Office of Immigration Statistics, *Yearbook of Immigration Statistics, 2008*

Figure 6A.2

Comparing Immigrants, the Second Generation and All US Adults, 2012

Median annual household income *(in dollars)*

1st gen. 45,800
2nd gen. 58,100
All US 58,200

College graduates *(% of ages 25 and older)*

1st gen. 29
2nd gen. 36
All US 31

Homeownership rate *(% of households)*

1st gen. 51
2nd gen. 64
All US 65

In poverty *(% of adults)*

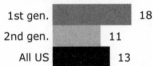

1st gen. 18
2nd gen. 11
All US 13

Note: Annual income figure is adjusted and standardized to a household size of three. College graduates include those with a bachelor's degree or more.

Source: Pew Research Center analysis of 2012 Current Population Surveys, IPUMS

Figure 6A.3

Characteristics of Hispanic Adults by Immigrant Generation, 2012

% (unless otherwise noted)

	Generation			
	1st	**2nd**	**3rd+**	**Total**
Population *(in millions)*	17.5	7.0	10.2	34.7
Share of population	51	20	29	100
Median age *(in years)*	41	28	39	38
Married	60	34	41	49
Fertility (*women ages 15–44***)**				
Had a birth in the past 12 months	9	7	7	8
Of these, share unmarried	29	52	49	39
Educational attainment (*ages 25+***)**				
Less than high school	47	17	21	35
Bachelor's degree or more	11	21	17	15
Median household income ($)	34,600	48,400	43,600	39,200
Average household size (*persons***)**	3.5	3.1	2.8	3.2
Homeownership (*householders***)**	43	50	49	46
Persons in poverty	23	16	20	21

Notes: Unmarried women include those who are divorced, separated, widowed or never married. Annual income figure is adjusted and standardized to a household size of three.

Source: Pew Research Center analysis of Current Population Surveys, IPUMS; fertility data from 2004–2010 CPS and all other data from 2012 CPS

Figure 6A.4

Which Term Do You Use to Describe Yourself Most Often?

% saying ...

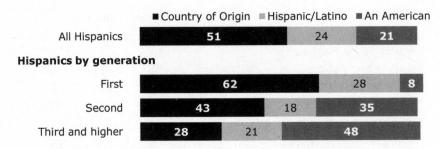

■ Country of Origin   ■ Hispanic/Latino   ■ An American

	Country of Origin	Hispanic/Latino	An American
All Hispanics	51	24	21

Hispanics by generation

	Country of Origin	Hispanic/Latino	An American
First	62	28	8
Second	43	18	35
Third and higher	28	21	48

Note: In this figure, first generation includes those born in Puerto Rico. Although individuals born in Puerto Rico are US citizens by birth, they are included among the foreign born because they are born into a Spanish-dominant culture and because on many points their attitudes, views, and beliefs are much closer to Hispanics born abroad than to Latinos born in the 50 states or the District of Columbia, even those who identify themselves as being of Puerto Rican origin.

Source: Pew Research Center National Survey of Latinos, Nov.–Dec. 2011, N=1,220 US Hispanic adults

---

Figure 6A.5

Trust in People

% in each group who say ...

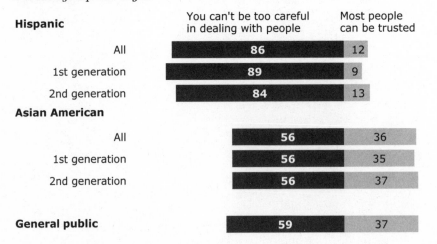

	You can't be too careful in dealing with people	Most people can be trusted
Hispanic		
All	86	12
1st generation	89	9
2nd generation	84	13
Asian American		
All	56	36
1st generation	56	35
2nd generation	56	37
General public	59	37

Note: Volunteered responses of "Other/Depends" and "Don't know/Refused" not shown.

Source: Pew Research Center National Survey of Latinos, Nov.–Dec. 2011 (N=1,220 US Hispanic adults); Pew Research Center Asian-American Survey, Jan.–Mar. 2012 (N=3,511 US Asian adults); and Pew Research Center survey of the general public, Apr. 2012 (N=3,008 US adults)

Figure 6A.6

Number of Children in Poverty, by Race and Ethnicity, 1976–2012

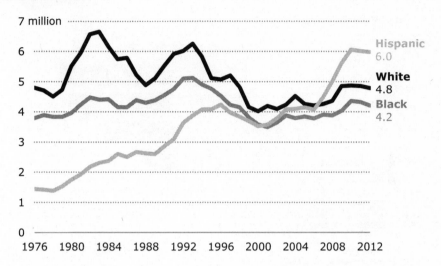

Share of Children in Poverty, by Race and Ethnicity, 2000–2012

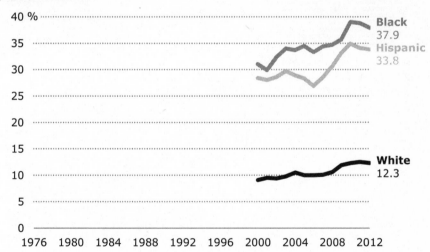

Note: Children include all individuals younger than 18. Whites include only non-Hispanics. Blacks include both Hispanic and non-Hispanic components of the black population. Hispanics are of any race.

Source: US Census Bureau data

Figure 6A.7

Education Characteristics of Recent Immigrants, by Race and Ethnicity, 2010

% among adults

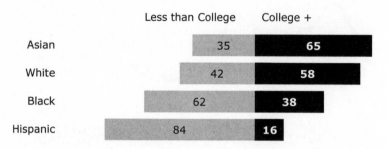

Note: Recent immigrants refer to those who came to the US in the past three years prior to the survey date (since 2007). "College +" includes those who are either currently in a four-year college or graduate school or have completed their bachelor's degree or advanced degrees. Asian includes mixed-race Asian population, regardless of Hispanic origin.

Source: Pew Research Center analysis of 2010 American Community Survey, IPUMS

Figure 6A.8

Attitudes about Work Ethic

% saying ...

"Most people who want to get ahead can make it if they're willing to work hard."

US Asians	69
General public	58

"Americans from my country of origin group are very hardworking"

US Asians	93

"Thinking about the country as a whole, Americans are very hardworking"

US Asians	57

Note: Those who did not provide a country of origin were asked about "Asian Americans."

Source: Pew Research Center Asian-American Survey, Jan.–Mar. 2012, N=3,511 US Asian adults

Figure 6A.9

For Most Asians, US Offers a Better Life

% saying ...

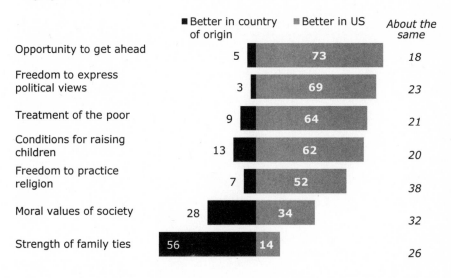

	Better in country of origin	Better in US	About the same
Opportunity to get ahead	5	73	18
Freedom to express political views	3	69	23
Treatment of the poor	9	64	21
Conditions for raising children	13	62	20
Freedom to practice religion	7	52	38
Moral values of society	28	34	32
Strength of family ties	56	14	26

Source: Pew Research Center Asian-American Survey, Jan.–Mar. 2012, N=3,511 US Asian adults

Figure 6A.10

Characteristics of Asian-American Adults by Immigrant Generation, 2012

% (unless otherwise noted)

	Generation			Total
	1st	**2nd**	**3rd+**	
Population *(in millions)*	9.2	2.4	0.9	12.4
Share of population	74	19	7	100
Median age *(in years)*	44	30	43	42
Married	72	37	56	64
Fertility (*women ages 15–44*)				
Had a birth in the past 12 months	8	4	5	7
Of these, share unmarried	10	***	***	16
Educational attainment (*ages 25+*)				
Less than high school	12	7	5	11
Bachelor's degree or more	50	55	53	51
Median household income *($)*	65,200	67,500	91,600	67,400
Average household size (*persons*)	3.1	2.6	2.7	2.9
Homeownership (*householders*)	58	51	65	57
Persons in poverty	12	12	8	12

Notes: Includes only single-race Asians, including Hispanics. The symbol *** indicates insufficient number of observations to provide a reliable estimate. Unmarried women include those who are divorced, separated, widowed, or never married. Annual income figure is adjusted and standardized to a household size of three.

Source: Pew Research Center analysis of Current Population Surveys, IPUMS; fertility data from 2004–2010 CPS and all other data from 2012 CPS

Figure 7A.1

Okay with Intermarriage

% saying they would be fine if a family member told them they were going to marry someone of a different race/ethnicity

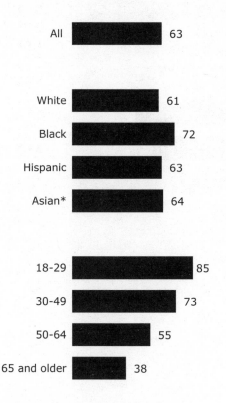

All	63
White	61
Black	72
Hispanic	63
Asian*	64
18-29	85
30-49	73
50-64	55
65 and older	38

Note: Respondents were asked how they would react if a family member was going to marry someone of three racial/ethnic groups other than their own: An African American, a Hispanic American, an Asian American and a white American. Results show those who say they would be fine with a family member marrying all three other racial and ethnic groups.*Sample size for Asian is 86.

Source: Pew Research Center survey conducted Oct. 28-Nov. 30, 2009, N=2,884 US adults

Figure 7A.2

Intermarriage Types, Newly Married Couples in 2010

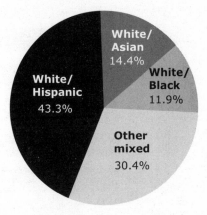

White/Asian 14.4%

White/Hispanic 43.3%

White/Black 11.9%

Other mixed 30.4%

Note: Asians include Pacific Islanders.

Source: Pew Research Center analysis of 2010 American Community Survey, IPUMS

Figure 7A.3

Earnings and Education, Newlyweds in 2008–2010

Median combined annual earnings, in 2010 dollars

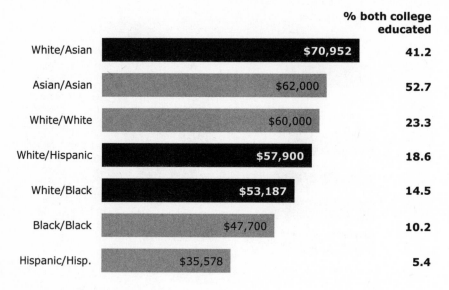

	Median combined annual earnings	% both college educated
White/Asian	$70,952	41.2
Asian/Asian	$62,000	52.7
White/White	$60,000	23.3
White/Hispanic	$57,900	18.6
White/Black	$53,187	14.5
Black/Black	$47,700	10.2
Hispanic/Hisp.	$35,578	5.4

Note: Asians include Pacific Islanders.

Source: Pew Research Center analysis of 2008–2010 American Community Survey, IPUMS

Figure 7A.4

Intermarriage among Asian and Hispanic Newlyweds, by Nativity, 2010

% of newlyweds married to someone of a different race/ethnicity

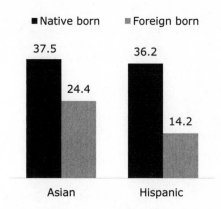

■ Native born   ▪ Foreign born

Note: Asians include Pacific Islanders.

Source: Pew Research Center analysis of 2010 American Community Survey, IPUMS

Figure 7A.5

Where Gaps Have Narrowed Where Gaps Have Widened

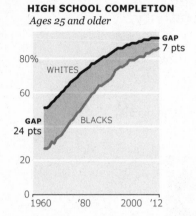

HIGH SCHOOL COMPLETION
Ages 25 and older

GAP
7 pts

80%

WHITES

60

GAP
24 pts

BLACKS

20

0
1960   '80   2000 '12

MEDIAN HOUSEHOLD INCOME
Household of three, in 2012 dollars

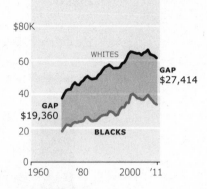

$80K

WHITES

60

GAP
$27,414

40

GAP
$19,360

20   BLACKS

0
1960   '80   2000 '11

LIFE EXPECTANCY
At birth

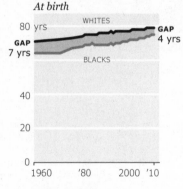

80 yrs   WHITES
GAP
7 yrs   GAP
4 yrs

BLACKS

40

20

0
1960   '80   2000 '10

MARRIAGE RATE
Ages 18 and older

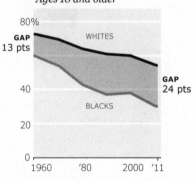

80%

GAP
13 pts   WHITES

GAP
24 pts

40

BLACKS

20

0
1960   '80   2000 '11

VOTER TURNOUT
In presidential election years

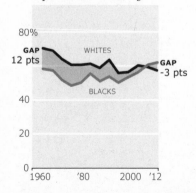

80%

GAP
12 pts   WHITES

GAP
-3 pts

40

BLACKS

20

0
1960   '80   2000 '12

MEDIAN HOUSEHOLD WEALTH
In 2012 dollars

$120K

100

WHITES

80

GAP
$84,960

60

GAP
$75,224

40

20

BLACKS

0
1960   '80   2000 '11

Source: Pew Research Center analysis of government data. For more details see Pew Research Center,
"King's Dream Remains an Elusive Goal; Many Americans See Racial Disparities," Aug. 22, 2013

Figure 8A.1

Share Married, by Race and Ethnicity, 1960–2011

% of adults 18 and older

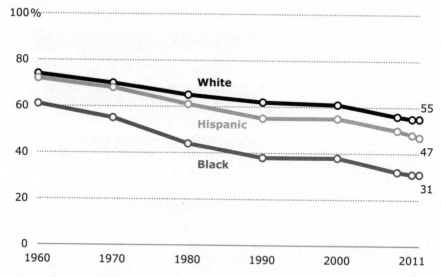

Source: Pew Research Center analysis of Decennial Census (1960–2000) and American Community Survey data (2008–2011), IPUMS

Figure 8A.2

Why Get Married?

% saying "very important" reason, by marital status

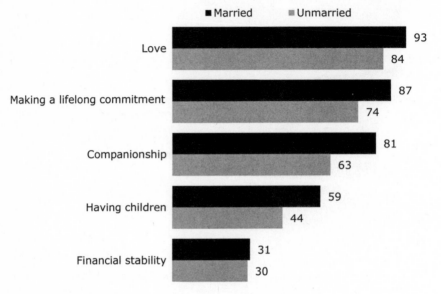

Note: Asked of married (n=1,306) and unmarried (n=1,385) separately

Source: Pew Research Center, Oct. 2010, N=2,691 US adults

Figure 8A.3

Marriage: It's Not about the Kids

Which of these is closer to your views about the main purpose of marriage?
Forming a lifetime union between two adults for ... (%)

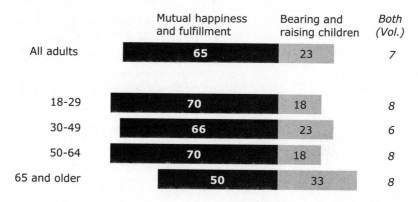

	Mutual happiness and fulfillment	Bearing and raising children	*Both (Vol.)*
All adults	65	23	7
18-29	70	18	8
30-49	66	23	6
50-64	70	18	8
65 and older	50	33	8

Note: Volunteered responses of "Neither" and "Don't know/Refused" are not shown.

Source: Pew Research Center survey, Feb.–Mar. 2007, N=2,020 US adults

---

Figure 8A.4

Share of Births to Unmarried Women, by Race and Ethnicity, 1960–2011

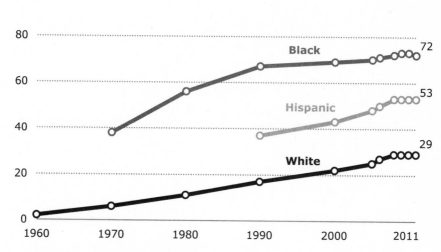

Source: National Center for Health Statistics data

Figure 9A.1

Worship Attendance Among the Unaffiliated and Affiliated

	Unaffiliated		Affiliated	
	2007	2012	2007	2012
Attends worship services ...	%	%	%	%
Weekly or more	7	5	44	45
Monthly/yearly	25	22	35	36
Seldom/never	68	72	20	18

Source: Aggregated data from surveys conducted by the Pew Research Center for the People & the Press, 2007 and 2012

Figure 9A.2

Trends in Disaffiliation, by Religious Attendance

% of each attendance category that is unaffiliated

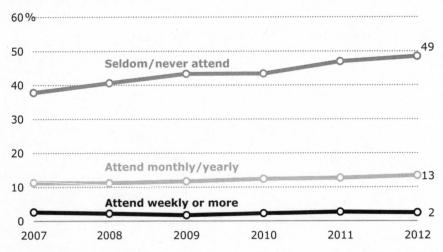

Source: Aggregated data from surveys conducted by the Pew Research Center for the People & the Press, 2007–2012

Figure 9A.3

Trends in Religious Disaffiliation, by Demographic Groups

% who describe themselves as religiously unaffiliated among ...

	2007	2012	Change
	%	%	
US general public	15.3	19.6	**+4.3**
Men	18	23	**+5**
Women	13	17	**+4**
White	15	20	**+5**
Black	13	15	+2
Hispanic	16	16	--
Bachelor's degree or more	17	21	**+4**
Bachelor's degree	15	22	**+7**
Post-grad	19	20	+1
Some college or less	15	19	**+4**
Annual family income			
$75,000 or more	16	21	**+5**
$30,000–$74,999	15	20	**+5**
Less than $30,000	17	20	**+3**
Married	14	14	--
Not married	20	24	**+4**
Region of residence			
Northeast	15	21	**+6**
Midwest	15	19	**+4**
South	12	15	**+3**
West	21	26	**+5**

Note: Hispanic figures based only on surveys that included Spanish interviewing. Changes that are statistically significant are shown in bold.

Source: Aggregated data from surveys conducted by the Pew Research Center for the People & the Press, 2007 and 2012 .

Figure 9A.4

Unaffiliated, But Not Uniformly Secular

	US general public	Unaffiliated	Affiliated
How important is religion in your life?	%	%	%
Very important	58	14	67
Somewhat	22	19	24
Not too/not at all	18	65	8
Believe in God or universal spirit?			
Yes, absolutely certain	69	30	77
Yes, but less certain	23	38	20
No	7	27	2
Other/Don't know	2	5	1
Frequency of prayer			
Daily	58	21	66
Weekly/monthly	21	20	22
Seldom/never	19	58	11
Think of self as ...			
Religious person	65	18	75
Spiritual, but not religious	18	37	15
Neither spiritual nor religious	15	42	8

Source: Pew Research Center survey, Jun.–Jul. 2012, N=2,973 US adults

Figure 9A.5

Views of Religious Institutions

% who agree that churches and other religious organizations ...

	US general public	Unaffiliated	Affiliated
	%	%	%
Are too concerned with money and power	51	70	47
Focus too much on rules	51	67	47
Are too involved with politics	46	67	41
Bring people together/strengthen community bonds	88	78	90
Play important role in helping the poor and needy	87	77	90
Protect and strengthen morality	76	52	81

Source: Pew Research Center survey, Jun.–Jul. 2012, N=2,973 US adults

Figure 9A.6

Differing Views over the Impact of Religion's Influence on Society

Is religion increasing or losing its influence on American life? Is this a good thing or a bad thing?

	US general public	Unaffiliated	Atheist/ Agnostic	Nothing in particular
	%	%	%	%
Increasing its influence	25	27	34	24
Losing its influence	66	63	59	65
Good thing	*12*	*28*	*43*	*22*
Bad thing	*49*	*26*	*10*	*32*
Other/Don't know	*5*	*9*	*6*	*11*
Same (Vol.)	2	2	2	2
Don't know	7	7	5	8

Source: Pew Research Center survey, Jun.–Jul. 2012, N=2,973 US adults

Figure 9A.7

Neither "Seekers" Nor More Inclined Toward New Age Beliefs Than the General Public

% of "nothing in particulars" who are …	US general public	Unaffiliated
	%	%
Looking for a religion that is right for them	n/a	10
Not doing this	n/a	88
% who believe in …		
Spiritual energy in physical things like mountains, trees, crystals	26	30
Astrology	25	25
Reincarnation	24	25
Yoga as a spiritual practice	23	28
% who often …		
Think about meaning and purpose of life	67	53
Feel deep connection with nature and the earth	58	58
% who say it is very important …		
To belong to a community with shared values and beliefs	49	28
% who have ever …		
Had religious or mystical experience	49	30
Been in touch with someone who has died	29	31
Seen or been in presence of a ghost	18	19
Consulted a psychic	15	15

Source: Pew Research Center survey, Jun.–Jul. 2012 (N=2,973 US adults) and August 2009 (N=2,003 US adults)

Figure 9A.8

Social and Political Issues

	US general public	Unaffiliated	Affiliated
Abortion should be ...	%	%	%
Legal in all/most cases	53	72	49
Illegal in all/most cases	41	24	46
Don't know	6	4	6
Same-sex marriage ...			
Favor	48	73	41
Oppose	44	20	50
Don't know	9	7	9
Prefer ...			
Bigger gov't, more services	39	42	38
Smaller gov't, fewer services	52	50	52
Depends/Don't know	9	8	10

Source: Abortion figures from aggregated data from surveys conducted by the Pew Research Center for the People & the Press, 2011–2012. Same-sex marriage figures from aggregated data from surveys conducted by the Pew Research Center for the People & the Press, 2012. Views on role of government from Pew Research Center for the People & the Press survey, January 2012.

Figure 9A.9

Trends in Religious Affiliation, 2007–2012

	2007	2008	2009	2010	2011	2012	'07–'12 change
	%	%	%	%	%	%	
Christian	**78**	**77**	**77**	**76**	**75**	**73**	**-5**
Protestant	53	52	51	51	50	48	**-5**
White evangelical	*21*	*19*	*20*	*19*	*18*	*19*	*-2*
White mainline	*18*	*18*	*17*	*17*	*17*	*15*	*-3*
Black Protestant	*8*	*8*	*9*	*9*	*9*	*8*	--
Other minority Protestant	*6*	*6*	*6*	*6*	*6*	*6*	--
Catholic	23	22	23	23	23	22	-1
Mormon	2	2	2	2	2	2	--
Orthodox	1	1	1	1	1	1	--
Other faith	**4**	**5**	**5**	**5**	**5**	**6**	**+2**
Unaffiliated	**15.3**	**16.0**	**16.8**	**17.4**	**18.6**	**19.6**	**+4.3**
Atheist	1.6	1.7	1.8	1.9	2.2	2.4	**+0.8**
Agnostic	2.1	2.3	2.6	2.6	3.0	3.3	**+1.2**
Nothing in particular	11.6	11.9	12.4	12.9	13.4	13.9	**+2.3**

Note: In the change column, figures that are statistically significant are shown in bold.

Source: Aggregated data from surveys conducted by the Pew Research Center for the People & the Press, 2007 and 2012.

Figure 9A.10

Which Religions Lead to Eternal Life?

% among respondents who are affiliated with a religion and who say "many religions can lead to eternal life"

	All	White evang.	White mainline	Black Prot.	White Catholic
Can **Catholicism** lead to eternal life?	%	%	%	%	%
Yes	73	75	77	69	n/a
No	14	14	11	19	n/a
Don't know	13	11	12	12	n/a
Protestantism					
Yes	74	n/a	n/a	n/a	83
No	13	n/a	n/a	n/a	6
Don't know	13	n/a	n/a	n/a	11
Judaism					
Yes	69	64	73	62	77
No	17	21	11	24	12
Don't know	14	15	16	14	11
Islam					
Yes	52	35	55	58	62
No	29	45	26	25	20
Don't know	19	20	19	17	18
Hinduism					
Yes	53	33	57	44	65
No	24	36	20	28	16
Don't know	23	31	23	28	19
Atheists					
Yes	42	26	46	--	49
No	46	68	41	--	38
Don't know	12	6	13	--	13
People with no religious faith					
Yes	56	35	62	--	66
No	31	53	22	--	20
Don't know	13	12	16	--	14

Note: "White Catholic" refers to white, non-Hispanic Catholics. Respondents were not asked about their own religion; e.g., Protestants were not asked if Protestantism can lead to eternal life, Catholics were not asked if Catholicism can lead to eternal life, etc. "Atheists" and "People with no religious faith" was asked of a random half of the sample. Sample size for these items is too small for black Protestants to produce reliable estimates.

Source: Pew Research Center survey, Jul.–Aug. 2008, N=2,905 US adults. See Pew Research Center, "Many Americans Say Other Faiths Can Lead to Eternal Life," Dec. 18, 2008

Figure 10A.1

Social Networking Site Use by Age Group, 2005–2013

% of internet users in each age group who use social networking sites

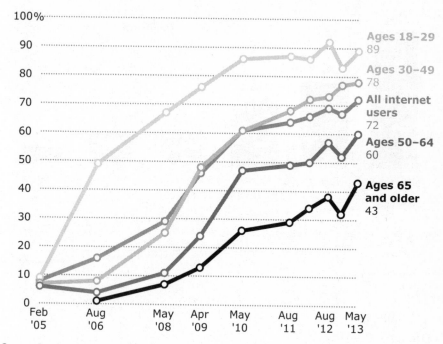

Source: Pew Research Center's Internet & American Life project surveys, 2005–2013

Figure 10A.2

Mean Size of Facebook Social Networks

(persons)

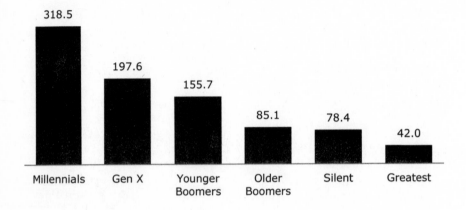

Source: Pew Research Center survey, Oct.–Nov. 2010, N=877 US adult Facebook users

Figure 10A.3

Digital Devices

% of adults who own each device

	All online adults	Millen-nials	Gen X	Younger Boomers	Older Boomers	Silent	Greatest
	%	%	%	%	%	%	%
Cell phone	91	97	95	91	87	80	62
Desktop computer	58	52	66	66	61	54	31
Laptop computer	61	73	70	62	49	39	20
iPod or MP3 player	44	70	60	36	24	10	5
Game console	42	62	59	41	21	10	3
e-Book reader	18	19	23	19	13	15	5
Tablet, like iPad	34	34	45	35	26	20	11

Source: Pew Research Center's Internet & American Life project Spring Tracking surveys, 2010–2013

Figure 11A.1

Who Wants an Extended Life?

% saying they personally would/would not want treatments for radical life extension

	Would	Would not	Don't know
All adults	**38**	**56**	**6**
Radical life extension			
Good for society	71	24	6
Bad for society	13	83	3
Men	43	52	5
Women	34	59	8
White	34	59	7
Black	46	49	5
Hispanic	46	48	6
18–29	40	57	3
30–49	43	51	6
50–64	35	58	7
65 and older	31	59	10
High school grad or less	41	54	5
Some college	34	60	6
Bachelor's degree or more	37	55	7

Note: This question was asked of half the survey sample, n=2,012

Source: Pew Research Center survey, Mar.–Apr. 2013, N=4,006 US adults

Figure 11A.2

What Would a Future With Radical Life Extension Hold?

% who agree/disagree with each statement

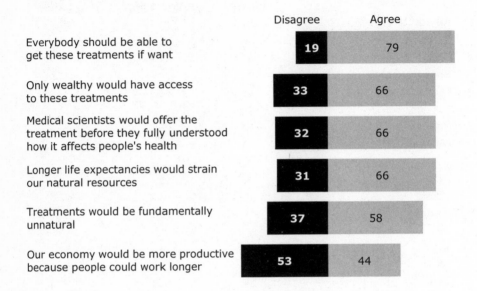

	Disagree	Agree
Everybody should be able to get these treatments if want	19	79
Only wealthy would have access to these treatments	33	66
Medical scientists would offer the treatment before they fully understood how it affects people's health	32	66
Longer life expectancies would strain our natural resources	31	66
Treatments would be fundamentally unnatural	37	58
Our economy would be more productive because people could work longer	53	44

Source: Pew Research Center survey, Mar.–Apr. 2013, N=4,006 US adults

Figure 11A.3

Most Markers of Old Age Differ for Young and Old

% saying that a person is old when he or she ...

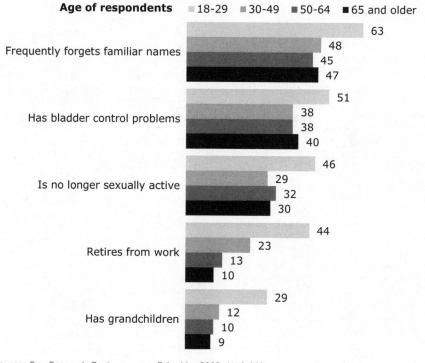

Age of respondents 18-29 30-49 50-64 65 and older

Frequently forgets familiar names
- 63
- 48
- 45
- 47

Has bladder control problems
- 51
- 38
- 38
- 40

Is no longer sexually active
- 46
- 29
- 32
- 30

Retires from work
- 44
- 23
- 13
- 10

Has grandchildren
- 29
- 12
- 10
- 9

Source: Pew Research Center survey, Feb.–Mar 2009, N=2,969

Figure 11A.4

At What Age Does the Average Person Become Old?

Mean age

Age of respondents 18-29 30-49 50-64 65 and older

Age of becoming old
- 60
- 69
- 72
- 74

Source: Pew Research Center survey, Feb.–Mar 2009, N=2,969

Figure 12A.1

Old-age Dependency Ratios, by Global Region

■2010 ■2050

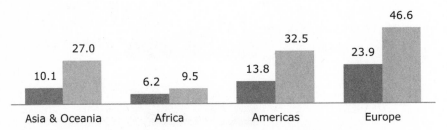

Child Dependency Ratios, by Global Region

■2010 ■2050

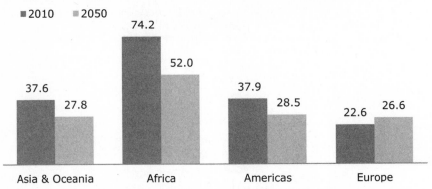

Total Dependency Ratios, by Global Region

■2010 ■2050

Note: The old-age dependency ratio is the population age 65 and over divided by population age 15–64. The child dependency ratio is the population age 0–14 divided by population age 15–64. The total dependency ratio is the population age 65 and over plus population age 0–14, divided by population age 15–64.

Source: United Nations, Department of Economic and Social Affairs, *World Population Prospects: The 2012 Revision*, June 2013

Figure 12A.2

Population Change in Selected Countries, 2010 to 2050

% change

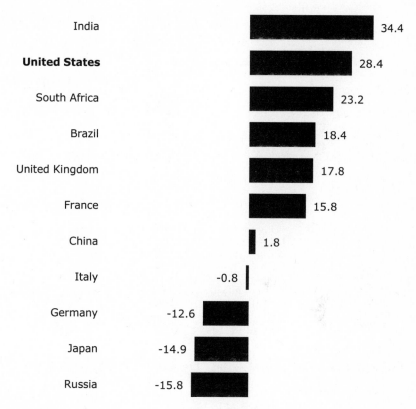

Country	% change
India	34.4
United States	28.4
South Africa	23.2
Brazil	18.4
United Kingdom	17.8
France	15.8
China	1.8
Italy	-0.8
Germany	-12.6
Japan	-14.9
Russia	-15.8

Source: United Nations, Department of Economic and Social Affairs, *World Population Prospects: The 2012 Revision*, June 2013

Figure 12A.3

Median Age in Selected Countries

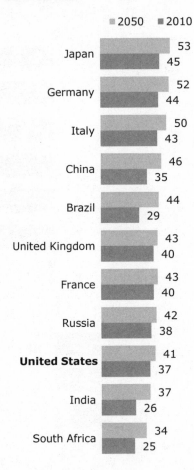

▪ 2050   ▪ 2010

Japan — 53 / 45

Germany — 52 / 44

Italy — 50 / 43

China — 46 / 35

Brazil — 44 / 29

United Kingdom — 43 / 40

France — 43 / 40

Russia — 42 / 38

United States — 41 / 37

India — 37 / 26

South Africa — 34 / 25

Source: United Nations, Department of Economic and Social Affairs, *World Population Prospects: The 2012 Revision*, June 2013

Figure 12A.4

Total Dependency Ratio in Selected Countries

Old-age Dependency Ratio in Selected Countries

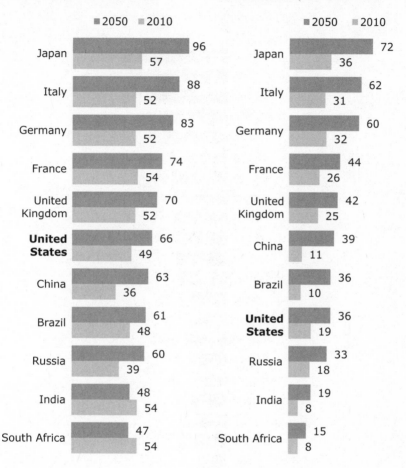

■2050 ■2010

	2050	2010
Japan	96	57
Italy	88	52
Germany	83	52
France	74	54
United Kingdom	70	52
United States	66	49
China	63	36
Brazil	61	48
Russia	60	39
India	48	54
South Africa	47	54

■2050 ■2010

	2050	2010
Japan	72	36
Italy	62	31
Germany	60	32
France	44	26
United Kingdom	42	25
China	39	11
Brazil	36	10
United States	36	19
Russia	33	18
India	19	8
South Africa	15	8

Note: The total dependency ratio is the population age 65 and over plus population age 0–14, divided by population age 15–64. The old-age dependency ratio is the population age 65 and over divided by population age 15–64.

Source: United Nations, Department of Economic and Social Affairs, *World Population Prospects: The 2012 Revision*, June 2013

Figure 12A.5

Is Aging a Problem in Your Country?

% saying it's a "major problem"

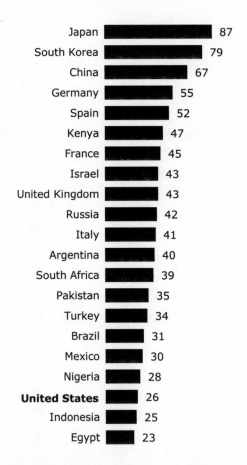

Country	%
Japan	87
South Korea	79
China	67
Germany	55
Spain	52
Kenya	47
France	45
Israel	43
United Kingdom	43
Russia	42
Italy	41
Argentina	40
South Africa	39
Pakistan	35
Turkey	34
Brazil	31
Mexico	30
Nigeria	28
United States	26
Indonesia	25
Egypt	23

Note: Question asked, "How much of a problem, if at all, is the growing number of older people in (survey country)...." Responses of "Minor problem," "Not a problem," and "Don't know/Refused" are not shown.

Source: Pew Research Center survey, Mar.–Apr. 2013, N=22,425 adults in 21 countries

Figure 12A.6

Who Should Bear the Greatest Responsibility for The Elderly?

% saying ... should bear the greatest responsibility for people's economic wellbeing in their old age

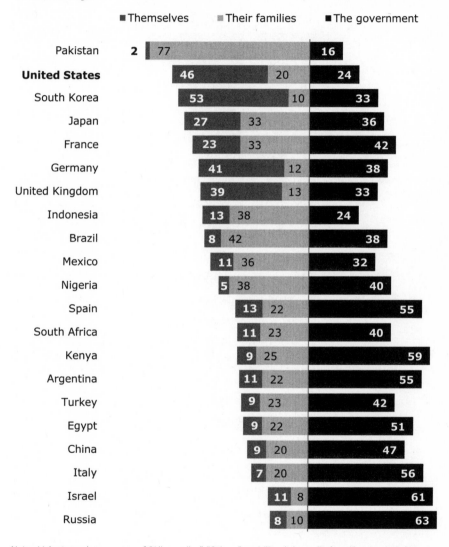

■ Themselves ■ Their families ■ The government

	Themselves	Their families	The government
Pakistan	2	77	16
United States	46	20	24
South Korea	53	10	33
Japan	27	33	36
France	23	33	42
Germany	41	12	38
United Kingdom	39	13	33
Indonesia	13	38	24
Brazil	8	42	38
Mexico	11	36	32
Nigeria	5	38	40
Spain	13	22	55
South Africa	11	23	40
Kenya	9	25	59
Argentina	11	22	55
Turkey	9	23	42
Egypt	9	22	51
China	9	20	47
Italy	7	20	56
Israel	11	8	61
Russia	8	10	63

Note: Volunteered responses of "All equally," "Other," and "Don't know/Refused" are not shown.

Source: Pew Research Center survey, Mar.–Apr. 2013, N=22,425 adults in 21 countries

Figure 12A.7

Will You Have an Adequate Standard of Living in Old Age?

% saying they are "very" or "somewhat" confident they will

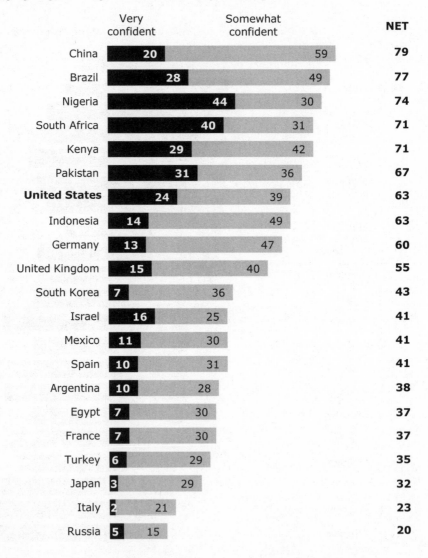

	Very confident	Somewhat confident	NET
China	20	59	79
Brazil	28	49	77
Nigeria	44	30	74
South Africa	40	31	71
Kenya	29	42	71
Pakistan	31	36	67
United States	24	39	63
Indonesia	14	49	63
Germany	13	47	60
United Kingdom	15	40	55
South Korea	7	36	43
Israel	16	25	41
Mexico	11	30	41
Spain	10	31	41
Argentina	10	28	38
Egypt	7	30	37
France	7	30	37
Turkey	6	29	35
Japan	3	29	32
Italy	2	21	23
Russia	5	15	20

Note: Question asked, "Thinking about yourself, how confident are you that you will have an adequate standard of living in your old age..." Responses of "Not too confident," "Not at all confident," and "Don't know/Refused" are not shown.

Source: Pew Research Center survey, Mar.–Apr. 2013, N=22,425 adults in 21 countries

NOTES

CHAPTER 1: INTRODUCTION

1. All long-term demographic projections in this book should be taken with a grain of salt—and the longer the term, the larger the grain. They're based on the best available data and analysis. But things change.

2. Fred Barnes, "America and Its Immigrants, A Hate-Love Relationship," *Weekly Standard,* July 29, 2013.

3. Pew Research Center, "The Lost Decade of the Middle Class," August 22, 2012. In this report, our analysis of long-term US Census data showed that the share of adults in the middle class declined from 61% in 1971 to 51% in 2011. We defined a "middle class" adult as one living in a household with an annual income between 67% and 200% of the national median—an income range of $39,418 to $118,255 in 2011 dollars (all incomes were scaled to reflect a three person household). We tested other middle income boundaries—some wider, some narrower—but always found the same pattern: the middle-income tier has been shrinking steadily for many decades. Our analysis also found that the share of adults in the upper and lower income tiers have each risen steadily over time—the lower tier to 29% in 2011 from 25% in 1971; the upper tier to 20% in 2011 from 14% in 1971. See http://www.pewsocialtrends. org/2012/08/22/the-lost-decade-of-the-middle-class/.

4. A 2011 cross-national analysis by the Organization for Economic Co-operation and Development (OECD) found that the United States ranked fourth from highest in income inequality among 34 of the world's most advanced economies—behind only Turkey, Mexico, and Chile. That study, which took into account the impact of taxes and public cash transfers, put the US Gini Coefficient at 0.38, lower than the measure of income inequality in the US before taxes and transfers. Both measures have risen more sharply in the US over the past several decades than in all but a handful of the world's other wealthy countries. See www.oecd.org/els/soc/49499779.pdf.

5. Julia B. Isaacs, "International Comparison of Economic Mobility," in *Economic Mobility in America,* Brookings Institution and the Economic Mobility Project of the Pew Charitable Trusts.

6. Based on a Pew Research Center analysis of wealth data from the Census Bureau's Survey of Income and Program Participation (SIPP).

7. Laurie Goodstein, "Christian Right Failed to Sway Voters on Issues," *New York Times,* November 9, 2012.

8. See, for example, Sara S. McLanahan, "Life without Father: What happens to the children?" Center for Research on Child Wellbeing, Princeton, NJ, 2001.

9. Pew Research Center, "The Decline of Marriage and Rise of New Families," November 2010.

10. Ezra Klein, "Good Riddance to Rottenest Congress in History," *Bloomberg,* January 2, 2013. See also Nolan McCarty, et al., "Polarization Is Real (and Asymmetric)," May 15, 2012, voteview.com.

11. Researchers at Yale and the University of California, San Diego, conducted a novel experiment and found they could cut the partisan gap on such questions by more than half if they offered survey respondents money for correct answers. Their finding suggests that some Democrats and Republicans know the right answers but choose to answer incorrectly anyway as a way to affirm their beliefs or stick it to the opposition. See www.nber.org/papers/w19080.

CHAPTER 2: MILLENNIALS AND BOOMERS

1. In this calculation by the Urban Institute's C. Eugene Steuerle and Caleb Quakenbush, it is assumed that the taxes paid by employee and employer earn interest each year at a rate 2% above inflation. See http://www.urban.org/UploadedPDF/412945-Social-Security-and-Medicare-Taxes-and-Benefits-Over-a-Lifetime.pdf.

2. It's no surprise that "selfie" was The Oxford Dictionaries 2013 Word of the Year (see http://blog.oxforddictionaries.com/2013/11/word-of-the-year-2013-winner/)—91% of American teens report they have posted at least one picture of themselves online. See the Pew Research Center's Internet Project report, "Teens, Social Media, and Privacy," May 21, 2013; http://pewinternet.org/Reports/2013/Teens-Social-Media-And-Privacy/Summary-of-Findings.aspx.

3. Robin Marantz Henig, "What Is It about 20-Somethings?" *New York Times Magazine,* August 18, 2010.

4. Arthur A. Stone, et al., "A Snapshot of the Age Distribution of Psychological Well-being in the United States," *PNAS* 107, no. 22 (June 1, 2010).

5. Yang Yang, "Social Inequalities in Happiness in the United States, 1972 to 2004: An Age-Period-Cohort Analysis," *American Sociological Review* 73, no. 2 (April 2008).

6. You never know what will strike the public's fancy online. "Charlie Bit My Finger" was for several years the most viewed YouTube video ever. It was posted in 2007 and by the end of 2012 had attracted more than 500 million views worldwide The 56-second video features 1-year-old Charlie biting the finger of his 3-year-old

brother, Harry, whereupon Harry announces, "Ouch." That's the whole of it. The young British lads now have their own blogs, video series, and fan clubs. But fame can be fleeting. Their world record has since been surpassed by a number of professional entertainers, among them Psy, the South Korean pop musician and reigning YouTube champ. His "Gangnam Style" video had drawn nearly 2 billion viewers by the end of 2013.

7. Volunteering is a difficult civic engagement activity to measure because measurement depends on survey question framing and context. According to an analysis of the Census Bureau's Current Population Survey September supplement, the Corporation for National and Community Service reports a much lower volunteering rate than the current survey (52%). In 2008, 26.4% of Americans say they had volunteered for an organization in the year prior to the survey (Corporation for National and Community Service, 2009).

CHAPTER 4: BATTLE OF THE AGES?

1. Sabrina Tavernise, "Whites Account for Under Half of Births in US," *New York Times,* May 17, 2012.

2. Ronald Brownstein, "The Gray and the Brown: The Generational Mismatch," *National Journal,* July 24, 2010. Ron has long been one of journalism's most astute observers of these demographic and political trends. He writes and edits a series of articles on this topic in the *National Journal* under the label, The Next America. (Good title! Imitation is flattery, my friend.)

3. Julia Isaacs, Katherine Toran, Heather Hahn, Karina Fortuny, and C. Eugene Steuerle, "Kids' Share 2012," Urban Institute.

4. Lynda Laughlin, "Who's Minding the Kids? Child Care Arrangements: Spring 2011," Current Population Reports, US Census Bureau, Washington, DC, 2013, pp. 70–135.

5. Joel Kotkin, et al., "The Rise of Post-Familialism: Humanity's Future?" Civil Service College, Singapore, 2012, p. 29.

CHAPTER 5: MONEY TROUBLES

1. Alicia Munnell, Center for Retirement Research at Boston College, Issue Brief 12-15, August 2012.

2. Teresa Ghilarducci, "Our Ridiculous Approach to Retirement," *New York Times,* July 21, 2012.

3. For Millennials, college may be a financial drag in terms of debt accumulation, but it has already begun to pay off on the employment front. Among young adults ages 25 to 32, the unemployment rate in 2013 was 4% for those with a BA degree or more—compared with 12% for their same-aged counterparts with no education beyond a high school diploma—according to a Pew Research Center analysis of US Census Bureau data. Looking back in time, our analysis found that 25- to 32-year-old

college graduates of previous generations had even lower unemployment rates—3% for Gen Xers in 1995, 2% for late Boomers in 1986, 2% for early Boomers in 1979, and 1% for Silents in 1965. (The national unemployment rate was also lower in the past. It stood at 7.6% in 2013, 5.4% in 1995, 7.2% in 1986, 5.8% in 1979, and 4.7% in 1965.)

4. Richard Fry, "Young Adults after the Recession: Fewer Homes, Fewer Cars, Less Debt," Pew Research Center, February 21, 2013.

5. In an effort to respond to critics, the US Census Bureau in November 2011 unveiled a Supplemental Poverty Measure designed, among other things, to make a more comprehensive tally of the non-cash government benefits that households receive and the out-of-pocket medical expenses they pay. While these adjustments have had little impact on the overall US poverty rate, they narrow the gap in the poverty rates for younger households and older households, reducing the former and raising the latter. This new supplemental measure represents the biggest change in the way poverty has been calculated since the federal government first began doing so in 1964, but it remains a methodological work in progress. For now, at least, the traditional measure remains the official measure. For more on the supplemental measure, see www.pewsocialtrends.org/2011/11/30/re-counting-poverty.

6. Quoted in Derek Thompson and Jordan Weissmann, "The Cheapest Generation," *Atlantic Magazine,* September 2012.

CHAPTER 6: THE NEW IMMIGRANTS

1. Michael Barone, "A Nation Built for Immigrants," *Wall Street Journal,* September 21, 2013.

2. Median household income figures have been standardized and adjusted to a household size of three so that comparisons can be made on an apples-to-apples basis.

3. In this 2012 Pew Hispanic Trends Project survey, which focused on identity and assimilation (see http://www.pewhispanic.org/2012/04/04/when-labels-dont-fit-hispanics-and-their-views-of-identity/), Puerto Ricans born in Puerto Rico were counted as immigrants, even though they are US citizens by birth. In the typical Pew Research Center survey, Puerto Ricans are not counted as immigrants.

4. Mark Lopez and Gabriel Velasco, "Childhood Poverty among Hispanics Sets Record, Leads Nation," Pew Hispanic Center, September 28, 2011.

5. The report was based on a Pew Research Center survey of a nationally representative sample of 3,511 Asian Americans, conducted by telephone from January 3 to March 27, 2012, in English and seven Asian languages.

6. Organisation for Economic Co-operation and Development (OECD), Education at a Glance 2011: OECD Indicators. Based on 2009 data.

7. The college data are for adults ages 25 and older. Household income is based on householders ages 18 and older and comes from Pew Research Center analysis of the Census Bureau's 2010 American Community Survey. Household wealth is based

on householders ages 15 and older and comes from Pew Research Center analysis of Wave 7 of the 2008 Survey of Income and Program Participation panel, conducted September–December 2010.

8. Jeffrey Passel, D'Vera Cohn, and Ana Gonzalez-Barrera, "Population Decline of Unauthorized Immigrants Stalls, May Have Reversed," Pew Research Center, September 23, 2013.

9. See, for example, Giovanni Peri, "The Effect of Immigrants on U.S. Employment and Productivity," Federal Reserve Bank of San Francisco, August 30, 2010.

10. Adam Davidson, "Do Illegal Immigrants Actually Hurt the US Economy?" *New York Times,* February 12, 2013.

11. In 2013 the US Senate passed a comprehensive immigration bill that included a provision creating a 13-year pathway to citizenship for immigrants who are in the US illegally. As this book was going to press, the fate of that legislation in the US House of Representatives was uncertain.

12. According to a 2012 survey by the Pew Hispanic Center, among Latino immigrants who are not US citizens or legal permanent residents (and therefore likely to be unauthorized immigrants), 54% identify with or lean toward the Democratic Party and 19% self-identify with or lean toward the GOP.

13. Karl Rove, "Immigration Reform and the Hispanic Vote," *Wall Street Journal,* June 6, 2013.

14. Partnership for a New American Economy, June 2011, www.renewour economy.org/sites/all/themes/pnae/img/new-american-fortune-500-june-2011.pdf.

15. According to the World Bank, Russia had 12.3 million immigrants in 2010, but the great bulk of them were residents of the former Soviet Union. Germany, with 10.8 million immigrants that year, is a more legitimate number two to the US, which had about 40 million in 2010.

CHAPTER 7: HAPA NATION

1. The de Blasios can give the Obamas a pretty good run for their money on the diversity front. I happened to be in Munich, Germany, last fall, two days after Bill de Blasio was elected mayor of New York City. Both Munich newspapers featured giant front page, above-the-fold photos of the winning candidate and his striking interracial family—his black wife, Chirlane McCray; their son Dante, sporting his massive Afro; and their daughter Chiara, who adorned her loose, kinky locks with flowers. Interest in the family was even more intense in Italy, the ancestral home of de Blasio's mother, where one restaurant near Naples named a dessert in their honor—a sponge cake filled with hazelnut and white chocolate. See http://www.nytimes.com/2013/11/15/nyregion/his-roots-in-italy-de-blasio-now-has-fans-there.html?hp&_r=0. Bill De Blasio had started out as a longshot in the mayor's race and wound up winning by a landslide. Some analysts credit the family itself (especially a TV ad featuring Dante and his huge Afro) for the turnaround. It's hard to imagine the

New York City of 1950—or, for that matter, of 2000—embracing that family. But in America, norms change. And the rest of the world watches with fascination.

2. For background information on intermarriage, see Pew Research Center Social & Demographic Trends project; and see Wendy Wang, "The Rise of Intermarriage," February 16, 2012.

3. M. D. Bramlett and W. D. Mosher, "Cohabitation, Marriage, Divorce, and Remarriage in the United States," *Vital and Health Statistics* 23, no. 22 (2002).

4. J. L. Bratter and R. B. King, "'But Will It Last?' Marital Instability among Interracial and Same-Race Couples," *Family Relations* 57, no. 2 (2008): 160–171.

5. Y. Zhang and J. Van Hook, "Marital Dissolution among Interracial Couples," *Journal of Marriage and Family* 71, no. 1 (2009).

6. Pew Research Center's Religion & Public Life Project, "A Portrait of Jewish Americans," October 1, 2013.

7. Prior to 1970, the US Census Bureau would have its enumerators make racial judgments about the identities of the people they counted, based on their in-person observations. Since then, Americans have been allowed to label themselves on their census form, and the bureau has adopted a you-are-whoever-you-say-you-are approach to racial labeling. So if an immigrant from Ghana, or a second-generation Chinese American, or a descendant of an Anglo-Saxon family that arrived on the *Mayflower* were, for whatever reason, to choose to identify as Hispanic, that's how he or she would be counted. And if a recent arrival from Mexico City decided to say she wasn't Hispanic, that's how she would be counted.

8. Peter Wallsten, "Obama Struggles to Balance African Americans' Hopes with Country's as a Whole," *Washington Post*, October 28, 2012.

9. Nia-Malika Henderson, "Blacks, Whites Hear Obama Differently," *Politico*, March 3, 2009.

10. Jodi Kantor, "For President, a Complex Calculus of Race and Politics," *New York Times*, October 21, 2012, p. A1.

11. For more information, see Pew Research Center Social & Demographic Trends project, "King's Dream Remains an Elusive Goal; Many Americans See Racial Disparities," August 22, 2013, http://www.pewsocialtrends.org/2013/08/22/kings-dream-remains-an-elusive-goal-many-americans-see-racial-disparities/#fn-17618-1.

CHAPTER 8: WHITHER MARRIAGE?

1. See Stephanie Coontz, *The Way We Never Were: American Families and the Nostalgia Trap* (New York: Basic Books, 1993).

2. See Stephanie Coontz, *Marriage, A History: How Love Conquered Marriage* (New York: Penguin Books, 2005).

3. Kay Hymowitz et al., "Knot Yet," the National Marriage Project at the University of Virginia, the National Campaign to Prevent Teen and Unplanned Pregnancy, and the Relate Institute, 2013.

4. Andrew Cherlin, "In the Season of Marriage, a Question: Why Bother?" *New York Times,* April 27, 2013.

5. For a summary of findings in this field, see the chapter on marriage (Chapter 8) in Charles Murray, *Coming Apart* (New York: Crown Forum, 2012).

6. Ibid., p. 158.

7. Sam Roberts, "Divorce after 50 Grows More Common," *New York Times,* September 20, 2013.

8. Susan L. Brown, "A 'Gray Divorce' Boom," *Los Angeles Times,* March 31, 2013.

9. Coontz was quoted in "Divorce after 50 Grows More Common," by Sam Roberts, *New York Times,* September 20, 2013.

10. Ross Douthat, "Marriage Looks Different Now," *New York Times,* March 30, 2013.

11. Isabel V. Sawhill, "Restoring Marriage Will Be Difficult," Brookings Institution, December 20, 2012.

12. Quoted at a Brooking Institution symposium, March 2013.

CHAPTER 9: NONES ON THE RISE

1. David Brooks, "The National Creed," *New York Times,* December 30, 2003.

2. Roger Finke and Rodney Stark, *The Churching of America 1776–1990* (New Brunswick, NJ: Rutgers University Press, 2005). Note that church membership is different from religious affiliation: a person can identify as a Presbyterian, for example, even if she does not belong to a Presbyterian congregation. Affiliation is measured in Pew Research surveys with the question, "What is your present religion, if any?" followed by a list of response options, such as, "Are you Protestant, Catholic, Orthodox such as Greek or Russian Orthodox, Jewish, Muslim, Buddhist, Hindu, atheist, agnostic, something else or nothing in particular?" Those who say they are atheist, agnostic, or nothing in particular are classified as unaffiliated.

3. Pew Research Center calculations based on the US Census Bureau's August 2012 Current Population Survey, which estimates 234,787,000 adults live in the US.

4. The term "nones" is often used to describe people who indicate in surveys that they have no religion or do not belong to any particular religion. See, for example, Barry A. Kosmin and Ariela Keysar, with Ryan Cragun and Juhem Navarro-Rivera, "American Nones: The Profile of the No Religion Population, a Report Based on the American Religious Identification Survey 2008," Trinity College, 2009, http://commons.trincoll.edu/aris/files/2011/08/NONES_08.pdf. See also Tom W. Smith, "Counting Religious Nones and Other Religious Measurement Issues: A Comparison

of the Baylor Religion Survey and General Social Survey," GSS Methodological Report No. 110, 2007, http://publicdata.norc.org:41000/gss/documents/MTRT /MR110-Counting-Religious-Nones-and-Other-Religious-Measurement-Issues.pdf.

5. See the November 2007 report by the Pew Research Center's Global Attitudes Project, "The American-Western European Values Gap: American Exceptionalism Subsides," www.pewglobal.org/2011/11/17/the-american-western-european -values-gap.

6. See Gallup, "In US, 3 in 10 Say They Take the Bible Literally," July 8, 2011, www.gallup.com/poll/148427/say-bible-literally.aspx.

7. See Mark Chaves, *American Religion: Contemporary Trends* (Princeton, NJ: Princeton University Press, 2011), pp. 14, 50–51.

8. Michael Hout and Claude S. Fischer, "Why More Americans Have No Religious Preference: Politics and Generations," *American Sociological Review* 67 (2002): 165–190; www.jstor.org/stable/3088891.

9. Robert Wuthnow, *After the Baby Boomers: How Twenty- and Thirty-Somethings Are Shaping the Future of American Religion* (Princeton, NJ: Princeton University Press, 2007), pp. 51–70.

10. By contrast, some measures of religious commitment—such as frequency of prayer and the degree of importance that people assign to religion in their lives—do tend to rise with age. See the Pew Forum's February 2010 report "Religion Among the Millennials," www.pewforum.org/Age/Religion-Among-the-Millennials.aspx.

11. Robert D. Putnam, *Bowling Alone: The Collapse and Revival of American Community* (New York: Simon & Schuster, 2000). In Robert D. Putnam and David E. Campbell, *American Grace: How Religion Divides and Unites Us* (Simon & Schuster: New York, 2010), p. 127, Putnam and Campbell also consider changing moral and social beliefs to be part of the mix.

12. See, for example, "A Bleak Outlook Is Seen for Religion," *New York Times*, February 25, 1968, p. 3. The article quotes sociologist Peter L. Berger predicting that by the twenty-first century, traditional religions would survive only in "small enclaves and pockets." Berger has since renounced his earlier position.

13. See Pippa Norris and Ronald Inglehart, *Sacred and Secular: Religion and Politics Worldwide* (Cambridge, UK: Cambridge University Press, 2004), pp. 216–217. They argue that "societies where people's daily lives are shaped by the threat of poverty, disease and premature death remain as religious today as centuries earlier. These same societies are also experiencing rapid population growth. In rich nations, by contrast, the evidence demonstrates that secularization has been proceeding since at least the mid-twentieth century (and probably earlier)—but at the same time fertility rates have fallen sharply, so that in recent years population growth has stagnated and their total population is starting to shrink. The result of these combined trends is that *rich societies are becoming more secular but the world as a whole is becoming more religious*" (emphasis in original), pp. 216–217.

14. See the 2007 report by the Pew Research Center's Global Attitudes Project, "World Publics Welcome Global Trade—But Not Immigration," www.pewglobal .org/2007/10/04/world-publics-welcome-global-trade-but-not-immigration.

15. Norris and Inglehart, *Sacred and Secular,* pp. 89–95. They offer a number of possible explanations for America's exceptional religiosity—asserting in particular that economic inequality and the perception of a porous social welfare net leave Americans feeling "greater anxieties" than citizens in other advanced industrial countries. They also mention "the fact that the United States was founded by religious refugees" and the continuing arrival of new immigrants who bring "relatively strong religiosity with them," pp. 107–108 and 225–226.

16. Evangelical Protestants are defined here as Protestants who say yes when asked, "Would you describe yourself as a born-again or evangelical Christian, or not?" Protestants who do not answer this question affirmatively are categorized here as mainline Protestants. Other research that sorts Protestants into evangelical and mainline categories based on denominational affiliation (e.g., Southern Baptist, United Methodist) finds that the long-term decline in American Protestantism is concentrated primarily among the Protestant mainline. See, for example, Chaves, *American Religion,* pp. 81–93.

17. Alan Wolfe, *The Transformation of American Religion: How We Actually Live Our Faith* (Chicago: University of Chicago Press, 2005).

CHAPTER 10: LIVING DIGITAL

1. Unlike Jane Smith, "Natalie Marks" is the pseudonym for a real person, as are other names in this chapter. Except for the name changes, no other details of their lives have been altered. All the quotes are real.

2. Kristen Purcell et al., "How Teens Do Research in the Digital World," Pew Research Center's Internet & American Life Project, November 1, 2012.

3. Janna Anderson and Lee Rainie, "Millennials Will Benefit and Suffer Due to Their Hyperconnected Lives," Pew Research Center's Internet & American Life Project, February 29, 2012.

4. Amanda Lenhart, Rich Ling, Scott Campbell, and Kristen Purcell, "Teens and Mobile Phones," Internet & American Life Project, Pew Research Center, April 2010, www.pewinternet.org/Reports/2010/Teens-and-Mobile-Phones.aspx.

5. A full explanation of networked individualism and the role of technology in abetting it can be found in Lee Rainie and Barry Wellman, *Networked: The New Social Operating System* (Cambridge, MA: MIT University Press, 2012).

6. These calculations come from the ongoing research of the University of Toronto's NetLab, run by Professor Barry Wellman; http://homes.chass.utoronto .ca/~wellman.

7. See www.kff.org/entmedia/8010.cfm.

8. See www.kff.org/entmedia/upload/8010.pdf.

9. See www.poynter.org/uncategorized/71347/our-complex-media-day.

10. See www.people-press.org/2012/09/27/
in-changing-news-landscape-even-television-is-vulnerable.

11. See www.pewinternet.org/Reports/2010/Online-News.aspx and
www.journalism.org/analysis_report/demographics_mobile_news.

12. See www.pewinternet.org/Reports/2011/Local-news.aspx.

13. See www.pewinternet.org/Reports/2013/Health-online.aspx.

14. Lee Rainie and Aaron Smith, "Politics on Social Networking Sites," Pew
Research Center's Internet & American Life Project, September 4, 2012.

15. Much of this framework for new literacies was inspired by the "networked
literacy" lecture of Howard Rheingold, University of Toronto, October 2010; the writings of Pam Berger on her Infosearcher blog, "Learning in the Web 2.0 World," http:
//infosearcher.typepad.com/infosearcher/2007/04/learning_in_the.html; and the
work of Henry Jenkins, especially "Confronting the Challenges of Participatory Culture: Media Education for the 21st Century," http://digitallearning.macfound.org
/atf/cf/%7B7E45C7E0-A3E0-4B89-AC9C-E807E1B0AE4E%7D/JENKINS
_WHITE_PAPER.PDF.

16. Danah Boyd, "Taken Out of Context: American Teen Sociality in Networked
Publics," PhD diss., University of California, Berkeley, 2008.

17. Ibid., p. 27.

CHAPTER 11: GETTING OLD

1. See testimony of Dr. Francis Collins before the Senate Appropriations Subcommittee on Labor, Health and Human Services, Education and Related Agencies on
May 11, 2011; http://appropriations.senate.gov/ht-labor.cfm?method=hearings
.view&id=8a1dcace-6f68-4e35-ad94-4409966e2ffb.

2. Calment (1875–1997) smoked until her 117th year and attributed her longevity
to the regular consumption of olive oil, port wine, and chocolate.

3. For more information on this theory, see Tom Kirkwood, *Time of Our Lives: The
Science of Human Aging* (Oxford, UK: Oxford University Press, 1999).

4. Quoted in "Who Wants to Live Forever?" *Financial Mirror*, July 6, 2010.

5. Quote from the film *Transcendent Man* (2009); http://transcendentman.com.

6. Joel Garreau, *Radical Evolution: The Promise and Peril of Enhancing Our Minds,
Our Bodies—and What It Means to Be Human* (New York: Broadway Books, 2005),
p. 104.

7. Holman Jenkins, "Will Google's Ray Kurzweil Live Forever?" *Wall Street Journal*,
April 12, 2013.

8. Quoted in Ker Than, "Would Life Extension Make Us Less Human?"
MSNBC.com, May 24, 2006, www.msnbc.msn.com/id/12953517/ns/
technology_and_science-science/t/would-life-extension-make-us-less-human.

9. Quoted in "Why We Age and How We Can Avoid It," at a July 2005 TED Conference in Oxford, England; www.youtube.com/watch?v=8iYpxRXlboQ.

CHAPTER 12: EMPTY CRADLE, GRAY WORLD

1. Even though China's gross domestic product has surpassed Japan's, the picture is quite different when one accounts for population size. The per capita income of the Japanese is still four times that of the Chinese.

2. Justin McCurry, "Let Elderly People 'Hurry Up and Die,' says Japanese Minister," *The Guardian,* January 22, 2013.

3. Chico Harlan, "A Declining Japan Loses Its Once-hopeful Champions," *Washington Post,* October 27, 2012.

4. Joel Kotkin and Harry Siegel, "Where Have All the Babies Gone?" *Newsweek,* February 15, 2013.

5. Hiroko Tabuchi, "Desperate Hunt for Day Care in Japan," *New York Times,* February 26, 2013.

6. Phillip Longman, "Think Again: Global Aging," *Foreign Policy,* November 1, 2010.

7. The median age divides the population into two equal parts, with 50% of the population older than the median age and 50% of the population younger than the median age.

8. In 2013 the health ministry reported that since the Chinese government introduced the one-child policy in 1971, doctors have performed 336 million abortions and 196 million sterilizations. By comparison, in the US, with a population about one-quarter the size of China's, an estimated 50 million abortions have been performed since the *Roe v. Wade* decision legalized abortion in 1973.

9. Dorinda Elliott, "The End of China's One-Child Policy?" *ChinaFile,* March 15, 2013.

10. Alternative measures of dependency ratios define the working-age population to be either ages 20–64 or ages 20–69.

11. Estimates of output are from the International Monetary Fund, World Economic Outlook Database, April 2012. Shares are based on purchasing power parity based evaluations of country gross domestic products.

12. Canada is excluded because it is not one of the countries in which surveys were fielded for this report.

13. See, for example, Robert J. Gordon, "Is U.S. Economic Growth Over? Faltering Innovation Confronts the Six Headwinds," National Bureau of Economic Research, Working Paper No. 18315 (August 2012); also, David E. Bloom, David Canning and Günther Fink, "Implications of Population Aging for Economic Growth," National Bureau of Economic Research, Working Paper No. 16705 (January 2011); also, Richard Freeman, "Is A Great Labor Shortage Coming? Replacement Demand in the

Global Economy," National Bureau of Economic Research, Working Paper No. 12541 (September 2006).

14. Norimitsu Onishi, "As Japan Works to Patch Itself Up, A Rift Between the Generations Opens," *New York Times*, February 12, 2012.

15. Alexandra Harney, "Without Babies, Can Japan Survive?" *New York Times*, December 15, 2012.

CHAPTER 13: THE RECKONING

1. Texas Governor Rick Perry road-tested the Ponzi metaphor in his campaign for president in 2012. It did not go well.

2. The most authoritative research that compares the return-on-contribution value of Social Security for different generations was done 20 years ago by Dean Leimer, an analyst at the Social Security Administration. His study found that in the aggregate, Americans born before 1938 either already have, or eventually will, receive a windfall of $8.1 trillion from Social Security—that's the excess of what they'll draw in benefits over the value of their contributions, accrued with interest. Leimer made those calculations based on 1989 dollars; updated to current dollars, that windfall would be valued at $18 trillion, according to a further analysis in 2012 by Sylvester J. Schieber, a former chairman of the Social Security Advisory Board. Who's paid for these windfalls? Leimer and Schieber spell out who: successive generations of taxpayers, in ever escalating amounts. They find that cohorts born from 1951 to 2010 will, in the aggregate, contribute $4.3 trillion more in Social Security taxes, accrued with interest, than they will receive in benefits. And for children not yet born, a $12 trillion bill awaits to help cover the Social Security windfalls that went to earlier generations of recipients. See Dean R. Leimer, "Cohort-Specific Measures of Lifetime Net Social Security Transfers," ORS Working Paper Series Number 59, Washington DC, Social Security Administration. Also see Sylvester J. Schieber, *The Predictable Surprise: The Unraveling of the U.S. Retirement System*, (Oxford: Oxford University Press, 2012), pp. 61–64.

3. Congressional Budget Office 2013, Long-Term Budget Outlook: www.cbo.gov/publication/44521; and Congressional Budget Office Historical Budget Data, August 2013: www.cbo.gov/publication/44507.

4. Another part of the Social Security system, the Disability Insurance Trust Fund, is expected to become insolvent even sooner—in 2016—because the disability rolls have nearly tripled since 1980. Critics say that lax eligibility standards have enabled some people with questionable claims to receive benefits.

5. A summary of the 2013 report of the Social Security and Medicare Board of Trustees, which includes long-term actuarial and financing projections, is available online at www.ssa.gov/oact/trsum.

6. For a compelling history of the political and policy debates over Social Security within FDR's own cabinet, see Schieber, *The Predictable Surprise*.

7. Milton Friedman's 10-minute exposition on "The Social Security Myth" is a YouTube favorite among conservatives, www.youtube.com/watch?v=rCdgv7n9xCY.

8. This analysis assumes that all contributions made by workers and employers earned 2% interest annually above the rate of inflation. It is based on a hypothetical average worker. The returns of actual Social Security recipients vary widely, depending on a range of factors, including wage levels, years of work, marital circumstances, timing of retirement, and longevity. See www.urban.org/UploadedPDF/412945 -Social-Security-and-Medicare-Taxes-and-Benefits-Over-a-Lifetime.pdf.

9. Jackie Calmes, "Misperceptions of Benefits Make Trimming Harder," *New York Times,* April 3, 2013.

10. In this example, the contributions are assumed to have earned 2% a year annually above the rate of inflation.

11. Some vivid examples from a 2013 report by the International Federation of Health Plans: an angiogram costs $218 in Switzerland and $914 in the US; bypass surgery is $22,844 in France and $73,420 in the US; hip replacements are $11,899 in Britain and $40,364 in the US.

12. As this book was going to press, the Affordable Care Act, aka Obamacare, was being implemented amid a blizzard of partisan rancor in Congress and many statehouses. Designed to both broaden health insurance coverage *and* reduce medical costs, it represents the largest expansion of the safety net since the 1960s. It's too soon to gauge what impact it will have on the future cost of health care.

13. Estimates from the Peter G. Peterson Foundation, based on data from the Congressional Budget Office; www.pgpf.org/Chart-Archive/~/link.aspx?_id=A0E17 E1FEBEE42BFA346F12F51DE4526&_z=z.

14. Jessica Perez, Gabe Horowitz, and David Kendall, "Collision Course: Why Democrats Must Back Entitlement Reform," Third Way, July 2012.

15. A 2011 Congressional Budget Office report estimated that Medicare's market power had enabled it to negotiate health care prices at an 11% discount from what would be available in a market made up only of private insurers. And for reasons that health economists don't fully understand, the overall rate of rise in health care costs has moderated significantly in recent years—perhaps in reaction to the Great Recession, perhaps in anticipation of the implementation of the Affordable Care Act (Obamacare). Whatever the cause, a hopeful sign.

16. Letter to the editor, *New York Times,* February 25, 2013.

17. Pieter Vanhuysse, "Intergenerational Justice in Aging Societies," A Cross-national Comparison of 29 OECD Countries, Bertelsmann Stiftung, 2013.

18. Rakesh Kochhar and D'Vera Cohn, "Fighting Poverty in a Bad Economy, Americans Move in with Relatives," Pew Research Center, October 3, 2011.

19. For an excellent account of how families handled generational relationships in primitive societies through modern times, see Chapter 1 by John B. Williamson and Diane M. Watts-Roy in *The Generational Equity Debate,* eds. Williamson, Watts-Roy,

and Eric Kingson (New York: Columbia University Press, 1999). They note that in primitive societies, anthropologists found that the question of what share of resources should be consumed by the elderly were sometimes resolved by considerations of power rather than need. For example, the elderly tended to be treated better in societies based on fishing and gathering than in nomadic societies based on herding and hunting, which placed a higher premium on youth and strength. Societal norms regarding relations between the old and young have shifted multiple times through different centuries and societies, but the overall drift has been toward a veneration of the old because of their moral and practical wisdom and their presumed physical and economic vulnerability.

20. "Growing Older in America: The Health and Retirement Survey," National Institute on Aging, published online March 2007, hrsonline.isr.umich.edu/index .php?p=dbook.

21. Michael Hurd, James P. Smith, and Julie Zissimopoulos, "Intervivos Giving Over the Lifecycle," Rand Labor and Population Working Paper WR-524-1, Santa Monica, California, October 2011, http://www.rand.org/pubs/working_papers /WR524-1.html.

22. "Grandparents Investing in Grandchildren," Metlife Mature Market Institute, New York, September 2012, www.gu.org/LinkClick.aspx?fileticket =jueWk9ubnyE%3D&tabid=157&mid=606; "Grandparents: Generous with Money, not with Advice," Metlife Mature Market Institute, Westport, Connecticut, 2009, www.metlife.com/assets/cao/mmi/publications/studies/mmi-grandparents -generous-advice-money.pdf.

23. This includes transfers from anyone, but the vast majority is composed of transfers from parents or grandparents.

24. Since these estimates are based upon respondents providing at least 100 hours of help, they are underestimates of the total share of respondents who provide help for their parents.

25. Hendrik Hartog, *Someday All This Will Be Yours* (Cambridge, MA: Harvard University Press), 2012.

26. Merril Silverstein and Roseann Giarrusso, "Aging and Family Life: A Decade Review," *Journal of Marriage and Family* 72 (October 2010).

27. Thomas Friedman, "Sorry, Kids. We Ate It All," *New York Times*, October 15, 2013.

28. To read the speech on this subject delivered by AARP CEO A. Barry Rand at the National Press Club on January 15, 2013, go to http://www.aarp.org/politics -society/advocacy/info-01–2013/rebuild-the-middle-class-speech.html.

INDEX

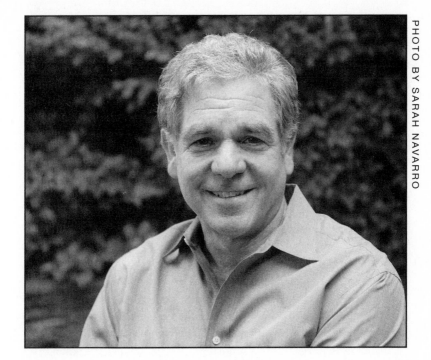

For the past decade Paul Taylor has served as executive vice president of the Pew Research Center, where he oversees the Social & Demographic Trends project, the Hispanic Trends project, and various center-wide research initiatives. From 1996 through 2003, he served as president and board chair of the Alliance for Better Campaigns, a nonprofit public interest group that sought to improve the formats and reduce the cost of political communication on television. Before that, he was a newspaper reporter for twenty-five years, the last fourteen at the Washington Post, where he covered three US presidential campaigns and served as the Post's bureau chief in South Africa during the historic transformation from apartheid to democracy. Taylor is the author of *See How They Run* (Knopf, 1990) and coauthor of *The Old News Versus the New News* (Twentieth Century Fund, 1992). He twice served as the visiting Ferris Professor of Journalism at Princeton University. He has a bachelor's degree in American studies from Yale University. He and his wife live in Bethesda, Maryland. They have three grown children and one grandchild (so far!).

PublicAffairs is a publishing house founded in 1997. It is a tribute to the standards, values, and flair of three persons who have served as mentors to countless reporters, writers, editors, and book people of all kinds, including me.

I. F. STONE, proprietor of *I. F. Stone's Weekly*, combined a commitment to the First Amendment with entrepreneurial zeal and reporting skill and became one of the great independent journalists in American history. At the age of eighty, Izzy published *The Trial of Socrates*, which was a national bestseller. He wrote the book after he taught himself ancient Greek.

BENJAMIN C. BRADLEE was for nearly thirty years the charismatic editorial leader of *The Washington Post*. It was Ben who gave the *Post* the range and courage to pursue such historic issues as Watergate. He supported his reporters with a tenacity that made them fearless and it is no accident that so many became authors of influential, best-selling books.

ROBERT L. BERNSTEIN, the chief executive of Random House for more than a quarter century, guided one of the nation's premier publishing houses. Bob was personally responsible for many books of political dissent and argument that challenged tyranny around the globe. He is also the founder and longtime chair of Human Rights Watch, one of the most respected human rights organizations in the world.

·   ·   ·

For fifty years, the banner of Public Affairs Press was carried by its owner Morris B. Schnapper, who published Gandhi, Nasser, Toynbee, Truman, and about 1,500 other authors. In 1983, Schnapper was described by *The Washington Post* as "a redoubtable gadfly." His legacy will endure in the books to come.

Peter Osnos, *Founder and Editor-at-Large*